Reading Franz Liszt

Portrait of Liszt by Henri Lehmann, oil, 1839.
Musée Carnavalet, Histoire de Paris (CC0 1.0).

Reading Franz Liszt

Revealing the Poetry
behind the Piano Music

Paul Roberts

AMADEUS
PRESS

Lanham · Boulder · New York · London

AMADEUS
PRESS

Published by Amadeus Press
An imprint of The Rowman & Littlefield Publishing Group, Inc.
4501 Forbes Boulevard, Suite 200, Lanham, Maryland 20706
www.rowman.com

86-90 Paul Street, London EC2A 4NE

British Library Cataloguing in Publication Information Available

Library of Congress Cataloging-in-Publication Data

Names: Roberts, Paul, 1949– author.
Title: Reading Franz Liszt : revealing the poetry behind the piano music / Paul Roberts.
Description: Lanham : Amadeus Press, 2022. | Includes bibliographical references and index. | Summary: "Paul Roberts immerses readers in the world of Franz Liszt, megastar of Romanticism, through a vivid exploration of his most beloved pieces and literature that inspired them—from Petrarch's love poetry to the sensibilities of Byron, Sénancour, and others. Roberts reveals the deeper essence of Liszt, recasting him as a composer of poetic feeling" —Provided by publisher.
Identifiers: LCCN 2022004277 (print) | LCCN 2022004278 (ebook) | ISBN 9781538143346 (cloth) | ISBN 9781538143353 (epub)
Subjects: LCSH: Liszt, Franz 1811–1886—Criticism and interpretation. | Piano music—19th century—History and criticism. | Music and literature.
Classification: LCC ML410.L7 R63 2022 (print) | LCC ML410.L7 (ebook) | DDC 780.92—dc23
LC record available at https://lccn.loc.gov/2022004277
LC ebook record available at https://lccn.loc.gov/2022004278

To Jenny

Directly, in itself, music signifies nothing, unless by convention and association. Music means nothing and yet means everything. One can make notes say what one will, grant them any power of analogy: they do not protest.[1]

—Vladimir Jankélévitch, *Music and the Ineffable*

The more instrumental music progresses, develops and frees itself from its early limitations . . . the more it will cease to be a simple combination of tones and become a poetic language, one that, better than poetry itself perhaps, more readily expresses everything in us that transcends the commonplace, everything that eludes analysis.

—Franz Liszt, *An Artist's Journey,*
Lettres d'un bachelier ès musique, 1835–1841[2]

People talk so much about music and they say so little. I am absolutely certain that words are not adequate to it, and if ever I found that they were, I should eventually give up composition. [Music] fills one's soul with a thousand better things than words. A piece of music that I love expresses thoughts to me that are not too imprecise *to be framed in words, but too* precise.

—Felix Mendelssohn, Letter to
Marc André Souchay, October 15, 1842[3]

Contents

List of Figures

Acknowledgments

*W*ithout the work of numerous scholars in my field and beyond, I could not have brought this book to fruition—I trust I have credited and thanked them all in my notes and bibliography.

To my students everywhere, I owe a deep debt of gratitude: to hear Liszt's music live in my teaching studio (and for a long period only over Wi-Fi), at whatever level of accomplishment, has provided an endless source of stimulation and insight.

My editor Michael Tan at Rowman & Littlefield has been unfailing in his advice, patient attention, and encouragement.

For help and expertise, I am grateful to Professor Barry Ife, Dr. Jennifer Rushworth, and Knut Maseide; to Glenn Moore not only for Shakespeare; to my son Ned Roberts not only for the index.

Very special thanks to my ideal reader, Oliver Bennett of Hunch Theatre, who read every single chapter as it emerged and returned to me essay-length responses.

Introduction

Making a Sound

*T*his book has arisen from a lifetime's fascination for literature and language that has paralleled my career as a pianist and piano teacher. The seed, planted a long time ago when I had just started out, was a brief conversation I had with an elderly and much-celebrated piano teacher. I introduced myself. I cannot remember quite how the topic came about, but within a few minutes we were talking about Liszt's great triptych of piano pieces known as the Petrarch Sonnets, inspired by the love poetry of the fourteenth-century Italian poet Francesco Petrarca. "Oh!" I enthused, "Those poems!" She entered her studio. "We don't need them," she said, and closed the door. I was deflated—and dumbfounded.

I trust that my lifetime still has a long way to go; but I feel I have lived long enough now to have something to say about the essential connections between literature and music, indeed about the *need* for these poems. After many decades I have formulated, at last, an answer to my colleague. This book is my answer. The first chapter I wrote was on Petrarch, which can be found here as chapter 3, "The Music of Desire."

Musicology over the past decades has at last turned to literary questions, but in my field of concert pianism the subject is still largely on the periphery. What has a piano recital to do with words on a page? What have the piano works of Franz Liszt to do with the canon of European literature? Actually, a considerable amount. That is what this book is about.

A mere glance at Liszt's piano music, from the beginning to the end of his life, reveals a large number of major works that are intimately associated with a variety of literary texts, above all poetry, often quoted at length. Liszt's practice takes the picturesque title to new heights, no longer "Romance" and "Nocturne," or "Raindrop" and "Moonlight," but quotations, taken from his voracious reading, whose purpose he passionately defended. For pianists and listeners who want to find a way into Liszt's music, who want to know more, who want to explore the extraordinary mind and achievement of one of the greatest composers of the nineteenth century, the literary background to his compositions provides a vital clue. Almost always the texts he drew on are displayed at the front for all to read.

In some ways this book is a kind of biography. Exploring what Liszt read, and how he reacted to what he read, inevitably leads to an understanding of central aspects of his life and the people he met. His long love affair with Marie d'Agoult, with whom he had three children, was the backbone of his formative years of the 1830s. She had a huge influence on his tastes and his reading, as did the prolific novelist, polemicist, and journalist George Sand. Liszt was for a time close to Heinrich Heine, Sainte-Beuve, Victor Hugo, and Alphonse de Lamartine, huge figures in European literature with whom he held his own. These were not mere acquaintances in the Paris salons, but writers with whom he engaged in the lively to and fro of debate, in letters, articles, and conversation.

I look at the nature of biography in chapter 1, and the processes by which a knowledge of an artist's life somehow impinges on our reception and interpretation of the art. "A writer should leave nothing behind him but his works," proclaimed Flaubert—nor perhaps should a musician. But the reality is often different. Flaubert had very strong views on the autonomy of art, the essentially impersonal nature of the creative process, as did Ravel. But Liszt didn't. Liszt's conviction that art and life were synonymous—the life he led and the life he fed off in the poetry and prose he read—was a fundamental belief of the far-reaching, pan-European phenomenon know as Romanticism. Defining Romanticism is a perilous undertaking, but an idea of it will emerge during the course of this book. I address the question directly in the chapter on "Vallée d'Obermann."

"If Byron and Victor Hugo had never lived, there would have been no Liszt,"[1] wrote Eleanor Perényi. It was her biography of Liszt, *The Artist as Romantic Hero*, published in 1974, which first drew me into Liszt's literary imagination and the nature of Romanticism. (It is a book much underrated today and deserves to be revived.[2]) Perényi's statement does not hold up logically, but as a provocation it had the same value for me as my esteemed colleague's dismissal of Petrarch's poems. Unaware of how Byron and Hugo could possibly fit into an understanding of Liszt, I aimed to find out.

Victor Hugo represents French Romanticism in all its glory. Constantly controversial, his life and work embodied his credo of the poet as prophet and guide. Liszt's literary milieu of the 1830s found the same poet-prophet in Lord Byron, whose narrative poetry, telling of the exploits of outcasts and heroes, became some of the most widely read literature of the age. Liszt aspired to achieve the same prestige for music—and himself.

One of his earliest letters, from 1832, begins with a nine-line quotation from a recently published poem by Hugo. "It is time. Let us get on! It is time," proclaims the poet, in a passionate exhortation not to delay life's offerings. Liszt's response is equally passionate:

> For the past fortnight my mind and fingers have been working away like two lost spirits. Homer, the bible, Plato, Locke, Byron, Hugo, Lamartine, Chateaubriand, Beethoven, Bach, Hummel, Mozart, Weber, are all around me. I study them, meditate on them, devour them with fury; and in addition I spend 4 to 5 hours practising exercises (thirds, sixths, octaves, tremolos, repeated notes, cadenzas etc. etc.). Ah! provided I don't go mad you will find an artist in me! Yes, an artist such as you desire, such as is required nowadays.[3]

Liszt had already befriended Hugo, who was nine years older, and played Beethoven sonatas to him. He was also sketching a piano étude based on the poet's narrative poem "Mazeppa" (which became one of the *Etudes d'exécution transcendantes* of 1851). He was to write several songs to Hugo texts (one of which would inspire Liszt's reading of Petrarch), and two symphonic poems, *Mazeppa* and *Ce qu'on entends sur la montagne*. In chapter 9, I will review Hugo's association with Liszt's Dante Sonata, whose title "Après une lecture du Dante" was taken from Hugo's poem of the same name. Liszt wrote to Marie d'Agoult in 1841, "Hugo is often very great, and very splendid. His conversation is powerful, rich, luxuriant, and yet a certain artificiality and theatricality is always mingled therein." He was "one of those rare men who attract one strongly to begin with," he wrote, "then stop one and make one retreat with bitter regret."[4]

Lord Byron was another matter. "He is the poet, as Liszt himself admits, whom he has embraced, to whom he has abandoned himself completely,"[5] a contemporary reviewer wrote. In chapters 7 and 8 we will see the major impact Byron had on the Swiss book of the *Années de pèlerinage*.

Reading the memoirs of the period when Liszt was first making his impact as a pianist and teacher in Paris (he was still living with his mother) is to realize how remarkable was his multiplicity of interests. Everyone who came across him had a similar story to tell. "Not to have heard him, you can have no idea what he's like," wrote one. "It is ecstasy and fatigue together, which at one and the same time consume and enchant.... Sometimes he reads us fragments of his favorite authors.... He links music to literature, leading us to one by way of the other."[6] It is this literature that is my concern in the following chapters, but this is not to overlook Liszt's deep musical erudition. As Susan Youens has observed, he "ceaselessly conducted a conversation from inside his own music" with the composers whom he admired, with Beethoven, Schubert,

Berlioz, Schumann—and later with Wagner. For Liszt these influences were "a singular form of collaboration with great musical minds."[7]

The literary side of Liszt is clearly discernible. It is there in his epigraphs and titles, in the company he kept, in the articles and letters he wrote. (Like Debussy's apparent desire to be a painter, it was reported that Liszt would rather have been a writer than a virtuoso pianist—see p. 101 below). The more complex issue is how our knowledge of Liszt's literary inspiration affects our experience of the music—to what extent is a pianist's interpretation, or a listener's reception of a performance, dependent on the accompanying texts? These are the questions I will explore in the following chapters as the story of Liszt's reading unfolds.

Toward the end of his life Liszt created the concept of the master class as we know it today. In his teaching, from what can be gathered from the surviving evidence, it seems he taught by means of analogy and metaphor. The skills of pianism (about which he said very little) were joined by considerations of other art forms, other modes of expression and communication. When we play and listen to music we constantly "link [it] to feeling, sensation, emotion, memory and desire."[8] For the cultural musicologist Lawrence Kramer that seems obvious, and we can confidently assume Liszt would have agreed. But my experience is that pianists struggling with the formidable technical demands of piano playing all too often miss such fundamental connections.

One analogy I draw in my own teaching is with theater. The British director Peter Brook wrote,

> When I hear of a director speaking glibly of serving the author, of letting a play speak for itself, my suspicions are aroused, because this is the hardest job of all. *If you just let a play speak, it may not make a sound.* If what you wish is for a play to be heard, you must conjure its sounds from it. [emphasis added] [9]

Brook identifies here the nature and practice of interpretation, for a director, an actor, and as I want to demonstrate, a pianist. In chapter 2, "The Pianist as Actor," I look at the parallels that might be drawn between musical performance and acting. Beyond the agility of our fingers how do we conjure the sounds from the music we are playing? What are our criteria? Once we have acquired our technique, what then? I am suggesting that a pianist's preparation of a Liszt score, with a literary quotation at its head, is analogous to an actor preparing a role. These questions were central for Liszt, both as performer and composer. In a widely read Parisian music journal, at the beginning of his career, he wrote,

> The musician exhales the more personal mysteries of his destiny in sounds. He thinks, feels, and speaks in music. But as his language, more arbitrary

and less explicit than any other, lends itself to a multitude of different in-terpretations . . . is it not without value . . . for the composer to give a brief psychological sketch of his work, for him to say what he intended . . . for him to state the fundamental idea of his composition?[10]

What is easy to overlook here, in this precisely reasoned argument for the validity of his literary references, is the unarguable statement that the musician "thinks, feels, and speaks *in music.*" Then follows the "but . . ." Liszt's epigraphs never invalidate the music as music, but his abiding concern for music to *mean* something, indeed everything, is what drew him to find common ground with the literature he so avidly read, literature in which the search for meaning—the examination and expression of the fundamental issues of existence—was the entire purpose. And Liszt read not just widely but with immense discernment. We might say he turned himself into a great literary critic, but one whose critiques were in the form of music not words. (He had the finest role models, for among the writers who were his friends and acquaintances were some of the greatest literary critics of the age.)

Liszt's reading was conducted in parallel with his formidable practice regime, his exercises in "thirds, sixths, octaves, tremolos, repeated notes, cadenzas etc. etc." When Liszt wrote the Paris article he had already, at the age of twenty-five, turned himself into one of the most celebrated pianists of Europe. Liszt as a virtuoso pianist is not the subject of this book, but we cannot overlook that during most of the period covered in the following chapters—his formative years in Paris in the 1830s, and the consolidation of his career in the following decade—he was in the process of inventing the art of the solo piano recital as we know it today. Indeed this was the Liszt whom his contemporaries knew and lauded, and for whose pianism they had to find a new mode of language to describe. For Marie d'Agoult his virtuosity was "prodigious, shattering, incomparable"; for Berlioz, he was "the pianist of the future," and his performance of Beethoven's "Hammerklavier" sonata "would have made the composer, had he heard it in his grave, thrill with pride and joy"; the pianist Charles Hallé "sat speechless for a quarter of an hour after-wards . . . in a stupor of amazement." And one further quotation will place the demonic element of his performing persona. Clara Schumann wrote in her diary for September 1851, "He played, as always, with a true demonic bravura. He lorded it over the piano like a devil (I cannot express it differently)."[11] She was deeply impressed and appalled at the same time, and her final remark (almost embarrassed in parenthesis) betrays a certain fear.

This Franz Liszt will appear, inescapably, in the following pages. For seven years from 1840, after having established himself at the forefront of the Paris cultural scene, he gave some one thousand concerts throughout Europe, traveling from the farthest corner of southwest Spain to the outer reaches of northeastern Russia. Then in early 1848, he gave it all up, never again to play in public for a fee, to devote himself to composition (which is not to say he gave up playing the piano). The immediate result was the union of literature and music in his programmatic symphonic poems, and his symphonies inspired by Goethe's *Faust* and Dante's *Divine Comedy*.

But it was in his piano music that he first began his exploration of literary texts, in his early collection from the late 1830s, *Album d'un voyageur* (later to become *Années de pèlerinage—Suisse*). Soon afterward he turns his early song settings of three of Petrarch's sonnets into pieces for solo piano, which in the 1850s became the celebrated "Tre Sonetti di Petrarca" in the second volume of *Années de pèlerinage—Italie*. This volume also contains the mighty Dante Sonata. The title of the collection *Harmonies poètiques et religieuses* is also borrowed from a poet, Lamartine, who supplied the title for the magnificent "Bénédiction de dieu dans la solitude" in that volume. The two St. Francois *Légendes* of the 1860s were published with long prefaces by Liszt in Italian and French, quoting religious authorities.

What do we do with all these texts that are presented to us as part of the score? What did Liszt expect us to do? The purpose of this book is to explore these questions, the "fundamental idea" that Liszt directs us toward, and then to see how it might be played back into our interpretation of the music.

What is here is not exhaustive. I have chosen seminal works that I believe best exemplify Liszt's achievement, which means three chapters are devoted to the Swiss volume of the *Années de pèlerinage*—merited by the extraordinary richness of the references in this collection, the unerring connections Liszt makes with the literary zeitgeist of his age. Byron is the main emphasis in *Années Suisse*, above all his narrative poem *Childe Harold's Pilgrimage*; but Etienne de Sénancour's epistolary novel *Obermann* had a crucial influence too, and so has a chapter of its own.

It might seem an anomaly that I have devoted a large space to the Sonata in B minor, among Liszt's greatest achievements in the realm of pure music (which I will define for the present as music without accompanying text). But this towering work cannot be avoided. My reasons for doing so can be found in detail in chapters 4 and 5, "The Question of Goethe's *Faust*" and "Music as Metaphor." My other seminal figures are Petrarch and Dante. In the appendix, I give brief commentaries on major pieces to which I have not given a fuller treatment.

My argument is that the texts are indeed needed, that they are an essential component of the art of Franz Liszt. No more than Peter Brook's play can Liszt's music, or any music, speak for itself. This is not to say that the music cannot stand alone; it is to say that music needs performing, interpreting, projecting. To make it sound we "must conjure its sounds from it," as Brook wrote. One way this can be achieved, in Liszt's case, is to pay serious attention to the literary quotations he took the trouble to provide. He was insistent on the place of these quotations, and angry with his publishers when they were missed out. He had to fight for the validity of his concept of "program music," which was often derided (and still is).

If nothing else, his epigraphs enable a conversation about music that avoids the inhibitions of musical analysis. One of the discoveries for me in writing this book has been how much easier it is to talk meaningfully (I hope) about poetry than it is about music. Poetry is about words and the meaning of words. Indeed poetry is about meaning. What is music about? I believe this was exactly Liszt's question. The answer is unfathomable, which is not to say it should not be asked. Answers will be speculative, but speculation can be immensely revealing. So in the first chapter I will explore, along with thoughts on biography, the nature of speculation and how it might be a necessary tool with which musicians arrive at an interpretation; and I call on the aid of a philosopher who wrote that "construction of meaning is always a hypothesis, that is a well meaning guess."[12]

The underlying theme throughout this book is how our literary inquiry affects our musical performance. What is to be gained for performance, for our interpretation, by an understanding of Liszt's literary sources? Perhaps the sheer delight we attain from trying to live inside his mind—trying to identify his reading habits and how they informed his creative demon—perhaps that sharpens our senses, alerts us more readily to the achievement, opens our imaginations to the wonders of his music. This is the paradox that Liszt himself articulates: the musician "thinks, feels, and speaks in music. But . . ." To understand and engage with the literature he read, to glimpse what we can of its deep meaning for him, is to come full circle back to the music as music. That is what I would have liked to say to my colleague all those years ago. I am sure she would have agreed with me.

· *1* ·

Life, Literature, and Music

Out of what can the artist create *if he does not create* out of life?[1]

—Wagner to Liszt

I've been reading about the death of Franz Liszt. Why does this draw me? Why should this be relevant to a book about the inspiration Liszt drew from European literature? This second question I can only answer as a kind of thought experiment, which I will come to. As for the first question, what death wouldn't draw us?

Alan Walker narrates Liszt's death at the age of seventy-six at the end of his indispensable three-volume biography; it is especially moving because when one has lived a life in the imagination for so long one feels at its end a sudden and terrible emptiness akin to grief. But Liszt, for Walker, clearly remained very much alive, so much so that a few years after the publication of the third volume, he addressed an open letter to his "highly esteemed Master." It began, "I have long cherished the notion of writing to you, and I am grateful beyond measure that I now have opportunity to do so."[2] Such a position might attract ridicule, but we know that stories of all genres, whether biography or fairy tale, soap opera or novel, the Bible or Shakespeare, have a deep and essential psychological impact on our well-being. For Walker, in the telling of his story—and there can be few stories from the nineteenth century more compelling than the life of Franz Liszt—his protagonist became a colleague and friend, and moreover someone to protect from fake news, a phenomenon to which Liszt fell victim repeatedly throughout his life.

I had a similar experience writing my short biography of Debussy, finding the moment of his death, and the act of writing about it, extraordinarily moving. And alongside the fact, the finality, came a sudden sense of wholeness. This is difficult to describe, and it is even harder to articulate the effect this might have had on my experience of the music. It was similar to the finality of a novel, indeed any story, even one that we have read before. This is what

9

stories do: they reconfigure time. With completion comes insight, a sense that everything one had previously known—about the life, the music—is now more concentrated, more vital, in a word more meaningful in some inchoate way. I did however resist writing Debussy a letter.

Now, immersed in Liszt's music, pondering its stature, its meaning, its expressive power—reaching for the means to perform it, as well as the words to articulate my thoughts—I find the fact of his death as profound as if he had died only yesterday.

LISZT OR "LISZT"?

Anyone experiencing this music, either as practitioner or listener, will have an image in their minds, an entity that goes by the signifier "Liszt." But the particular signifier I am concerned with contains not just the music but a wide paraphernalia of literary references specific to Liszt's interests, to the world of his imagination, to his creative demon, his life. When I play my particular "Liszt," I am playing—performing and recreating—the world of his titles and his epigraphs, the fountains of the Villa d'Este, the sonnets of Petrarch, the valley of Obermann. I don't have to think this way—the music after all has a life of its own—but I choose to. More to the point, Liszt proffers an invitation to do so. The title is there at the head of the score; the poems are there; and because of Liszt the novel *Obermann* by Etienne de Sénancour is on my desk. The music is its own entity, but the "Liszt" I perform and teach, in relation to the poems and prose excerpts attached to it, is a different entity. This entity connects somehow to Liszt's life.

I recognize that this attempt to distinguish two entities is problematic. It risks weakening the validity of the music as music, which is the very opposite of my intention. But it is worth a try, not only to grasp the specific phenomenon of Liszt, but to be able to talk about music at all.

One can access Liszt's total command of the art of musical composition through analysis. His greatest compositions withstand scrupulous analytical scrutiny in the same way as Beethoven's or Wagner's. But analysis cannot reveal that other dimension, that ineffable expressive power that is the nature of artistic experience; something remains unexplained, and possibly that something is everything. To simplify, analysis reveals the brain not the heart—we might say the workings not the purpose. My thought experiment is an attempt to understand how a performer might grasp what this is, how we might articulate the ineffable. What is it that reaches our listeners? How can we judge its effectiveness if we can't somehow articulate what "it" might be?

It seems the young Liszt was also asking these questions. Just at the time he was compiling his *Album d'un voyageur*, a collection of some of his earliest piano pieces with descriptive titles and long quotations attached, he was writing the article from which I quoted in the introduction. It was in the form of an open letter, in the *Gazette musicale de Paris*, to his close friend George Sand, with whom for a number of years he had an immensely creative engagement. Sand challenged his intellect. "You think and talk not badly for a musician," she said to him.[3]

As we saw, it was in this article that he began to work out his ideas on musical meaning. Given that the language of music is "more arbitrary and less explicit than any other, [and] lends itself to a multitude of interpretations," would it not be valuable for the composer, at the outset, "to state the fundamental idea of his composition"?[4]

For Liszt, life, literature, and music were extraordinarily interwoven. His titles and epigraphs were his way of indicating this, his way of "talking about" the music he had written. "To interpret music verbally is to give it a legible place in the conduct of life,"[5] writes Lawrence Kramer, arguing for his own extensive verbal interpretations. But his remark is equally applicable to Liszt's need to express, verbally, his fundamental idea.

Kramer's field is what is known as musical hermeneutics, a forbidding expression for a wholly illuminating and accessible approach to musical meaning and interpretation. Does music have a meaning in the way language does, can it *say* things, and if so how do we identify what it says? Hermeneutics identifies joined-up experience (known as the hermeneutic circle), the manner in which a larger context influences how we react to a particular part. An example would be how our experience of Liszt's late piano music is affected by our reading about his life and death; or more simply how a composition's title or attached epigraph influences our experience of the music. In our everyday lives most of us practice hermeneutics all the time without realizing it.

I am suggesting in this book that this way of thinking, for the performer, is fundamental to the way we arrive at an interpretation of a work. The process is probing, open-ended, and necessarily speculative; and it takes us beyond the safe ground of the three fundamentals of teaching and preparation that are the staples of the conservatoire: stylistic understanding, analytical understanding, and the technical fluency we attain through arduous practice. "For hermeneutic thinkers construction of meaning is always a hypothesis, that is a well-meaning guess," writes Jens Zimmermann.[6] But the speculation is far from arbitrary. It is informed by knowledge and experience, and in the context of this book by the literature with which Liszt deeply engaged. It might also be informed by reading Liszt's biography. How else did we discover that for him life and literature were interwoven?

Why does that matter? Hermeneutics is about understanding; it is also about how we make ourselves understood.

ILLUSTRATING HERMENEUTICS

As an example of hermeneutics in practice, we can look at the third book of *Années de pèlerinage*, Liszt's "late" style. I've always experienced this visionary music as a parallel to self-portraiture, akin to the all-seeing, bleakly truthful gaze of Rembrandt in old age. On the manuscript of "Les jeux d'eaux à la Ville d'Este," Liszt has written a biblical quotation in Latin from the book of John, which the King James Bible translates as follows: "But the water that I shall give him shall be in him a well of water, springing up into everlasting life." Liszt we recall was a devout Catholic, and he took holy orders in 1863.

When Busoni drew attention to the huge influence this piece had on subsequent composers, calling it "the model for all musical fountains which have flowed since then"[7] (Ravel's youthful *Jeux d'eau* is an example), he would have had in mind Liszt's effortless gift for musical imitation, for tone painting, his characteristic keyboard style that creates hitherto unimagined sounds from some eighty-five tones, ten fingers and two (if not three) pedals. But Busoni's remark hardly does justice to the full symbolic power of the piece, or to Liszt's quotation, which has a far greater reach. The opening pages can certainly be compared to the energy, sound, and even visual appearance of fountains—the music is exultant, uplifting, dazzlingly colored with dissonance. We know water does not sound anything like this, but the imagination has no trouble at all with the analogy once we are given the prompt "fountains." (I've overheard a comment after a performance of impressionist piano pieces: "I was totally soaked from the watery spray of those fountains and lakes.") But the piece develops far beyond this illusion. A fine performance can set off reactions in a listener comparable to the emotive force of drama, a novel, a poem, a great work of visual art or architecture—perhaps feelings of wonder, ecstasy, and catharsis. The music is moving in that inexplicable way that we know music can be.

Liszt's tone painting, originating in his contemplation of the fountains in the grounds of his retreat near Rome, is the stage upon which he enacts a play of ecstatic religious devotion. If we want to hunt for the explicable, the "meaning" of his title, then we can find it here, if we choose to, and in his quotation on the manuscript. But it is the nature of music that it doesn't require the permission of a quotation or title for its full power to be felt. The quotation is a parallel experience of comparable intensity. The music is something else.

Joined together we have something else again. The title and quotation draw an analogy. Without them, without our knowledge of what they meant for Liszt, the music would still communicate in the way of music. Within certain parameters—the notes on the score being the most essential, and the instructions which indicate the composer's intentions—the piece is open to multiple interpretations. The literary context of Liszt's music is the one we are exploring in the following chapters, but it is not the only one available.

In the third book of the *Années de pèlerinage*, "Les jeux d'eaux à la Ville d'Este" follows the two pieces titled "Aux Cyprès de la Villa d'Este"—Liszt's meditations on the ancient cypress trees that stood near the fountains. As the third piece of this triptych, "Les jeux d'eaux" takes on a different meaning. Whether this is a richer meaning is not the issue; what matters is that when we hear "Fountains" following on from "Cypresses" our experience of "Fountains" alters.

Figure 1.1. Cyprus trees at the Villa d'Este, painted by Jean-Honoré Fragonard.
The ALBERTINA Museum, Vienna.

The two Cypress pieces are each subtitled "Threnodie." A threnody is a song or poem of mourning. The word asks us to experience the music as an enactment of grief. If we have read Liszt's biography, our interpretation also takes in his own experiences of mourning and grief, his contemplation of his own mortality, his fear and acceptance of death. And we know that for the aging Liszt his personal suffering was assuaged by the act of musical expression. It is almost impossible to demonstrate how the music conveys all this. But experiencing it, playing it, hearing it, with the knowledge of Liszt's life at this point, is to gain an incomparable insight into the motivations of his art. It is part of the methodology of preparation, of the way we develop an interpretation, that we should want to know about Liszt's fountains, his cypress trees, about his life and death. What did the cypress trees represent for him, what did their presence stir in his psyche?

Figure 1.2.   Liszt in 1886, the year he died.
Photo: Atelier Nadar (Public Domain).

Traditionally the cypress is a symbol of mourning, but its shape, reaching upward into a point, like the fountains (though dark and dense rather than light and translucent), can also symbolize hope, a spiritual aspiration beyond death. During the process of performance, the music expands the traditional symbolism into the person of Liszt himself, the mythic is enacted as the experience of an individual consciousness. The performer plays a crucial role in this process. For the duration of the music, molded and revealed under our fingers, Liszt's cypresses become the performer's. We become part of the hermeneutic circle.

This is the context of "Les jeux d'eaux à la Villa d'Este" if the three Villa d'Este pieces are heard as a triptych (which they clearly are, even though they don't depend on each other). The ineffable beauty of the tentative F sharp major section in the second threnody echoes throughout "Les jeux d'eaux" as a fully conceived resolution, as catharsis. But it is not only through the simple means of motivic echo that our awareness is awakened. The "Cypresses" create the mental condition in which we hear the "Fountains." In the final piece of the triptych grief is assuaged, yet none of its profundity, none of its darkness, is minimized. Liszt's "Les jeux d'eaux à la Villa d'Este" bears little relation to the impressionism of Ravel's *Jeux d'eau*—the magnificence and power of Liszt's fountains, the colossal dimensions of his vision, is of a different order of intention.[8] Following the two threnodies this is confirmed beyond doubt, we receive meaning as part of a continuum of multiple, linked experiences. Liszt's achievement is comparable to Beethoven's in his piano sonata Op. 111. The catharsis of the final pages of this sonata, resolving onto C major, not only relies on the preceding variations, but on the rugged dissonance and oppositions set up in the opening movement. And before that we might have experienced the two preceding sonatas, Op.109 and Op. 110. It is in this manner the hermeneutic circle operates.

The French philosopher Vladimir Jankélévitch wrote, "Meaning in music, for the composer, crops up as the music is being written; for the performer and listener it is manifested during the performance."[9] The art of performance is the art of being surprised in the moment by the material under our fingers, just as an actor is taught to speak words as if they have only just occurred. But we could argue that the fountains and the cypress trees for Liszt were sources of such deep meaning that their musical existence was manifested in the very act of meditation, prior to composition. Liszt, we recall, said that the musician "thinks, feels, and speaks in music" (which is not to say that setting down the music, composing it, is other than an arduous intellectual task).

Such intimations about the effect of music, the experience it creates for each of us, are difficult to articulate, and always have been. The meaning of music has been debated by philosophers ever since the ancient Greeks. Our duty as interpreters is to make as plausible a hypothesis as possible, remove ourselves from speculation that is merely fanciful, but recognize nevertheless that speculation has every chance of illuminating our understanding and deepening our art. The struggle for meaning, for validation, is worth the guess work, as long as we guard against excess. As Lawrence Kramer has observed, "Interpretation by its very nature is always in excess of whatever facts may be at its disposal. . . . This art is easy to abuse."[10]

THE HERMENEUTIC CIRCLE

When I first began my musings on the nature of interpretation, I saw the film *The White Crow*, the story of the Russian ballet dancer Rudolf Nureyev.[11] The film is a vibrant example of how the context of our lives governs who we are, how part and whole, detail and complete picture, are continually interacting. The film dramatizes how an artist reaches maturity through a growing awareness of joined-up experience.

Nureyev's formation as a man and a dancer—his and our own understanding of Nureyev—is conveyed through a combination of experiences from his childhood and early adulthood: Nureyev then and Nureyev now, examined simultaneously through the characteristic techniques of cinema. One of the means by which the film captures this sense of "becoming" is through its focus on Nureyev gazing at pictures, his intense concentration on images of arms and muscles and shapes; we see him touching the marble sculptures in the Paris Musée du Louvre, his reactions to the straining of limbs. We see Géricault's great oil painting *The Raft of the Medusa*; we see Greek sculpture and Rembrandt portraits; we see a scene where Nureyev's father is holding him as a little boy, which morphs into an image from a painting in which this same scene is distilled, frozen in time. We are inside Nureyev's head, and we become part of his thought process. As he dances (acts) as an adult on stage he remembers (becomes) moments from his past as images available to us, the viewers: a scene with his mother, a forest in the snow, a train. A toy train and a real train become leitmotifs. Nureyev as a young adult had a passion for toy trains, a familiar trope of childhood but also an image that focuses the real circumstances of his birth—he was born on a train. As a dancer he finds the "story" of himself and relives it, becomes it; the story is, and must be, the vital end product. Nureyev's teacher connected his pupil to this story and to his "play," to the vital experiences that made up his early life, its emotions, joys, and traumas. "For hermeneutic thinkers this is how knowledge works," writes Zimmermann. "Objective understanding of the world, others, and ourselves requires personal engagement and passionate curiosity."[12] Through the story of Rudolph Nureyev, *The White Crow* demonstrates how we see and make art—dance, music, painting, film, fiction—and how we interpret it.

BIOGRAPHICAL FALLACY

The relevance of Liszt's life and death, his biography, to my theme might simply be seen in terms of Zimmermann's "passionate curiosity." We read an author, gaze at a painting, listen to a piece of music, and we at once want to know about the life of its creator. But we are also mindful of the biographical fallacy: that art can be created without any reference to the circumstances in which it was created, that the life of the artist need not (some say should not) be relevant; that to believe one can find the life in the art is a fallacy. But the opposite can also be true, and Liszt exemplifies this. In purely musical terms the movement from the early Liszt of the *Etudes* and the *Album d'un voyageur* to the Liszt of the third book of the *Années de pèlerinage* and beyond embraces a remarkable creative journey, ever changing, ever experimenting. But to see this journey only as a history of music, of an evolving style, is to subtract it from a context that can only enrich our understanding of the art. I accept there are strong arguments for treating an artist's work as autonomous. In the introduction, I quoted Flaubert's dictum, "A writer should leave nothing behind him but his works." With every word and sentence in *Madame Bovary*, Flaubert aimed to remove himself from view, he sought an almost militant objectivity. Liszt as an artist did the opposite. "Liszt's music . . . projects the man," writes Alfed Brendel. "With rare immediacy it gives away the character of the composer as well as the musical probity of his executant."[13]

Liszt's journey from those early piano compositions to the end of his life, embracing over fifty years, was governed by a consistent belief in the transcendental power of music to express the experiences of his own life—galvanized by the life of others, his contemporaries and those whom he revered from the past. And to a considerable degree his imaginative life was filtered through his avid experience of literature. "It is utterly impossible for me," Liszt wrote, "to enjoy anything that appeals only to my ears, without my mind and my emotions also taking a part, a very large part, in my enjoyment." He was twenty-seven. It might be a remark that could have been said, self-servingly, by any of us. But for Liszt it meant much more. He had just witnessed a performance of Donizetti's *Lucrezia Borgia* in which he found "pleasant, flowing, and melodious music that one can listen to effortlessly and remember easily; music, that is, that pleases nearly everyone"[14]—but which, crucially for Liszt, fails to honor the gravity of Victor Hugo's story, the Hugo whose writing Liszt admired at this point in his life to the point of idolatry. David Trippett has suggested that Liszt's remark is a sign of the way his creative brain worked, its "need to engage the other hemisphere, as it were, which we might interpret as a yearning for literary fulfillment."[15] This might seem too complex an analysis of a somewhat self-regarding remark on the young Liszt's part, especially as we find him, a few years later, indulging his own penchant for crowd pleasing: in his mighty *Grande Fantaisie Réminiscences de Lucrezia Borgia*, he transcribes the very same "pleasant" melodies for the pleasure of his own audiences. But we should not scorn his idealism just because of his weakness for applause. (And the *Grande Fantaisie*, crowd pleasing or not, is an outstanding achievement.) Much of Liszt's music manifestly arises from a need for "literary fulfillment," from a quest for musical meaning of the kind embodied in the greatest imaginative literature.

In his preface to the *Album d'un voyageur*, those early pieces that became the great collection *Années de pèlerinage—Suisse*, Liszt suggested that music would "become a poetic language, one that, better than poetry itself perhaps, more readily expresses everything in us that transcends the commonplace, everything that eludes analysis."[16] Under his hands that is what it became.

• 2 •

The Pianist as Actor

The rise of the actor in music: a momentous event which not only leads
me to think but also to fear. In a word: "Wagner and Liszt."[1]

—Friedrich Nietzsche

$\mathcal{T}$he remark I quote here comes at the end of Nietzsche's notorious attack on Wagner in his extended essay *The Case of Wagner* (1911), first published in 1888. Why did he fear the actor in music? Why has Liszt been thrown into the mix?

Nietzsche was a fine musician (composer, pianist, improviser). Along with Schopenhauer, whose work had an immense influence on him, he considered music to be the most exalted and meaningful of all the arts. His philosophy constantly returns to the nature of music, captured in his celebrated aphorism "Without music human life would be a mistake."[2] Initially he was a follower of Wagner to the point of idolatry, an early habitué of the Wagner circle in Bayreuth—it was here, in 1872, that the twenty-eight-year-old philosopher met the sixty-one-year-old Liszt.

In his seminal book *The Birth of Tragedy*, published that year, Nietzsche argued that Greek drama was born "out of the spirit of music."[3] He sent Liszt a copy. Liszt, while praising its "astonishing lucidity" and "glorious language," graciously pointed out that his own concerns were Christian and not Hellenic; but that he had read the book with great interest, twice. "In its pages there glows and blazes a powerful spirit which stirred me profoundly."[4] Nietzsche was initially a great admirer of Liszt's music, telling him that he exemplified what he termed the Dionysian aspect of art—the spontaneous, energetic, uninhibited:

> When I look around me for the few people who have grasped with true
> instinct the phenomenon I have described . . . it is to you above all that
> my eyes turn to again and again: you in particular must be familiar with

19

the most recondite mysteries of that phenomenon to such a degree that I consider you one of its most remarkable exemplifications, and observed you time and again with the greatest theoretical interest.[5]

In his later work, Nietzsche turned against both Liszt and Wagner. He came to see Wagner's operas as "theatrical," at the expense of genuine feeling. "With drums and fifes, Wagner marches at the head of all artists in declamation, in display and virtuosity." He came to regard Liszt as an exemplar of a similar kind of virtuosity: "The musician is now becoming an actor, his art is developing ever more and more into a talent for *telling lies*."[6]

VIRTUOSITY AND ELECTRICITY

Wherever questions of virtuosity raise their head, Liszt is in full sight. It is well known that he brought a sense of theater, of entertainment, to the concert hall; and that he brought opera on to the concert stage through innumerable, and magnificent, transcriptions. But this was far from all he did as a performer. Theater need not mean "theatrics," though for Liszt it sometimes did. And anyway, why not? Liszt's playing was electrifying.

"Electricity" was a frequently used term in contemporary accounts of Liszt. The connection between his playing, its reception, and the new phenomenon of electricity is a fascinating subject in itself. The 1830s saw huge advances in the science of electricity and magnetism, including the first electric motors, all inspiring new metaphors of wonder, as in this account of a recital in Britain in 1840:

> The thunder [of Liszt's performance] after muttering at a distance, gathered in strength till it crashed in dreadful peals around our ears commingled with coruscations of the electric fluid, struck out from the highest notes of the instrument, then gradually dying away.[7]

The history of this side of the Liszt phenomenon—Liszt as a charismatic performer, the adulation he received as well as denigration, the hysterical reactions, the jealous sneering, the fear of the tawdry—lies largely outside the scope of this book, but it does have some bearing on my theme of the pianist as actor.

> After he annihilated the Erard Grand Piano in the first piece, he played the Fantasy on a different instrument, broke two bass strings, fetched himself the second walnut Graf from the corner—an inestimably fine instrument—and played his etude, after which he, having once again broken

two strings, said aloud to the public that it—the etude—had not succeeded and he would like to play it again. As he entered he vehemently threw his gloves and handkerchief on the ground in front of the piano. It was the strangest concert of our life.[8]

It is not, however, this aspect of Liszt's theater, recounted by Clara Schumann's father, Friedrich Wieck, that is my concern here. The meaning of the word acting, like the word fiction (and storyteller), contains within it the opposite pole, the paradox that Picasso identified in his celebrated aphorism "art is a lie that makes us realize the truth."[9] My pianist-actor is Picasso's truth teller, not Nietzsche's liar. I urge my students to identify with the music they perform in the same way actors identify with the characters they are playing. An actor taking on the role of Lady Macbeth immerses herself in the character, in the motivation and the psychology of Macbeth's wife and partner in crime, forgetting herself and becoming the character—or opening herself and finding the character within. Cannot a pianist similarly take on the role of a piece of music, of Beethoven's Appassionata, for example, or Liszt's B minor Sonata? The parallel is not direct—it raises the question as to precisely what the "role" might be—but it is far closer than it at first appears.

Early commentaries on Liszt's playing clearly identified this aspect of his art. Theatricality, charisma, electricity were not the only ingredients that Liszt offered his audiences. The god-like virtuoso who thrills by the apparent impossibility of his playing, the facial expressions, the tossing of the hair, the glances to heaven, the breaking of pianos—these were not the only ingredients that caused what Heine called Lisztomania.[10] In addition Liszt, it seems, from contemporary accounts, *acted*—not theatrically but through the music:

> As he played the arias from Don Juan, they [the characters] stepped palpably forward into the scene, the tones became action as though the figures, Zerlina and the others, wanted to emerge out of them.[11]

Liszt's complete grasp of the character and style of the music, his identification with Mozart's meaning, enabled the listener to imagine the palpable presence of the characters. The complexity of this experience is remarkable. It would not have been possible without the listener's prior knowledge of the opera; yet neither would it have been possible without Liszt's characteristic interpretation—it seems that in this respect, from the contemporary memoirs, he was unique. Even allowing for the prejudicial nature of Marie d'Agoult's relationship with him, her recollection of his presence on the concert platform pinpoints this aspect of his art. "How can I describe what I felt at that moment? It was Franz I saw, and yet it was not Franz. It was as though someone were portraying him on the stage with much skill and verisimilitude, but who for all that had nothing in common with him except in physical appearance."[12] Marie relates how Liszt had caught her eye, "by either a strange chance, or by some secret magnetism," at the moment he had started playing. She claims an intimacy with him that she suddenly realizes is not there. The actor has taken over. He is no longer Franz.

It was not only in his transcriptions of operas, and the consequent presence of stories and characters in the listener's mind, that Liszt manifested this phenomenon. He didn't need to rely on operatic characters—he subsumed their role into his own persona on stage. His self-identification with the music, and his electrifying communication of it, had the force of a writer's invention of a character or an actor's projection of a role. Leon Botstein has observed how nineteenth-century music, not only Liszt's, was analogous to the new art of the realist novel.[13] Liszt on stage created dramatic narratives that had an emotional, visceral, and intellectual effect on the listener; and which didn't require the precision of language. "After the first blank astonishment with which he is listened to," a contemporary account relates, "the mind as well as the ear are perpetually on the alert, to enter into the story he means to tell."[14] (Heinrich Heine called Liszt "the modern-day Homer."[15])

The point to be emphasized is that this experience did not require a given story, a "program" (or the presence of operatic characters). The unspecified narrative released from within the music takes place, privately, in the listener's imagination.

"BEHIND A SCREEN"

It is easy to overlook that before the age of recording the only way to hear music was to attend a performance—in the opera house, salon, or stage—and that music was not only heard but *seen*. Schumann had this to say about Liszt's performances:

> First he played with the public as if to try it, then gave it something more profound, until he had enmeshed every member of the audience with his art and did with them as he willed.... Within a few seconds tenderness, boldness, exquisiteness, wildness succeed one another; the instrument glows and flashes under the master's hands. All this has already been described a hundred times, and the Viennese, especially, have tried to catch the eagle in every way—through pursuits, snares, pitchforks, and poems. But he must be heard—and also seen; for if Liszt played behind a screen, a great deal of poetry would be lost.[16]

This is a vivid, firsthand account of the Liszt phenomenon from a highly reputable source. But we need to dwell for a moment on the curious final comment. When I first came across Schumann's critique, it was only that single phrase that was quoted: "If Liszt played behind a screen a great deal of poetry would be lost." I concluded that Schumann was being ironic at Liszt's expense. As a student I knew little of either composer, and what I knew of Liszt was laced with prejudice; Schumann's comment fitted the stereotype of Liszt as a showman. I imagined it meant that without the antics there would have been no Liszt. I assumed Schumann was jealous. In fact he meant his comment in profound homage. Schumann had discerning musical judgment and his critical acumen was acute, yet here he is articulating a concept of live music-making that relies on more than the music itself. He is experiencing music as a quintessentially holistic experience, sound, sight, and presence as one. Had Schumann perhaps got carried away? Was he too in thrall to the power of Liszt on stage? Possibly so, for that is the profound effect of theater. But Schumann had glimpsed, almost in passing, in a remark that was meant to capture for his readers what otherwise couldn't be explained, the extraordinary force and originality of the Lisztian phenomenon—not just a virtuoso, not just a poet of the keyboard (Chopin was already that), but "the emergence of the actor in music." Unlike Nietzsche however, Schumann applauded.

FORM AND FEELING

There are other parallels to be drawn between the actor's craft and the performing musician's, especially parallels with verse speaking, and specifically the blank verse of Shakespeare. In much the same way as a performer obeys the indicated rhythm and structure of a musical motif, so an actor follows the indelible instructions embedded within Shakespeare's line. Blank verse uses unrhymed lines that contain ten syllables divided into five stresses (known as iambic pentameter). What in theory might seem over-formal and restricting, from the mouth of a trained actor sounds effortlessly natural and musical. Shakespeare's blank verse embraces wit and pathos, comedy and tragedy, the nuances of everyday conversation and the sublime insights of poetry. Indeed it is poetry, but a poetry that is able to contain everything.

Peter Hall, the founder of the Royal Shakespeare Company, spent his life revealing to actors the nature of iambic pentameter and its crucial role in conveying the meaning and expression of Shakespeare—he proudly wore the label "the iambic pentameter fundamentalist." Hall insisted that the form of Shakespeare's line, the rhythm and structure of the stresses, is paramount. Within his line structure,

> Shakespeare tells the actor when to go fast and when to go slow; when to come in on cue, and when to accent a particular word or series of words. He tells the actor much else; and he always tells him when to do it (provided the actor knows where to look). But he never tells him why. The motive, the why, remains the creative task of the actor. He has to endorse feelings in himself which support the form that Shakespeare's text has given him.[17]

Once this relationship between form and feeling is understood, the actor is presented with "an almost infinite number of choices . . . and form and feeling interact on each other and become one." The analogy with music is striking. In music, too, form is intimately related to expression. The familiar injunction to "play in time" is not only about playing the rhythm the composer has written (and certainly not about playing in metronomic time), but about discerning the pacing and life of the music. The rhythm as written is our first point of call, as it were. It is the composer/poet telling us what to do, and "when to do it," but we are not told *why*. "The motive, the *why*, remains the creative task" of the pianist/actor.

Without a total sense of the form of Liszt's B minor Sonata, for example, a pianist cannot capture, or control, its expressive power other than in passing moments, in localized, disconnected vignettes. Without the form there is no emotional strength—the expression becomes either hysterical or sentimental, or indeed no expression at all, just empty gesture. It is Liszt's command of the structure of his massive edifice that enables its expressive power. Form works within the localized structures too. Each motif has the formal strength to draw attention to itself, to exist in the moment. Liszt's material is never less than transfixing, moment by moment, but the pianist must also sense, and then demonstrate, how a motif can transform itself, and how it links effortlessly to the material around it like a sequence of DNA.

I suggested in the previous chapter that structural analysis can reveal how this operates, but that something still remains to be found. It is found not only *by* the performer but *within* the performer. It is for the performer, as Peter Hall writes, "to endorse feelings which support the form that [the] text has given." But before we can begin to grapple with what these feelings are, the structure of Liszt's score needs scrupulous attention, just as Shakespeare's iambic pentameter does for the actor. Hall's constant refrain was "first comes the form, second comes the feeling."

As we turn now to the writers with whom Liszt engaged, we will keep Hall's refrain in mind. Inescapably "feeling"—which remains to be defined—will be foregrounded; this is not a book about about "how to play Liszt"; least of all is it about the Lisztian equivalent of iambic pentameter. But it should go without saying that before any interpretation can be arrived at that takes into account the poetry behind the music, the music itself needs to be in place—the music, that is, in terms of its structure and the pianistic skills required to realize this structure.

I am not, however, confident that Hall's hierarchy of first and second is actually necessary. I would rather see our approach to Liszt as moving simultaneously on two fronts, form and feeling together. It also seems logical to me that while tackling Liszt's Petrarch Sonnets at the keyboard we can, at the same time, be reading Petrarch's *Canzoniere*. We don't have to wait. Petrarch's Laura can be envisioned before a note of Liszt's music is heard; as pianist-actors we need to be acquainting ourselves with the story of our play, not only the role we are playing in it. Once we begin, we can be honing our technique with the very material that lies under our fingers and speaks to our ear. A first reading, whether of verse or music, can be aligned with the embedded rhythms and sounds at the very point where those rhythms and sounds start to reveal their emotional identity.

Nietzsche had his own furrow to plough. He saw Wagner and Liszt as less than musicians because of the literary dimensions they so determinedly embraced. One can say of Liszt what Nietzsche said of Wagner: that "he increased the powers of speech of music to an incalculable degree—he is the Victor Hugo of music as language, provided always we allow that under certain circumstances music may be something which is not music, but speech."[18] We can applaud. Nietzsche was actually appalled.

• *3* •

The Music of Desire

Petrarch Sonnets

If music be the food of love, play on,
Give me excess of it, that, surfeiting,
The appetite may sicken, and so die.
That strain again! It had a dying fall;
O, it came o'er my ear like the sweet sound
That breathes upon a bank of violets,
Stealing and giving odor.

—Shakespeare, *Twelfth Night*[1]

In 1835 Liszt and the countess Marie d'Agoult left Paris for Geneva where, avoiding scandal and shielded from the glare of Liszt's celebrity, they planned for her to give birth to their first child. After several return visits to Paris, not least to vanquish the pianist Sigismund Thalberg in the famous contest of March 1837 (verdict: "Thalberg is the first pianist in the world, Liszt the only one"), Liszt and d'Agoult settled in Italy for two years.[2] It was here that Liszt became exposed to Italian renaissance art and poetry—to Dante, Raphael, Michelangelo, and to the great love poetry of Francesco Petrarca. From the songs and piano pieces Liszt subsequently wrote in response to the poet's story of unrequited love, we know that Petrarch held a central place in his creative imagination. This chapter is about the extraordinary creative engagement of two major artists born five hundred years apart.

Music and desire, music and love: such conjunctions have a long history. "If music be the food of love, play on"—indeed musicians have rarely stopped, from the troubadours of early renaissance Europe to the popular music of our own day. Songs of desire and heartache, of the joy of possession and the pain of loss, have dominated the European classical and popular musical traditions. In the literary sphere it was Francesco Petrarca, called variously "the first troubadour" and "the first modern man," who established the foundations of European love poetry.[3]

27

Born in 1304, Petrarch was by any standards an extraordinary figure: poet laureate, fashionable diplomat, devout man of letters, and hugely celebrated in his lifetime for a large body of religious and philosophical writing in Latin. But it was his *Canzoniere*, a collection of 366 poems (including 317 sonnets)—one for every day of the year—in the vernacular Italian, that was to have the most far reaching influence on European literature. Petrarch's "Sonnets" are the principle reason we know of him today. Written over a period of forty years, to his death in 1374, they are addressed to the mysterious and ever unattainable Laura with whom the poet was in love.

For Liszt, in the Romantic milieu of 1830s Paris, Petrarch couldn't be avoided. The huge admiration for his *Canzoniere* (like the rediscovery of Dante's *Divine Comedy*, as we shall see in chapter 9), was a feature of European Romanticism. Petrarch's influence over the centuries since his death had already been immense. To take a few examples: *Twelfth Night* is one of Shakespeare's most profoundly Petrarchian plays; Shakespeare's own sonnets are a homage to Petrarch's (the famous line of Sonnet 130, "My mistress's eyes are nothing like the sun," is a parody of Petrarch's obsessive praise of Laura); Thomas Wyatt, the major poet of Elizabethan England just prior to Shakespeare—granted renewed fame today as a character in Hilary Mantel's trilogy of novels about Cromwell and Henry VIII—wrote some of the finest translations of Petrarch's sonnets in the English language; in eighteenth-century France Rousseau's novel *Julie; ou la nouvelle Héloïse* drew heavily on Petrarch, while Voltaire, in a single, and partial, translation of one of Petrarch's *canzoni* (beginning "Clear, fresh and sweet water") "ushered in a new era of Petrarch translation."[4] The poets and novelists of French Romanticism, many of whom were Liszt's friends—Hugo, Sainte-Beuve, Lamartine, Balzac, de Musset—were constantly alluding to Petrarch, imitating Petrarch, reinventing Petrarch; Lamartine, a major influence on Liszt, even claimed lineage from Laura herself.[5] There is a direct line from Petrarch to Shakespeare and thence forward nearly 250 years to French Romanticism, and to Liszt.

SONGS AND SONNETS

By far the largest number of poems in the *Canzoniere* are sonnets, which is why the whole collection, in the English-speaking world at least, is usually referred to as Petrarch's Sonnets (echoing Shakespeare's). The word *canzoniere* can refer both to songs or to poems—one of the many instances in which language shows that poetry and music have a common root. The question at the center of Petrarch's *Canzoniere* (as in Shakespeare's *Twelfth Night*) might be formulated as "What is love?" At risk of repeating the tiresomely familiar, and often erroneous stories of Liszt's numerous love affairs we cannot help but notice that this question was central to his identity.

The line from the opening of *Twelfth Night* makes a startling claim: music is not just the accompaniment to love, not just the expression of love, but the food which nourishes it. Through his character Count Orsino, Shakespeare is saying that music keeps love alive. The irony contained in that first word "If" has not prevented the famous line entering the lexicon as one to which we all give assent. Do we really notice the suggestion that perhaps music *isn't* the food of love? Do we remember that moments later the love-sick Count Orsino, who has languidly proclaimed these words, petulantly denounces them: "Enough! No more. Tis not as sweet now as it was before"? There is a Petrarchian irony at work here. In the *Canzoniere* Petrarch bewails his inability to write fine poetry at the very point when inspired to write poetry at its finest. So too Orsino expresses his self pity, in imitation of Petrarch, in the sweetest, loveliest sounding verse—he reaches for the music of rhyming words at the very point of disowning music:

> *Enough, no more!*
> *'Tis not so sweet as it was before.*
> *O spirit of love, how quick and fresh art thou,*
> *That, notwithstanding thy capacity,*
> *Receiveth as the sea.*

We will return to the music of rhyming words later in this chapter.

I intend to look at Liszt's Petrarch Sonnets as solo piano music, but the question is complicated by the fact that he first wrote the pieces as songs: the "Tre Sonneti di Petrarca" are transcriptions. But are they? Certainly nearly every phrase has a line of poetry associated with it—it only takes a few minutes to ascertain from the original vocal score what specific moments in the piano transcription "mean." But this is not quite what the pianist does or is expected to do. By the time Liszt finalized his "Tre Sonetti di Petrarca," the sonnets had become epigraphs, the music had loosened its moorings from the songs. So what does the pianist do with Petrarch's Sonnets? That is the question I will endeavor to answer.

My own fascination for the poems and the music began long ago when as a student I came across Sacheverell Sitwell's biography of Liszt. Published in 1934 it is out of date today, based on much discredited information and full of errors. This does not mean that Sitwell is without judgment, and his pioneering study is still worth reading. He did much to redress, for British audiences of the 1930s, the popular image of Liszt as a composer of extravagant Romanticism and empty virtuosity. His ringing endorsement of Liszt's Petrarch Sonnets remains entirely valid today:

They form the most perfect examples of Liszt's art. His genius was of the sort which has to act upon suggestion, so that, in this instance, the circumstances were most favorable to its fruition. In their early version, they form an astonishing transformation into musical form of the atmosphere, the sentiments, the shape, even, of Petrarch's sonnets; while the transference of these songs into pieces for piano solo, an art of which Liszt was the supreme master, has resulted in an extraordinary fusion, for they have their own perfection as piano pieces . . . typical of Liszt at his best . . . and have the sunburnt and fiery romance of the rhymed words from which they took their origin.[6]

"Sunburnt and fiery romance" might be a little too redolent of an Englishman's rose-tinted view of renaissance Italy. The Petrarchians of Liszt's milieu would have found it perfectly appropriate. But in every other respect Sitwell was spot on. Even his focus on "rhymed words" draws attention to what is so easily missed in translation: the rhyming of Petrarch's Italian is central and unmissable, all part of the incantatory music of meaning. For me, as an impressionable student, Sitwell's seductive words spoke of Liszt's first vital experiences of Italian art, poetry, and sunlight. And I discovered Petrarch's *Canzoniere.*

This was not Petrarch's title, and nor was the other title by which his collection has come to be known: *Rime sparse*—Scattered Rhymes. In the first line of Sonnet 1, Petrarch exhorts his readers, his listeners, to hear his "scattered rhymes" of love, and to pardon him and pity him. Petrarch simply referred to his poems as *Rerum vulgarium fragmenta*, "fragments of things in common speech." He worked on them for over forty years, distributing them among his friends (as Shakespeare was to do over two hundred years later with his own sonnets) from the early 1330s onward, completing the definitive version just before his death in 1374. His constant revision belies his remark a few years before he died that his poems were "trifles" that he hoped would not outlive him.[7] Indeed one of the central themes of the *Canzoniere* is the fame that the poet foresees his muse will bring.

ART AND FAME

It is easy to see the attraction for Liszt, who knew all about fame and all about muses. For Liszt, in the vanguard of the new Romantic consciousness, seeing Petrarch as a kind of Romantic Hero would have been irresistible—the poet/artist struggling with opposing forces of desire and virtue, ambition and humility, the worldly and the divine. We might even speculate that Liszt knew Petrarch's real-life story, his profligate youth, his conversion, his taking of minor orders in the church. There is ample evidence for his feeling of kinship with Petrarch.

It is wholly appropriate that Liszt chose "Benedetto sia 'l giorno"—Blessed Be the Day—as one of his three settings, for the sonnet is central to Petrarch's idea. Here we find the poet not only praising the day, the month, the year, and the season when first he "was struck by the two lovely eyes that have bound me"; but also extolling the many words he has uttered "calling her name," and all the pages of poetry he has written that will bring her fame—by which he clearly means fame for himself. The name Laura becomes the center of a complex web of symbolism and word play that runs through the poems, not least the association of Laura with laurel, a symbol of renown. A laurel crown was the greatest honor awarded to poet "laureates," of whom Petrarch was one. Poetry is the route to a kind of immortality.

The leaves of the laurel tree figure among the many lavish illustrations in the first edition of *Années de pèlerinage—Italie*. Each of the Petrarch pieces is preceded by a colored etching of a twining laurel branch (laurel for Petrarch would have been the highly fragrant Mediterranean bay tree), with the punning words *Ed il suo lauro cresceva col suo amor per Laura* engraved on the stem and leaves: "And his fame [laurel] grew with his love for Laura."[8] To Liszt's annoyance the texts of the sonnets were not included in the first printing, but his wish prevailed in later reprints.

Figure 3.1.   Illustration for Liszt's Petrarch Sonnets, from an edition of 1858, showing *Ed il suo lauro cresceva col suo amor per Laura* engraved on the laurel stem and leaves.
(Public Domain).

Our knowledge of Liszt's exultant responses to Italy at the end of the 1830s, above all to its art and literature, comes principally from his open letters in the *Gazette musicale*.[9] We see taking shape his passionate convictions about the nature of art and the artist's relation to the world, and we witness the deeply serious engagement of a young, alert, and open mind with problems of meaning. The letters range from the naive to the profound, from a traveler's innocent delight in new sights and sounds, to quasi-philosophical observations on art and culture. Liszt's imaginative world in these formative years was shaped by the writers and thinkers he met in Paris, and through the ideals and aspirations delineated in the literature he was reading. As Heine had written (also in the *Gazette musicale*), not entirely with a straight face, Liszt had "an indefatigable thirst for divinity and enlightenment."[10] As Liszt gradually came to discover Petrarch, he would have responded to the poet's need, which was very much his own, to reconcile spiritual fulfilment with worldly desire. In the *Canzoniere* the "thirst for divinity and enlightenment" is experienced in both spiritual and worldly terms: the artist aspires to an immortality conferred by the works he leaves to posterity. Woven into the fabric of Petrarch's self-analysis is a forensic examination not only of what it means to love—"understanding love through experience" as the poet says in Sonnet 1—but of what it means to live. For Liszt this would have meant what it means to live as an artist.

The concept of the "artist" as we understand it, and as Liszt's Romantic generation understood it, was not Petrarch's. But it is fair to say that the part of Petrarch's psychology recognized today as "modern" was the part that looked toward our own concepts of artistic imagination and self-awareness. In Petrarch's meticulous making of his story, and the pride with which he pursues it, we recognize our own conception of an artist at work; and we recognize a work of art. Dante, a generation before Petrarch, had led the way in his *Divine Comedy*, his story of a human soul seeking knowledge and spiritual salvation, recounted in the triptych "Inferno," "Purgatorio," and "Paradiso." But the crucial difference in Petrarch's case is not only the context he chooses for his own story—life on earth rather than the "life" of heaven and hell—but its subject, a love story that expresses desire in human terms, present life not afterlife. Although the spiritual dimension for Petrarch remains central to his world view—as it did for Liszt—in the *Canzoniere* he manages to speak with a recognizably modern, humanist voice.

For Petrarch's readers it was for his esteemed works in Latin that he was awarded the laurel crown of Poet and not the vernacular poems that were to secure his place in the canon of European literature. And yet it is in these, in the poems of the *Canzoniere*, that his ambition as an artist—in the sense we now understand it—reveals itself through his unrelenting self-scrutiny

and self-absorption. One is aware throughout the whole long sequence that despite the poet's self-pity (later parodied by Shakespeare)—despite the way he berates himself for his backsliding and for allowing his love for Laura to prevent him from living—the experience is wholly creative, inspiring, and self-transforming. Above all it enables him to be a poet. Liszt had found a soulmate. He wrote in one of his open letters for the *Gazette musicale* in 1838,

> The acclaim they lavished on me [in Milan] was enough to satisfy a far more exacting ego than my own. I will not deny there is an indescribably powerful enchantment, a proud yet loving delight, in exercising a faculty that draws the thoughts and hearts of others to us. . . . [The artist] feels like the king of all minds; he senses an indescribably small particle of creative force inside him because he has created emotions, feelings and ideas with his sounds. It is a dream that ennobles his existence.[11]

Yet, like Petrarch, he could also be appalled at his own craving for applause. The year before, in one of his open letters to the *Gazette* addressed to George Sand, he defines this as a response to a kind of loneliness. "Whatever he does, wherever he goes [the artist] always feels himself an exile. . . . What then must he do to escape this vague sadness, and undefined regrets?" He answers his own question with a series of images that have distinct echoes of Petrarch:

> He must sing and move on, pass through the crowd, scattering his works to it with without caring where they land, without listening to the glamor with which people stifle them, and without paying attention to the contemptible laurels with which they crown them. What a sad and great destiny it is to be an artist.[12]

And there is an echo too in a private journal—for his and Marie's eyes only—from 1839, in which his frustrations with his current mode of living, his increasingly fraught relationship with Marie, his sense of thwarted destiny, spill out in the darkest terms:

> There is thunder in the air, my nerves are irritable, horribly irritable. . . . Two opposing forces are fighting within me; one thrusts me towards the immensity of space, higher, ever higher, beyond all suns, up to the heavens; the other pulls me down towards the lowest, the darkest regions of calm, of death, of nothing . . . equally miserable in my strength and my weakness.[13]

The whole passage could be taken for a loose prose translation of one of Petrarch's most dramatic exemplars of "opposing forces," the sonnet "Pace non trovo," which became Liszt's Sonnet 104:

I find no peace, and I am not at war,
I fear and hope, and burn and I am ice;
I fly above the heavens, and lie on earth
and I grasp nothing and embrace the world.[14]

Liszt's diary entry at this point also has echoes of his reading of Dante's *Divine Comedy*. It seems that he articulated moments of emotional extremity by reaching for tropes from both poets. He writes, in the vein of Dante's "Hell," of "images of desolation, of deep disenchantment which hover over my entire destiny" and then quotes a line, in Italian, from the opening canto: "I am like Dante's she-wolf: *Che di tutte brame ... Sembiava carca nella sua magrezza.*" The wolf is thin, hungry, and ravenous. (Allen Mandelbaum's translates the lines as "She seemed to carry every craving in her leanness."[15]) The animal is one of three that assail Dante at the opening of "Inferno" as he struggles his way through a dark wood toward what he discovers to be the gate of hell. Whether Liszt knew or not that the wolf was a symbol of avarice, his intention was to express his own desolate sense of under nourishment, the futility he felt at this point in a life with Marie that was thwarting his artistic fulfillment.

Six years earlier, the young Liszt had quoted an Italian line from Petrarch in a letter to Marie d'Agoult, just after they had met. A single line does not mean that he would have fully read and understood Petrarch's archaic Italian from five hundred years in the past—it would have been as difficult as the medieval English of Chaucer is for us today. Liszt was only just setting out on his literary education. It would, however, have been characteristic of him to want to grapple with the Italian, which he did eventually. Initially he would have relied on French translations. In a letter from early 1838, in which he makes fun of his easy life in Italy, he writes of breaking out from "two months of work and solitude ... going to balls, and paying umpteen visits to La Scala; ... further, I go riding, and am even learning a little Italian, without giving too much thought to it."

HUGO'S PETRARCH

Liszt would have read the *Canzoniere*, as would his contemporaries, as the expression of a passionate erotic love, albeit one hedged around with ideals of religious purity and selfless devotion. But the immediate spur for the music he began to write seems likely to have been a contemporary poem by Victor Hugo, *Oh! quand je dors* (published in 1840 in his collection *Les rayons et les ombres*). Liszt set the poem as a song in 1842 and the first sketches of the

Petrarch music come from the following year.[16] Hugo's take on the love story is overtly sexual:

> *Oh! quand je dors, viens auprès de ma couche,*
> *Comme à Pétrarque apparaissait Laura,*
> *Et qu'en passant ton haleine me touche . . .*
> *Soudain ma bouche*
> *S'entr'ouvrira!*

> Ah, while I sleep, come close to where I lie,
> As Laura once appeared to Petrarch,
> And let your breath in passing touch me . . .
> At once my lips
> Will part!

Laura did not actually appear to Petrarch in this way—the *Canzoniere* barely mentions any meetings with Laura. Hugo is weaving a fantasy from the last line of the first sonnet: "worldly joy is a quick passing dream." Eroticism is only an implication in Petrarch, barely a possibility, though it is never fully denied. Laura represents for the lover, whose advances she never returns, a spiritual aspiration, an unattainable vision of perfect femininity. But Laura is drawn in such a way as to provoke infinite conjecture. Although the fact of physical love is evaded, its absence is clearly responsible for the narrator's ever-changing emotional states—bitter, pained, hysterical, resigned, accusatory. The name Laura, the syllables of which the poet continually interweaves and hides within other words in the text, becomes a metaphor of a desire that he cannot name.[17] Victor Hugo most certainly names it. Such was the interpretation of the *Canzoniere* that prevailed among the French Romantics.

By 1846 Liszt had grappled enough with the language to be able to complete his vocal settings, in Italian, of three of the sonnets. In a letter to Marie d'Agoult from 1846 (despite their estrangement they still communed by letter), he wrote,

> Among my next publications, if you have the time to look at them (after dinner) are three song settings of Petrarch's sonnets [he names them], also very freely transcribed for piano in the guise of nocturnes. I consider them to be especially successful and the most fully achieved in form than anything else I've published.[18]

"After dinner" is a nice touch—it arises from a train of thought that leads to the final word of his sentence, "nocturnes," as well as a gracious concern for not giving her too much trouble. But the most interesting part of this comment is the phrase "very freely transcribed." Already Liszt was sensing that the piano version was taking on a life of its own. Ten years later, in *Années de pèlerinage*, this was fully achieved. And by then they were hardly the "nocturnes" that Liszt had first thought them to be.

Liszt returned to the *Canzoniere* many times, though his compositions remained fixated on the three sonnets he had first chosen. (Rena Mueller tells us that "he penned no fewer than nine complete versions of the *Benedetto sia 'l giorno* melody alone over some fifty years."[19]) He published his final setting of the songs only a few years before he died—compositions which owe nothing to the music first conceived in the 1840s. By this time his knowledge and understanding of the poems had broadened considerably. It seems likely that in the 1840s, like many of his contemporaries, he only concerned himself with the first part of the *Canzoniere*, which was often published separately and labeled "During the Life of Laura." Liszt's three sonnets all come from Part 1. The second part of the *Canzoniere*, "After the Death of Laura," focuses on the poet coming to terms with bereavement and the meaning of mortality. Although for his later settings Liszt uses the same three sonnets, the music is bleaker, attenuated, the torrid passion has been severely pruned. He had experienced the death of his two eldest children, Daniel in 1859 at the age of twenty, and Blandine in 1862, a few months before her twenty-seventh birthday. Walker deals with these events in detail and his account is harrowing.[20] One of Liszt's greatest piano compositions comes in the months after Blandine's death, the variations on the first movement of Bach's cantata "Weinen, Klagen, Sorgen, Zargen"—"Weeping, Wailing, Mourning, Trembling." There is no finer example in Liszt's output of words (of grief) becoming music.

PERFORMING LISZT'S PETRARCH SONNETS

Why does it matter how Liszt came upon Petrarch, at what point he read him, how well he grasped the Italian? In what way do all the issues we have discussed so far in this chapter affect the way we understand the music, how we play it and communicate it? Once started on this path of questioning and discovery we come to realize that the finished canvas—the interpretation and understanding we arrive at—can only be an assemblage of details, some central to our understanding, not all of them of the same degree of relevance, but every one of them enabling the picture's overall strength of perspective, color, and space. This returns us to the nature of interpretation with which we began in chapter 1, the hermeneutic circle and joined-up experience. Each of Liszt's sonnets is part of a triptych, a single work in three parts that takes its place in the larger context of *Années de pèlerinage*; the second book of which was born from Liszt's engagement with Italian art, poetry, and music. *Années de pèleri-nage* was also born from the context of his life within the European Romantic movement. We know there is no simple answer to the question of why context matters—no easy assessment of the effect our inquiry has on the music we will perform—but we are permitted to rely on an instinct, strengthened as the process proceeds, telling us that the part relates to the whole, Petrarch relates to Liszt, poetry to music, art to life.

Bringing the focus closer to the music itself, we can now ask what it is the pianist does with the poems that Liszt was at pains to place at the head of his compositions. Clearly he intended the performer to begin with the son-nets themselves, with Petrarch's story of unrequited love. There is no doubt that Liszt wished the poems to be close at hand, for the performer to read them, know them, to sense their meaning in the music.

Over the centuries different publications of Petrarch's *Canzoniere* have had no standard numbering system. In Liszt's early songs and their transcrip-tions, the sonnets are not numbered. Later he would have consulted French and Italian editions of the poems, and he gave them the numbering he found there—but even in the nineteenth century, the poems did not have the num-bers by which they are known today. The confusion has arisen because some editions treated the sonnets separately from the other verse forms. Today the poems that make up the *Canzoniere* are numbered in the chronological order of their original publication—interspersed throughout the 360 poems are 317 *sonetti*, 29 *canzoni*, 9 *sestine*, 7 *ballate*, and 4 *madrigali*. Liszt's Sonnet 47 is now found as *Canzoniere* 61; Sonnet 104 is *Canzoniere* 134; and Sonnet 123 is *Canzoniere* 156.

In Liszt's original publications of 1846, "Benedetto sia 'l giorno" (what became Liszt's opening Sonnet 47 in the *Années de pèlerinage*) came second in both the song and solo-piano versions. "Pace non trovo," Liszt's Sonnet 104, was placed first. Liszt reversed this ordering for the *Années de pèlerinage*. It is a small but vital change of emphasis, at once musically and narratively stronger. It also points to Liszt's deepening understanding of Petrarch. To plunge in at the opening of the triptych with the high passion of "Pace non trovo" is to make a fine gesture, but it places too great an emphasis on this aspect of the *Canzoniere* at the expense of more nuanced meanings. Placed second the hysteria becomes recognized as just one element of the poet's psychological state, enabling the narrative moment to take its due place within the poet's journey of discovery. And the reordering also mirrors Petrarch's structure across the first part of the *Canzoniere*: from the moment when he first sees Laura (Sonnet 47—"the day, the month, the year, the season"), to his unassuaged desire (Sonnet 104—"I am in this state, Lady, on account of you"), to resigned and wondering acceptance of the unattainable (Sonnet 123—"Whatever I look upon seems a dream"). Liszt's chosen sonnets give in microcosm the narrative structure of the whole of Part 1, "The Lady Laura in Life," and the psychological journey of the protagonist. The healing process of time is central to Petrarch's conception.

All three pieces suggest a narrator and a tale, an introductory preparation, a settling down, an unfolding story. We don't need to know these were originally songs in order to imagine we are singers as well as story tellers. The introduction to Sonnet 47 is a musical equivalent of the curtain rising in the theater—our attention is at once caught and we watch as the singer/narrator takes the stage. Liszt's antennae are alive to the context of Petrarch's "Songbook" and the ancient tradition of song-making and storytelling: the accompaniment figure that begins at bar 12 suggests a lute, perhaps a prelude to a troubadour's song (figure 3.2). A musical narrative now unfolds that expresses the complexity of feeling not only of this particular sonnet but of the sonnets as a whole. Liszt's Sonetto 47 is at once innocent, loving, tender, wistful, and deeply troubled. It is a translation of feeling—the meaning of words, Petrarch's poem—into music.

Figure 3.2.   Petrarch Sonnet 47, mm. 1–19.
Editio Musica, 1974.

The pianist needs to imagine a wide theatrical context, both metaphorically and physically. Liszt's music is literally for a space much larger than the salon (Chopin's milieu), requiring a more pronounced projection. Liszt's inauguration of the solo piano recital—freeing the pianist from accompanying performers and collaborators—meant in effect he took upon himself the roles he had usurped. In addition, especially in his function as transcriber and performer of operatic and symphonic scores, Liszt (as pianist-actor—see chapter 2) became the embodiment of the orchestra, singer and conductor.

SONNET 47

In Sonnet 47 the juxtaposition of a grand orchestral introduction (*Preludio, con moto*) and the intimacy of a lute-accompanied song (*intimo sentimento*) creates a scene in which the curtain of a nineteenth-century theater rises on a fourteenth-century narrative of unrequited love. The transition from the one to the other (bars 1–15) is masterly, as is the unification of the musical ingredients. In figure 3.2 we can notice the way the recitative at bar 6 is born from the upper line of the opening four chords; and how the restless separation of the parts between the hands in bars 1–5 is carried over into the song's lute-like accompaniment. Yet by this point, just before the singer/narrator begins, the theatrical dynamic has changed in every respect, the excitement of instability has given way to the solace of security (the delayed modulation into the home key is exquisite), and the listener is prevailed upon to attend. We are expectant, ready to enter into the play.

The rest of the story unfolds naturally from here, partly expected, partly unforeseen. The poet blesses the sheer existence of Laura. Time has long passed since that moment he first saw her, and in his memory he is so in thrall to the delight of her that he can even accommodate the pain of rejection. Pain is ameliorated by the thrill of writing about her. By this stage of the sequence—it is not until Petrarch's poem 61 (Liszt's Sonnet 47) that Petrarch describes this first meeting, from afar—we have learned how the poet's delight repeatedly gives way to despair. In "Benedetto sia 'l giorno," this delight, unerringly captured by Liszt, is in the foreground.

One of the themes of Petrarch's *Canzoniere* is the nature of time as it impinges on the lover's psychological state—"the incomprehensible changeability of the self in love," writes the Petrarch scholar Robert Durling, "which is so violent as to call its very identity into question."[21] At the simplest level, Liszt captures changeability in the three iterations of his melody, which act like the verses of a song but which also present the protagonist's changing state through changes of key and inflections of harmony. The violence of this change, to be experienced in full in the following Sonnet 104, is not present in Sonnet 47. But one hint of what is to come is conveyed by the almost constant separation of the melodic line and the accompaniment—what at first seems a lilt we start to recognize as unease, like the tremor in a heartbeat, which hovers on the edge of the tender delight of the poet's prevailing mood. Change is also presaged in the cadenza at bar 59, which conveys a sense of bittersweet pain culminating in the *dolente* of bars 60–61 (figure 3.3). Here it is as if the poet is staring at his own grief.

Figure 3.3.   Petrarch Sonnet 47, mm. 60–63.
Editio Musica, 1974.

I suggested earlier that our interpretation of these pieces does not rely on following the word setting line by line, that by the time Liszt found the final form of his "Tre Sonetti," he had moved beyond his word setting. Yet there are several moments, as we would expect, where coordination of music and text remain. Even without text it is not at all difficult, given the theme of the story, to imagine the descending figurations of the cadenza as tears of longing. It is at this point in the song that Liszt sets the words "The sighs and the tears and the desire." What I suggested as the moment where the poet stares at his grief is the actual moment where Liszt placed the word *desire*. The pain of unrequited love is concentrated here, and in the silence that precedes the realization (bar 60). The repeated G sharp that follows extends the thought, hovers on it, and enacts—dramatizes—the continuing process of change. The music now shifts into E major and the poet returns to his tender song of meditation, the same but different.

SONNET 104

Sonnet 104 repeats the idea of introduction, recitative and song, although this time, when the accompaniment begins at bar 21 (*cantabile con passione*), the music is redolent of a nineteenth-century nocturne, just as Liszt originally stated to Marie d'Agoult. The recitative on the opening page also acts as one of the verses of the song—the melody and harmony are fully worked out, to be repeated when the nocturne gets underway, but here with fragmented *fermatas*, *ritenutos*, and interjecting arpeggiated chords. There is a suggestion of a harpsichord and even a hint of strummed guitars—this connects back to the minstrel's lutes of Sonnet 47, and forward to the accompanying arpeggiated chords of Sonnet 123. Liszt's art employs a variety of allusions, which it is the pianist's task to notice and to unify across the whole triptych. Sonnet 104 is the most operatic, not only stylistically but also in the sense that it is the most fulsome, the largest, the most richly orchestrated.

Figure 3.4.   Petrarch Sonnet 104, mm. 5–20.
Editio Musica, 1974.

Liszt makes no attempt to scale back his translation to suit the attenuated, concentrated dimensions of a fourteenth-century sonnet. This is Lisztian piano writing at its peak of projection. What he takes from the sonnet is precisely its passionate rhetoric, but it is translated into what we recognize as the expressive style of nineteenth-century Romanticism. It is challenging for the pianist, who has to find an extravagance that is believable, a rhetoric that is not overblown, a massive scale of sound that without strain embraces the scale of the passion expressed.

Despite Liszt's initial description of the first piano versions of his Petrarch Sonnets as nocturnes, I have never thought of Sonnet 104 as a nocturne in the manner of Chopin, even though the second verse might look like that on the page. To play it this way weakens and sentimentalizes Liszt's final purpose. In expressly indicating *forte* for the melody and *piano* for the arpeggiated accompaniment, markings often overlooked, he is asking for a dramatic and emotional tension that is entirely apposite to the explicit oppositions of the poem—peace and war, fear and hope, burning and freezing. Every line of the sonnet sets up these oppositions, sometimes twice in the line. In the last line it is Laura and the poet himself—"you and I," he says—who are presented in opposition: "Because of you, lady, I am this way."

The first half of Liszt's melodic line begins with a four-times repeated note culminating in a strong accent; nothing could be less melodic, less shaped (bars 7–8, figure 3.4). If it is vocal it is more like a cry, or shout, the sound of speech rather than song. Later this is reinforced *fortissimo*. The opposing fragment, which completes the phrase, is highly contoured, angular, leaping up an octave and falling down an augmented fifth (declaimed speech morphs into the declamation of opera, bars 9–10). We sense a faltering at the end of each fragment, as the melodic line falls in pitch, as if the will is failing (*ritenuto*—held back). We might also adduce a different form of theater by drawing an analogy between these melodic lines and the shapes of ballet (we can appeal to Rudolf Nureyev again as we did in chapter 1). The rising and falling gestures of arms, legs, and bodies when we witness ballet stir in us memories of love and grief, joy and pain—meanings that accompany the aesthetic pleasure we find in the proportions of lines and curves, or in the choreographer's supreme art of manipulating movement in space. Certainly Liszt's melody pleases by its shape, his harmony arrests us by its delineation of structure, but we also respond emotionally by association, as we do when watching ballet. Spontaneously we draw analogies, almost unnoticed, almost subconsciously.

SONNET 123

"I'vidi in terra," the sonnet Liszt sets for his Sonnet 123, is one of the most beautiful of the many that are beautiful. It expresses the poet's vision of Laura separated from him, and us, by a distance of both time and space; her death is prefigured. The sonnet encapsulates the pervasive theme in the *Canzoniere* of recollection, the poet's meditation on what is past and his gradual acceptance of the unattainable. Laura is identified as a spiritual entity, inevitably so because she can now only exist for the poet in his mind. Memory is identified with spirit. He finds solace in this identification, he accepts his pain through visualizing Laura as a source of wonder, removed from him but ever present. Petrarch and Liszt give spirituality a palpable presence, which I translate as follows:

I saw upon the earth the grace of an angel
I saw heavenly beauties so unmatched in this world
that to recall them now is both joy and pain
a memory shrouded in dreams, shadows and mist.

And I saw her weeping, and I saw tears falling
from eyes that have outshone the envious sun,
and I heard words mingled with sighs such as
would move mountains and stay the motion of streams.

Love and sadness, pious wisdom and valour
blended there into a sweeter harmony
than was ever heard on this earth.

And so intent was Heaven to hear these sounds
that not a leaf lifted on the boughs
As her sweet music drifted upon the air.

Figure 3.5.   Petrarch Sonnet 123, mm. 1–14.
Editio Musica, 1974.

Liszt responds to these words with tone painting that foresees musical impressionism. It is not only that we hear "her sweet music drifting on the air" but that we seem to sense the air itself, "dreams, shadows and mist" (which we can compare to the celebrated *enveloppe* of light in impressionist painting). Petrarch's actual word is *fumi*, "smoke," but in English this sounds too harsh for the fragrance and sweetness he wants to evoke. All the ingredients of piano sound come together to achieve this at the opening (figure 3.5): the disembodied harmony, hovering unresolved for fourteen bars, resonating in the pedal and articulated by means of a rocking triplet accompaniment. And space is evoked by the bell-like F (*dolcissimo*), creating both aural and spatial perspective. Ravel and Debussy learned from this aspect of Liszt's piano writing. The rhythm of this motif, on the offbeat, holds the musical narrative in suspense—the masterly effect is of a held breath, a transfixion of wonder: "I saw upon the earth the grace of an angel." It is this image that pervades the whole poem, present in every subsequent image in variation—the poet saw Laura and holds the memory forever in his mind in varying forms, her "heavenly beauties," her weeping, her eyes. At exactly the halfway point the memory shifts from the sight of her to the sound of her voice, and the vision becomes almost pantheistic: the effect of the sound of Laura's words and sighs reverses the course of nature so that mountains move and streams stand still. In the final lines the evocation of Heaven anchors the vision in Christian theology, but even now the poet suggests that the heavens (without a capital H) are as equally transfixed as the earth.

RHYME AND TRANSLATION

It is fascinating to hear Petrarch's poetry read aloud in the original Italian. It becomes immediately apparent that Liszt's music was not only a response to the meaning of the poems, but also to the sound of the language, its characteristic inflections, its musicality, and the manner in which Petrarch creates rhymes. The sound of rhyme in Petrarch's Italian is a sensuous experience. Sonnet 61 (Liszt's 47) begins,

> *Benedetto sia 'l giorno, e 'l mese, e l'anno,*
> *e la stagione, e 'l tempo, e l' ora, e l' punto,*
> *e 'l bel paese, e l' loco, ov'io fui giunto*
> *da duo begli occhi, che legato m'hanno*

> Oh blessed be the day, the month, the year,
> the season and the time, the hour, the instant,
> the gracious countryside, the place where I
> was struck by those two lovely eyes that bound me

And for the sake of the rhyme alone, which we can see on the page and hear in our ear irrespective of whether we understand Italian, I will quote the second quatrain too.

> *et benedetto il primo dolce affanno*
> *ch' i' ebbi ad esser con Amor congiunto,*
> *et l'arco e le saette ond i' fui punto,*
> *et le piaghe che 'nfin al cor mi vanno*

> and blessed be the first sweet agony
> I felt when I found myself bound to Love,
> the bow and all the arrows that have pierced me,
> the wounds that reach the bottom of my heart[22]

In the Italian we can see and hear at once the rhyme scheme across these two quatrains—incantatory, melifluous, musical—and how the rhyming of the second quatrain interlocks with the first. Throughout his triptych Liszt alludes to this rhyming in the shaping of his melodic phrases. We can hear how this is achieved in bars 11–19 of figure 3.2 above—every two-bar fragment ending with the same stress on the downbeat followed by either a falling minor 3rd or major 2nd. This is a feature of the melodic line throughout.

With the two languages side by side, it becomes obvious that the sound of the original cannot be carried across into English. Mark Musa's sensitive translation wisely doesn't attempt rhyme. Italian rhymes far more easily than English (there are many more rhyming words); attempts to capture the sound of Petrarch's rhyme tip easily into banality and bathos. (Thomas Wyatt in the sixteenth century succeeded, but he was a great poet and he changed the rhyme scheme to suit the language of Elizabethan England—his translation of Liszt's Sonnet 104 is reproduced in the appendix.) All that can be done is to make the meaning clear with a certain elegance and an ear for sound and cadence, but inevitably much is lost. Petrarch's Italian is the essential vessel for the fulness of this experience.

I have suggested that Liszt's music is itself a mode of translating Petrarch, but how close is it to Petrarch's intention? Translation is itself a change of form, a metamorphosis, and it will have varying degrees of contact with the original. We can say that the great translations of Wyatt transformed Petrarch's Italy into Elizabeth I's England. Wyatt created a new poem by Wyatt rather than a faithful reproduction of Petrarch. Liszt himself was a master of such transformations in his operatic transcriptions and paraphrases, sometimes using the original to create a new Lisztian composition, suited to his titanic keyboard virtuosity. At other times, in the case of his transcriptions of Beethoven's symphonies, or Berlioz's *Symphonie fantastique*, he would endeavor to reproduce the original in as faithful a manner as possible. But it remained nevertheless a new entity, the piano replacing the orchestra. We might see the sounds and rhymes of words as the equivalent of the sounds and textures of orchestral instruments. We can appreciate how much is lost in translation.

Mendelssohn thought music more precise than words—as we have seen in the famous letter quoted at the front of this book. Charles Rosen mused on this phenomenon in one of his last books, *Music and Sentiment*:

> The communication of information is one of the most important of the many different functions of language, but not of music (you cannot, for example, by purely musical means, ask your listeners to meet you tomorrow at Grand Central Station at 4 o'clock). However language must seek out poetic methods even to approach at a distance the subtlety and emotional resonance of music.[23]

As one who has spent most of my life manipulating words and fascinated by poetry, I cannot agree with Rosen about the nature of poetic language. But when wearing my musician's hat, I am not so sure. Debussy, even though an ardent admirer of poetry, said all the same that "music remains for all time the finest means of expression we have"[24]—he could only have been thinking of what Rosen calls its "emotional resonance." And if we accept that Liszt's music is one way of translating Petrarch then certainly an argument can be made for its greater emotional resonance, in as much as Liszt creates a Petrarch for the nineteenth century (as Hugo had). Whether this is faithful to Petrarch's intentions is another matter. Liszt's translation creates a profoundly different entity.

Our acquaintance with Petrarch's *Canzoniere* is an acquaintance with a story, just as it was for Liszt. It is the story that informs what we feel and what we do when we perform the music—in addition, of course, to everything else we do as pianists when performing. With his quotations at the outset of each, Liszt draws our attention to the story. "When we hear the music of one of the great narrative musicians," the American poet Wallace Stevens wrote, "we identify it with the story and it becomes the story and the speed with which we are following it. When it is over, we are aware that we have had an experience very much like the story just as if we had participated in what took place. It is exactly as if we have had listened with complete sympathy to an emotional recital. The music was a communication of emotion. It would not have been different if it had been the music of poetry."[25]

Stevens suggests that our responses to music are governed by an instinct for narrative time, "not by any sense"—by which he means not by the kind of sense we get from stories expressed in words. His detailed description of the process of listening captures the excitement of the narrative taking place, the changing dramatic pace and rhythm, and the imaginary world we inhabit emotionally inside our heads as we give ourselves to the experience (in an ideal world exactly the experience we desire in the concert hall and the theater). It is "just as if we had participated in what took place." Stevens then turns this around and makes the same plea for poetry: "It would not have been different if it had been the music of poetry." For Stevens, poetry works in a similar way to music—or at least that is one way it works—in that it can by-pass semantic sense and communicate meaning through sound, rhythm, and time. T. S. Eliot said similarly, and more famously, "Poetry can communicate before it is understood."[26] Like all of us, Stevens is a little vague on what this experience actually is, because it is beyond language, it makes sense beyond the sense of words. Which is why music is so difficult to talk about (and why many prefer not to try).

Stevens the poet helps us understand the process by which Liszt the composer translates Petrarch. Liszt undertakes to create a musical equivalent of unrequited love, initially by setting Petrarch's words to music but then by realizing that the music itself can loosen its mooring from the words and become a separate mode of expression, an equivalent, an analogy—a translation. The experience of music for Stevens "would not have been different if it had been the music of poetry." Poet and composer both hear and understand meaning beyond the "sense" of language. Their greatness lies in their ability to make art in their own medium from this realization: Liszt approaches poetry, Stevens approaches music.

And so does Shakespeare. For Count Orsino, music came to his ear "like the sweet sound that breathes upon a bank of violets, stealing and giving odor." The poetry of Shakespeare and Petrarch (and Stevens) approaches music not only through the sounds and rhythms of words. Metaphorical language has the ability to set off a chain of responses that take us beyond the bounds of logical meaning. In the opening lines of *Twelfth Night*, sound and metaphor coalesce to produce an extraordinary subtlety and emotional resonance (that Rosen believes to be only the preserve of music). What is "the sweet sound" that breathes on the violets, and to which music is compared? It is not identified. It can only be the sound of the poetry, the five sibilant *S*s that echo the unnamed breath of wind that both takes and brings the violet's perfume. The words "stealing and giving" not only state an action but encapsulate it in the language itself: we experience a swinging motion and the enactment of kissing, we sense the odor of the violets, we identify with Orsino's languorous delight. And all in a single line describing the sound of music.

"If music be the food of love play on." We don't need to argue that Liszt knew the opening lines of *Twelfth Night* to appreciate how his Petrarch Sonnets are a manifestation of Shakespeare's metaphor, how they act out a transfixing and deeply moving experience of desire. Pianists are fortunate to be in possession of this music, and thereby to experience the love poetry of Petrarch. Through Petrarch we can attain a deeper engagement with Liszt. Through Liszt we can attain a deeper engagement with Petrarch.

• 4 •

The Question of Goethe's *Faust*

Sonata in B minor

Let us plunge into the rush of things,
Of time and all its happenings!

—Faust[1]

Whoever he was, Dr. Faust is a figure admirably suited to symbolize
the birth of modern Europe and of the modern European mind.[2]

The inclusion of the B minor Sonata in my exploration of Liszt's debt to literature might seem an anomaly. It is a work with no program, no descriptive title, and no epigraph, with all the hallmarks of an autonomous work in the sonata tradition. After initial neglect and dismissal—the influential critic Eduard Hanslick proclaimed that "he who has heard it and found it beautiful cannot be helped," and Clara Schumann found in it "only blind noise"[3]—it now holds a central place as one of the greatest works of nineteenth-century piano music: for its monumental proportions, its colossal emotional breadth, and for its masterly reconstruction of a classical sonata structure that combines four movements into one.

But a programmatic context for the B minor Sonata has long been fought over and above all its relation to one of the pinnacles of European literature, Wolfgang von Goethe's verse drama *Faust*. Many pianists have made this connection—among them Alfred Cortot, Louis Kentner, Claudio Arrau, and Alfred Brendel; many other commentators have refuted it, notably Liszt's first major biographer Lina Ramann, who worked with him closely and devotedly for over a decade at the end of his life, and Liszt's current major biographer Alan Walker.

My purpose in this chapter is to lay out the evidence and examine the reasons why *Faust* is seriously considered to have relevance to a performer seeking to master Liszt's greatest piano work. Those who make this connection have not done so unthinkingly, and the ironic (and sometimes rude) dismissal of a

49

Faustian interpretation is unmerited. In order to address this question, I will need to introduce the play itself in some detail. In the next chapter I will apply the Faustian themes—or I might say the Faustian conjectures—to the music.

There is no question that *Faust* was central to Liszt's imaginative and philosophical view of the world and to himself. One of Liszt's piano students recalled him saying that "when traveling he always took Goethe's *Faust* and [Dante's] *Divina Commedia* with him, and that without these two master-works, which he read again and again, he could not live. . . . No work, he said, had caused such a revolution in his views as Goethe's *Faust*."⁴ Liszt's direct programmatic engagement comes in the Faust Symphony, written, as was the Sonata in B minor, after he had taken up residence in Weimar, in February 1848, as Court Kapellmeister to the Grand Duke Carl Alexander. In September of the previous year, he had given up his virtuoso career, one month before his thirty-sixth birthday.

Liszt's ambition in taking the post at Weimar, apart from wanting to devote himself to composition, was to revive the spirit of Goethe, whose residence in the duchy until his death in 1832 had created a magnificent flowering, now wilting, of German literature, art, and music. (Liszt's ambitious plan, laid out in his essay of 1851, *De la fondation Goethe à Weimar*, was for an annual prize to promote, in turn, poetry, painting, sculpture, and music.) Sketches for both the symphony and the sonata exist from the 1840s, and even an early version of the sonata from 1849, which Liszt played to his friends. But serious work on the B minor Sonata we know today was not begun until 1852; the symphony was completed the following year.

"THE WORLD-RENOWNED MAGICIAN AND MASTER OF THE BLACK ARTS"

Faust has not fared well as a drama for English-speaking audiences owing to the difficulty of translating its heavily rhymed verse and because no tradition of understanding the play in translation was established early on. The English Romantic poet Coleridge, some twelve years younger than Goethe and a close reader of German poetry and philosophy, published a watered-down translation under a different name, fearful that the blasphemies of the text would damage his reputation. In a letter to Byron he appears to deny he had ever undertaken the task:

> I had the open-heartedness to dissuade [my publisher] from hazarding any money on the translation of the Faust of Goethe, much as I myself admired the work on the whole, & tho' ready to undertake the translation—from

the conviction that the fantastic character of its Witcheries, and the general Tone of its morals & religious opinions, would be highly obnoxious to the Taste & Principles of the present righteous English Public.[5]

This is not to say there weren't many other translations into English, but as Osman Durrani points out in his exhaustive study of the innumerable "Fausts" from the middle ages to the early twenty-first century, "Modern translators have been known to use trendy sounding prose . . . which entirely destroys the flavor of the original, and only partly preserves its significance; older attempts often result in a quaintly antique pseudo-Shakespearian idiom, whose uncomfortable linguistic contortions raise too many smiles to be taken seriously."[6]

The play is also very difficult to stage, even in German. (In the year 2000, the German director Peter Stein mounted a production of the uncut text that lasted twenty-one hours.) It is nevertheless for Germans a touchstone, a storehouse of images, signs, and sayings as well as an archetypal story. In the same way as lines from Shakespeare have found their way into everyday English, so have lines from Goethe into everyday German. I am told that in Germany there is a quotation from Faust in some form, unwittingly or knowingly, on social media, a newspaper, or a broadcast almost every day. During World War I, it was common for German soldiers to carry *Faust* in their rucksacks;[7] Peter Stein's production of the play was front-page news all over Germany, and tickets were sold out within hours of going on sale.

Goethe conceived the play as a young man, in the 1770s, and continued rewriting and revising it all his life. Part 1, the part that is most widely known, was published in 1808; Part 2 was not published until just after he died in 1832. His theme was a well-known German folk tale depicting the exploits of a certain Dr. Faust who dabbled in alchemy and the black arts and made a pact with the devil. In return for a life of uninhibited luxury and sensuality he would give his soul to eternal damnation. Faust was based on a real figure at the time of the Reformation, around whom the superstitious mind wove tales of fantasy that reflected the reality of people's lives. The populace of Lutheran Germany, as of Tudor England, lived with a genuine fear of hell, but such is the human spirit—and the lure of money and sex—that the consequences of transgression are easily postponed.

Before Goethe, Faust in the popular imagination was a grubby, sometimes comical Everyman who provided the thrill of an anti-hero thumbing his nose at the authority of the church. This is his incarnation in the first printed account, whose full title gives a synopsis of the tale, complete with moral:

> The History of Dr Johann Faustus, the World Renowned Magician and
> Master of the Black Arts, relating how he pledged himself to the devil

for a fixed period of time, and the strange adventures that he experienced, brought about and committed, until he finally received the wages that he had earned. Collected in several parts from among his own surviving papers, and prepared for publication as a terrifying example, a case-study of debauchery, and a well-intentioned warning for the benefit of all arrogant, overbearing and godless individuals.[8]

The tale was published in Frankfurt in 1587 as a chapbook—a cheaply produced publication with woodcut illustrations of the kind that flooded the European market once inexpensive printing had been mastered. (It was picked up almost at once, in 1590, by Christopher Marlowe in London for his hugely popular play *Doctor Faustus*.) The tale of Faust was intended as an admonition to those not leading a Christian life; at the time of Luther, it was also anti-Catholic, with the devil easily aligned with all things papist. In America once the first Puritan settlers had established themselves in New England, *The History of Dr Johann Faustus* became the most widely read book after the Bible and the hymnal.

In Goethe's version, some two hundred years later, the essential story remains but is hugely amplified. Goethe imbues his character with all the characteristics of the Enlightenment; he is portrayed as a serious scholar, a thinker, and a sceptic. The Faust that gripped the European mind in the nineteenth century, and which has continued to resonate into the twenty-first in innumerable films and adaptations,[9] is one who probes the experience of life and death, of love and betrayal, of human idealism, degradation, and nihilism. Above all Faust is the hero with a divided self. The drama not only portrays "the conflict of a human soul with the might of hell,"[10] but the struggle between thought and action within the psyche of a supremely intelligent but flawed human being.

Faust's agony, amid his pleasure seeking, is expressed with an intensity of insight and feeling that persists throughout the play—whenever he is onstage his predicament is palpably dramatized:

> *In me there are two souls, alas, and their*
> *Division tears my life in two.*
> *One loves the world, it clutches her, it binds*
> *Itself to her, clinging with furious lust;*
> *The other longs to soar beyond the dust*
> *Into the realms of high ancestral minds.*[11]

For the generation of Romantic writers and musicians in the first decades of the nineteenth century, the experience of Goethe's drama was no less than life changing. Faust represented the zeitgeist, he represented the new concept of "genius," the word Goethe popularized to describe the tortured

Figure 4.1.　Delacroix, *Faust in His Study*. Lithograph. The caption reads, "You poor hollow skull, what does your grinning say?"—from *Faust Part 1*, l.664

John H. Wrenn Memorial Collection (CC0).

soul of Romanticism, of which Faust was the archetype. As one commentator has observed, Faust was "learned, passionate, curious, tender, courageous, bewitched and desperate."[12] The idea of genius, represented in the fictional characters of literature, was then shifted onto to the artists themselves across all genres, to Delacroix, Hugo, Byron, Berlioz, Beethoven—and to Liszt. For the Romantics, the artist lived the art.

Elements of the folk tale are always in the background in *Faust*, arising from Goethe's interest in traditional German literature. But the play employs a wide diversity of verse styles and rhyme schemes that extend far beyond the tropes of the traditional ballad, ranging from doggerel to sublime lyricism. "This not wholly worthless poetic monstrosity," as Goethe described it,[13] embraces tragedy, satire, philosophical exposition, and obscene humor. *Faust* is long but it moves at great speed, carried by the almost ceaseless regularity of the rhythm and rhyme, at once seductive, enthralling, incantatory. While the play employs scenes of devil worship and necromancy, witches and potions—what Coleridge called "the fantastic character of its Witcheries"—it contains within its irrealism a story that is profoundly human. Goethe promised to "ensure that the parts are pretty and entertaining and a little thought-provoking."[14] The thoughts it provokes are existentialist. Goethe presents us with an updated and more complex version of the questions about Love and Life with which Petrarch grappled, at the dawn of modern consciousness five hundred years earlier, in the *Canzoniere*.

THE TRAGEDY OF GRETCHEN

Goethe not only created a new Faust, but also changed the whole axis of the story by introducing the character—and the tragedy—of the beautiful peasant girl Gretchen, entirely his own invention. Thus was created the trinity of Faust, Mephistopheles, and Gretchen that dominates the structure of Part 1 (hence the "Three Character Sketches" of Liszt's Faust Symphony).

Faust, with the aid of his alter ego Mephistopheles, seduces Gretchen, and then abandons her when she is pregnant. The denouement of Part 1 is Gretchen's incarceration for infanticide and her refusal to be freed by Faust who, through the magic of Mephistopheles, has the power to release her from her cell. The final scene, "A Prison," is among the most harrowing portrayals of love and grief, of betrayal and remorse, in the whole of dramatic literature. In Goethe, women were "now demanding their rights as creatures of flesh and blood, rather than as glamorous phantoms. . . . Gretchen herself represented a triumph for girlhood in the modernisation of the myth."[15]

Figure 4.2.   Peter von Cornelius: *Faust and Gretchen,* **lithograph.**
Ulrich Christoffel: Die romantische Zeichnung von Runge bis Schwind, Mit 84 Abbildungen. Verlag Franz Hanfstaengl, München 1920. (Public Domain).

Gretchen's tragedy in my synopsis might seem far from a triumph. But Goethe's portrayal of her is psychologically acute, and her essential goodness and simplicity (in keeping with the values of *sturm und drang* literature in which lack of sophistication was prized) prove to be the very qualities that enable her strength of purpose. Mephistopheles, as the symbol of negation, cannot negate Gretchen. He arranges her seduction for Faust, but because the devil is incapable of recognizing anything other than lust, he cannot foresee that Gretchen and Faust will make a free choice to fall in love. Equally, for all his powers, he cannot foresee that Gretchen will refuse the proffered freedom from prison. She renounces Faust's love at this point because of the devil's presence. Innocence recognizes evil. Faust, by contrast, compromises with evil. He is diminished in the final prison scene, reduced to the role of victim—

"I wish I had never been born,"[16] he cries—whereas Gretchen is raised from victimhood and survives. At the last moment she calls on God to judge her and "a voice from above" is heard saying, "She is redeemed." It seems neither Faust nor Mephistopheles hear it. The voice is for us, the witnesses; it is in our own heads, confirming our awareness of Gretchen's ultimate triumph.

FAUST AND MEPHISTOPHELES

Faust Part 1 is not just the tragedy of Gretchen, but her story has such an intensity of realism that for the first admirers of the play it came to dominate. Yet three quarters of Part 1 centers on Faust and his relationship with Mephistopheles, a pairing that we can interpret as a single entity made of opposites. Oppositions of light and dark, day and night, action and contemplation, life and death are the binding images of the drama, both in the action and the language. Faust at times speaks some of the most beautiful poetry of the German tongue, and his antagonist some of the most brutally cynical. Mephistopheles functions partly as a jester and truth teller, and in puncturing the lofty thoughts of Faust, he constantly asks us to examine our own moral position. Unlike the devil of the chapbooks, Goethe's devil is not meant to be frightening and Faust constantly gets the better of him.

Gretchen's strong reaction to Mephistopheles is not fright but rather intense disgust. She refuses to be intimidated. What is shocking in the play is not so much the devil's careless nihilism and obscenity—which is portrayed to great comic effect—but Faust's. When we witness Faust being loving and gentle with Gretchen, we cannot believe that he will hurt her. But he does. Mephistopheles puts it very simply when Faust turns on him after the seduction, trying to cast blame: "Who was it who ruined her, I or you?" The stage direction at this point is "Faust glares about him in speechless rage."[17]

The play is often referred to as the tragedy of Faust, but it might be more accurate to see it as the damnation of Faust (as Hector Berlioz does)—not a biblical damnation but a moral condemnation. In the final scene Faust is damned in his own eyes and in ours. We and he are the accusers.

What then is positive about Faustian man?[18] Why did so many artists, from Liszt in the nineteenth century to Orson Welles in the twentieth, identify with him?[19] Faust represents not so much a figure of nobility to be admired, but rather one who contains within himself all the possibilities of human experience, both creative and destructive. In that sense he is perfectly recognizable. Goethe's *Faust* presents the world we live in, as relevant today as it ever has been, and one man's striving to make sense of it.

One of the central motifs of Goethe's poem, the most pervasive and the most celebrated, is proclaimed by Faust early in the play: "In the beginning was the deed."[20] Man, for Goethe, is a creature who should be endlessly active in his desire for life, in constant motion. Life is not endowed by outside forces, it is created from within the self. It is this life-force that Faust believes will win through in his wager with Mephistopheles. He believes he cannot lose:

> *If ever I lie down in sloth and base inaction*
> *Then let that moment be my end!*
> *If by your false cajolery*
> *You lull me into self sufficiency,*
> *If any pleasure you can give*
> *Deludes me, let me cease to live!*
> *I offer you this wager!*

The pleasure Mephistopheles procures for him is Gretchen. But the temptation Goethe dramatizes is not simply sexual, it is the "inaction" that true sexual fulfillment brings, and which neither Mephistopheles nor Faust had anticipated. Faust says to Gretchen,

> *Don't be afraid. Oh let my eyes,*
> *My hands on your hands tell you what*
> *No words can say:*
> *To give oneself entirely and to feel*
> *Ecstasy that must last forever.*
> *Forever!—For its end would be despair.*
> *No never ending! Never ending!*[21]

Many commentators have pointed out that while Faust insists on action, he also craves the opposite, the moment that is motionless and eternal. Ecstasy can be simultaneously active and inactive. If ecstasy lasts forever nothing else need be sought. Action ceases. This paradox is central to the play.[22] It was also central to Liszt's experience, as we shall now see.

LISZT'S *FAUST*

Liszt first got to know Goethe's *Faust* through Hector Berlioz in 1830. Liszt was nineteen when he first met the twenty-six-year-old Berlioz in Paris, the day before the premier of the *Symphonie Fantastique*. "Liszt called on me," Berlioz wrote in his *Memoirs*. "I spoke of Goethe's *Faust*, which he confessed that he had not read, but which he soon came to love as much as I."[23] The

French translation by Gérard de Nerval of *Faust Part 1* had only recently appeared, and this exchange was very much *à la mode* of these young lions. (Liszt as a famous virtuoso was certainly the bigger lion at this stage, notwithstanding that Berlioz had just won the highly coveted prize for composition, the *Prix de Rome*.) Liszt and Berlioz became close friends—Liszt was one of the very few Berlioz addressed by the intimate pronoun *tu*—and they shared the same views on literary inspiration and the evocative power of music post Beethoven. The new concept of "program music" was coming into being.

Faust has the dramatic quality of storytelling, the compelling power of ballad, the regular thrum and motion of folk song. From the start, even before the story begins, one can immediately see what drew Liszt in, how the verse spoke to his own sense of his place and role in the world. In the opening "Dedication," written long after the play was first conceived, Goethe ruminates on the poem he wants to bring into being, and the act of imagination that will draw in threads and visions from his past. He recalls his youth: "They cannot hear my present music, those / Few souls who listened to my early song." When Liszt took up *Faust* again in Weimar these words would have deeply resonated.

Turn the page and we find "Prelude on Stage," a superbly crafted comic scene between the Director, the Poet, and the Clown, representing the three key stereotypes of theater. Liszt, we might say, is all three. The Director has "to please the mob" to earn his living. The Clown, for whom acting is his life blood, enthusiastically agrees: "They must be entertained, it's what one owes." Goethe's Poet, in the cliché role of misunderstood artist, is aghast. He makes a plea for a quiet place in which to develop the perfection of his craft away from the crowd; it is only a poet who can achieve "true gold that lives for posterity." Who else can do it but an artist of genius?

> *Who divides up this dull monotonous drift*
> *Into living rhythm? Who can lift*
> *Particular things into a general sense*
> *Of some great music's congruence?*[24]

Liszt gave up his virtuoso career in order to be this kind of poet.[25]

There are two aspects to verse drama: language and plot; the way it is read as poetry and the way it is read as narrative. This is as true for Goethe as it is for Shakespeare. Goethe's language in *Faust* has a resonance, a musical actuality, that seems to ride above considerations of plot, or the motivations of character and the enigma of meaning. One reads Faust's long monologues transfixed by the beauty of the language (which David Luke's translation superbly evokes). Take for example the famous "sunset" passage. Faust has been exulting in the fecund beauty of the natural world:

Evening has come, our sun is westering now—
But it speeds on to bring new life elsewhere.
Oh if some wings would raise me, if somehow
I could follow its circuit through the air!
For then as I strove onwards I would see
A silent sunset world forever under me,
The hills aglow, the valleys lost in dreams,
The silver brooks poured into golden streams;
No mountain-range would stop me, not with all
Its rugged chasms; at divine speed I fly,
The sea already greets my wondering eye
With its warm gulfs where now the sun's rays fall.[26]

This has a life of its own as lyric poetry. But Goethe's vibrant touch here also presents one of the principal themes of the play with which Liszt would have identified. The monologue articulates Faust's colossal aspiration, his desire for a godlike quality within himself, for a power that is able to circumnavigate the world. Amid the lyricism of Faust's vision lies a profound danger. The moment is at once followed by his recognition of his two souls in conflict, whose "division tears my life in two." The division is at once exploited by Mephistopheles who now makes his first appearance disguised as a poodle. Faust takes the animal back to his study. The transcendent beauty of the natural world provides no defense. Faust falls victim to simple frivolity.

The human archetype Goethe defines in the play is also the archetype of the artist. There is no doubt that Liszt was in thrall to *Faust* because he recognized in its protagonist not only the wellsprings of his own creativity, his genius, but also the conflicts within his own psyche. This has always been the allure of Goethe's *Faust*.

THE FAUST SYMPHONY:
"FAUST," "GRETCHEN," "MEPHISTOPHELES"

There is no better preparation for a pianist coming to grips with the Sonata in B minor than to get to know the Faust Symphony. Motifs and moods echo each other across the two works, and the huge scale of the symphony, at well over twice the sonata's length, enables the pianist to gain some sense of proportion. At the very least a knowledge of the Faust Symphony creates for us a vocabulary of sound and texture, reminding us of the reality of orchestral sonority, which on the piano can only be a suggestion, an aspiration that we trust our listeners will take up and magnify. In the symphony we can notice, for example, the sense of desolation imparted by the oboe at its first entry (figure 4.3). It is not only the stark falling seventh that suggests a soul in dislocation (Faust's), but the very texture of the oboe's keening G sharp, which morphs into the desolate sound of a high bassoon. This is not a range of tone color that is available to the pianist, though the piano can offer a variety of ways, through pedaling and touch, through which we can create the illusion of orchestral sounds.

Figure 4.3. Faust Symphony, mm. 1–5.
Reprinted Ernst Eulenburg, n.d. (after 1947).

We are told the three movements are "character sketches" of the three protagonists, and if we know the story, as Liszt expects us to, we enter into it much as we would when reading a novel. We visualize the characters in our minds. But there is no way in which instrumental music can even attempt the philosophic dimension of Goethe's *Faust*; music by itself cannot ask questions of life and death and morality; it cannot literally tell a story. But it can distill a complexity of feeling, and even the dramatization of feeling as lived experience, in a way that the greatest poetry can. The union of music and poetry in the Faust Symphony is achieved by the presence of Goethe's characters in our minds. It is us, the listeners, who create the program, the story; but at the same time, as Liszt wrote in his essay *Berlioz and His "Harold" Symphony*, the music is granted "its supreme power of self-sufficiency."[27]

A great performance of the Faust Symphony can be an overwhelming experience in the way opera can be. To experience the music in terms of the story and characters of the play is to give it a parallel expressive intention, the two lines of which coalesce. Liszt wrote in his Berlioz essay that a program defines "the psychological moment which prompts the composer to create his work" and "the thought to which he gives outward form."[28] Music, for Liszt, is an outward form of thought. The stimulus in many cases was the literature he read. But it could equally include responses to other kinds of music (the Hungarian Rhapsodies for example, or the Swiss mountain songs in *Années de pèlerinage*), to landscape, or to paintings.

FAUST AND THE SONATA IN B MINOR

If Liszt had intended a program for his sonata, the reasons for his silence are not hard to find. It is also possible that he was not quite so silent on the subject as has been believed.

For Claudio Arrau the sonata's Faustian context was self-evident, and moreover "was taken for granted among Liszt's pupils."[29] Arrau's teacher, Martin Krause, was one of these pupils. The difficulty with this information is that it is not corroborated anywhere else, least of all in the memoirs of those who took notes during Liszt's famous master classes (notably Lina Ramann's *Pädagogium*, and the diaries of August Göllerich and Carl Lachmund). But then the sonata was barely played in the classes, and there were few public performances during Liszt's lifetime. In Göllerich's diary, which records in meticulous detail all the pieces performed for Liszt over a period of two years from 1884 to 1886 in Weimar, Rome, and Pest, the sonata is not mentioned once. In Ramann's *Pädagogium* there are a few references, all of which have entered into the literature, but not one mention of *Faust*.

So what are we to make of Arrau's remark? He could only have had it from his teacher Krause, who was an important presence in the Liszt entourage during those later years. Krause founded one of the first Liszt Societies in Leipzig, he was a pall bearer at Liszt's funeral, and he gave an address by his graveside. He seems a thoroughly credible witness, despite the fact that he figures not at all in accounts of the master classes. (Krause was thirty-three when Göllerich's diary starts, a good deal older than most of the participants at this time, so his absence is unsurprising. He was also heavily involved with his teaching in Leipzig.) Are we to impugn the reliability of Krause or Arrau himself? If we accept their recollections, then from whom did Liszt's pupils gain their knowledge? If not from Liszt, then we can only assume that the pupils themselves, among themselves, indulged in the same kind of speculation that has been conducted ever since the sonata was first discussed. Certainly the question of Faust began at the beginning, and won't go away.

Goethe and *Faust* were all around Liszt at Weimar. "Anything connected with Goethe is dangerous for me to handle," he wrote to Carolyne von Sayn-Wittgenstein.[30] No doubt as an outsider he would have feared creating resentment by associating himself with the most revered figure of German literature. (It seems it was because of resentment, the politics of the tiny community that made up Weimar, that his plans for an annual Goethe competition foundered.) But there is a sense too that he felt the danger of self-identifying as Faust. It was not a story he could escape or would ever escape.

Whatever the danger, Liszt was "handling" Goethe constantly, along with everything else. The outpouring of compositions at Weimar was extraordinary. Liszt's termination of his hectic activity as a virtuoso hardly ushered in a time of contemplation; Faustian action was Liszt's raison d'être. In the early years he was working on the two piano concertos, *Totentanz*, the symphonic poems *Tasso* (after Goethe), *Ce qu'on entend sur la montagne*, and *Mazeppa* (both Hugo) the Dante Sonata and *Funérailles*. He was also trying to get to grips with an opera on Byron's *Sardanapalus*. The year following his move he conducted Schumann's large-scale oratorio *Scenes from Goethe's Faust*. Then in 1850 he discussed plans with Gérard de Nerval, the French translator of *Faust*, for a Faust opera, which in the event came to nothing. In 1852 he invited Berlioz to Weimar to conduct *The Damnation of Faust*. He also mounted Spohr's opera *Faust*. It is reasonable to conclude that the vivid story of Goethe's three protagonists, a story of love, violence, human tragedy, and the vicissitudes of heaven and hell, would have been dominant in his mind during the composition of his sonata, which took shape between 1849 and February 1853.

There are strong reasons to believe that Liszt himself questioned the need for literary paraphernalia, and that this was the question in his mind during the sonata's composition. When it reached publication in May 1854, he wanted it to be his final say in the realm of piano composition: "I will finish with the piano, for the time being, in order to occupy myself exclusively with orchestral compositions, and to attempt a number of things in this area that for quite some time have become an inner necessity for me."[31] The inner necessity was of course his desire to explore the union of poetry and music, what would become his Faust and Dante Symphonies and his symphonic poems. But his sonata would be the opposite, a proud demonstration that he could write an extended work of pure music, unadorned by title, epigraph, or program, a perfectly formed sonata structure that could stand comparison with the greatest piano works of Beethoven. The literary context, if there was one, he would keep to himself so as to prove music's "supreme power of self-sufficiency."

Liszt suffered from repeated critical denigration of his music, and a widespread ridicule of his programmatic intentions. Richard Strauss "once got so worked up in the course of a conversation on how much Liszt had been misjudged that the people around him became seriously concerned about the state of his health." Strauss described Liszt as "tragically misunderstood in Germany."[32] Liszt mostly suffered in silence other than to his closest friends and pupils. But the refusal of his publishers to append his literary quotations to his scores angered him (as was the case with the Faust Symphony, the Petrarch Sonnets, and the *Two Scenes from Faust*—one of which was the "Mephisto Waltz"), because, he said "the so-called competent critics do not want it, and because program music is so much despised. The publishers do not dare act against the censor's veto and allow the poems to be left out again and again."[33]

Anticipating the reception of his *Harmony poètiques et religieuses*, piano pieces inspired by the religious poetry of Alphonse de Lamartine, he was bitterly ironic: "Yes, when nothing comes to mind, then one takes a poem from somewhere and it works; one need understand nothing about music and one produces—program music!"[34] To his closest confidant of all, Carolyne von Sayn-Wittgenstein, he wrote that the hugely influential critic Edouard Hanslick "will soon be taking the trouble to pass on his good advice to me, and I, as befits me, will be told of my total incompetence in matters of musical composition."[35] To another correspondent he wrote, in the spirit of the damned souls of Dante's hell, of the "learned criticisms . . . which declare in unison a truth which is truer than true: that LISZT has never been and never will be capable of writing four bars . . . that he is sentenced without remission to drag around the ball and chain of piano transcription in perpetuity."[36]

It does seem that the Sonata in B minor and the Faust Symphony were present at some level in Liszt's mind simultaneously, whatever the precise chronology of setting them down. While he was sensing and planning a full response to Goethe in symphonic form, the sonata was taking shape, we can argue, as the antidote to the foreseen programmatic treatment in the symphony. The sonata would be the antithesis. With the Faust Symphony to come, already settled in his mind in a manner that would deal with his inner "necessity," he was able in the sonata to divest the story of its outer garments so as to distill its poetic core.

• *5* •

Music as Metaphor

Sonata in B minor

The field, here, is wide open to the imagination of the performer.

—Alfred Cortot, "Liszt Sonata in B minor"[1]

$\mathcal{T}$he French pianist Alfred Cortot, who was the first to record the B minor sonata, never concealed his own belief that the sonata was directly related to Faust. In his commentary for his 1934 edition for Salabert, however, he concentrates almost exclusively on issues of pianism and structure: "No program underlies this gigantic composition," he writes, "in which all the resources of the piano are exploited through writing of prodigious novelty and ingenuity. . . . But the themes confront each other with such dramatic plasticity that one cannot help but attach a symbolic meaning to them." We experience the themes, he writes, "not as abstract constructs but as purely human sensibility," and throughout we "glimpse the strife of emotions beneath the clash of musical propositions."[2]

For me this says it all, tying together the intense emotional charge of the music with Liszt's supreme control of his material. We know the themes are "abstract constructs," we can analyze their workings, yet we can effortlessly experience the music in terms of "human sensibility." The manner in which Liszt presents and then transforms his themes is clearly and thrillingly discernible to the ear, creating for the listener an experience analogous to a play or a novel (see p. 108 below).

Alfred Brendel is also a *Faust* proponent. In his 1981 essay on the sonata, he wrote that "the Faust-Mephisto-Gretchen constellation . . . remains a working hypothesis and my personal luxury."[3] How interesting that forty years on, in a lecture at the Goethe Institute in London (January 2021), his hypothesis becomes certainty. He speaks now of the sonata and symphony as "companions" and of how the sonata "can safely be located in *Faust*'s orbit."[4]

Liszt scholar and pianist Kenneth Hamilton, whose short book on the B minor sonata should be essential reading for anyone embarking on a performance (as should Brendel's essay), aims to refute its connection with *Faust*. But during the course of his argument, he shifts his position. He is himself a fine performer of the sonata and his comments are not only those of a musicologist but of a pianist who responds to the emotional power of the score under his fingers: "I feel compelled to admit, in blatant contradiction to everything I have written about the sonata and programmaticism, that when playing this page [the build up to the magnificent B major of bar 600] I cannot avoid thinking of the final defeat of Mephistopheles and the redemption of Faust."[5]

What stands out in Hamilton's account is the way he is able to bring his reactions to the music alive in language, even while believing that language is inadequate. "This prose description may seem—indeed is—a pedantic and laboured peroration of some tremendously exciting music," he writes.[6] All he means is that the music has to be experienced in itself; but in fact his description of it—always attempting to be grounded in the verifiable facts of the score, but inescapably manifesting an emotional response—is far from pedantic for the very reason that his language is constantly interwoven with metaphor. He describes the introduction as a "thematic womb," the repeated Gs as "tentative groping," the opening descending scale motif as "pensive, brooding," and he writes of the "chattering, sardonic counterpoint" of the fugue.[7]

Liszt taught "in an allegorical way, or by metaphor," his student August Stradal recalled[8] (for example, to the pianist Arthur Friedheim, who was playing *Harmonies du soir*, Liszt exclaimed, pointing outside to the sunset, "Play that!"[9]). Writing and talking about music, the experience of music rather than its construction, can hardly avoid metaphor. Hamilton employs a familiar literary metaphor when he comments on the strange presence of the key of E flat in the sonata's tonal scheme—he calls it "a sort of 'Banquo's ghost' . . . turning up in the most unexpected places."[10] Banquo's ghost repeatedly appears in *Macbeth*. It is not only unexpectedness that the metaphor captures, but the palpable sense of something awry in the scheme of things—the key of E flat as Liszt uses it in his tonal structure is "wrong." The metaphor is even more appropriate than Hamilton perhaps intended. Macbeth on seeing Banquo's ghost dares to "look on that / Which might appall the devil." The odd presence of E flat in the sonata might not be as intense as the effect of Banquo's ghost on Macbeth, but with this image in mind in the context of our Faustian metaphor the performer can possibly make it so.

One of the few comments we have from Liszt (though indirectly) on the sonata comes from a recollection by his student August Stradal—this too employs metaphor:

> With respect to [the second theme of the sonata's opening bars] the master mentioned . . . that he had Beethoven's "Coriolan" Overture in mind. "Why

should I show you my sufferings? I carry them in my inner being and lock them away proudly from you."[11]

This throws up all kinds of questions. The metaphor here is multiple: not only alluding to repressed suffering and pride, but more specifically to those emotions as expressed by another piece of music beloved by Liszt. So the metaphor is also a musical one: the student is being asked to express one piece of music in terms of another. The reference is also literary, a quotation from a play by Heinrich Joseph von Collin based on the same story Shakespeare used for his Roman play *The Tragedy of Coriolanus*. Beethoven wrote his *Coriolan* music for a staging of Collin's play in Vienna in 1807. Liszt gave a spontaneous performance of the overture one evening at the piano, saying afterward that, had he made a transcription, "That's roughly how I would have done it."[12] This was just at the time when he was about to begin substantial work on an early version of the B minor Sonata and it looks highly probable that the opening of Beethoven's overture was in his mind. We can even detect in the opening bars of the sonata elements of the overture that Liszt has employed as a structural model.[13] This is an intriguing conjunction in the context of a programmatic interpretation of the B minor Sonata. For Liszt, Beethoven was revered not only as the master of the sonata tradition but as the precursor of program music. In the Berlioz essay from which I quoted in the previous chapter, he wrote of "how close Beethoven came to the idea of connecting poetry with instrumental music."[14]

Where does this leave our *Faust* narrative? As a working metaphor it leaves it intact. Liszt was drawing attention to a musical idea, and to an alliance with Beethoven that was part of his identity. One of the first characteristics of the sonata that can be noticed after coming to it via Beethoven's sonatas—as was my experience—is the extent to which, without sounding like Beethoven, it makes the same demands, emotionally and intellectually, pianistically and structurally—indeed the extent to which it feels like Beethoven under one's fingers.

EXPERIENCING *FAUST*—SYMPHONY AND SONATA

I have suggested, in relation to the Petrarch Sonnets, that Liszt's music can be seen as a kind of translation. Another way of seeing it is as metaphor—the Faust Symphony can be understood as a metaphor for Liszt's response to Goethe's play. Liszt clearly saw it this way. As listeners, especially if we know *Faust*, the music becomes a metaphor for our own responses to Goethe. We might even ponder whether we can learn about Faust, Gretchen, and Mephistopheles from the music alone. I think we can—not the facts of the story, not what the characters do to each other—but the emotional moods, the *kinds* of characters that the music intends to bring into being. Liszt's delineation in the Faust Symphony of three distinct personalities, even if we do not know who they are but for their names, is palpable. As Hamilton says, the themes "function as characters in a drama, and we can experience their variation as the vicissitudes of their lives."[15] There is a sense in the concert hall that we are witnessing an opera without a setting or a stage. We imagine willingly, lacking all inhibition *not* to, because of the invitation from Liszt in the title of his work and the titles of the movements. The colossal experience of Goethe's *Faust* is staged in our heads.

On one level, to adapt the metaphor of the symphony's subtitle "Three Character Sketches," the brush strokes of Liszt's portraits are very broad: the Faust movement paints uncompromising psychic disturbance and a palpable sense of struggle, allied to the characteristic heroic manner of Lisztian Romanticism; the Gretchen movement delineates exquisite tenderness (Liszt, as Faust, seems to be in love with his Gretchen), a sense of innocence and yearning; the Mephistopheles movement is mercurial, unsettling, broken-surfaced. In the Gretchen movement Faust is present; in "Mephistopheles" all three protagonists are present, and we experience them in interaction—but here Mephistopheles is not given a theme of his own, but rather, through Liszt's characteristic thematic transformations, he is present as a distortion of the Faust themes, a negation of Faust; while Gretchen's themes remain undisturbed. The musical processes, at the service of Liszt's dramatic intentions, are unmistakable to the ear. Broad brush strokes are a necessity for program music to achieve the precision of storytelling. The processes are thrillingly clear, but the emotional resonances are extraordinarily subtle.

What I am leading to is that there is a kind of viewpoint that inhibits such responses in the case of the B minor Sonata, "because Liszt said nothing about it." This ignores so many questions about the nature of music as well as the nature of the creative process; it ignores all the historical and biographical details in the background of the sonata's creation; it ignores what we know about Liszt's responses to literature's "union" with music, and the way he composed it, conducted it, and taught it. Above all it ignores the nature of music as metaphor.

In a similar way to an actor grappling with the enormities of a tragic character in Shakespeare—or Arthur Miller's Joe Keller, or Goethe's Faust—performers of Liszt's Sonata in B minor (the pianist as actor) need to find some correspondence for the vast scale of its emotional landscape—not only in ourselves but outside ourselves. In this way we will have reference points by which to control the intensity and strength of the music, and to enable us not to flinch from it. *Faust* can be this reference point. For some it will be "a private indulgence" (Brendel); for others (as for Arrau) it will be a specific matching of motif to story. Even the agnostic Kenneth Hamilton refers to the themes of the sonata as "discrete *dramatic personae*, starkly recognizable even under their myriad future disguises."[16] Equally there are others who refer to different stories (the Bible, Milton's *Paradise Lost*), or to none. One would hope that the end results, in performance, will all be essentially the same, a rendering that brings the experience of Liszt's sonata alive, off the page; and essentially different, in as much as all performances of the sonata can only be a personal response from within one's own imagination. As Cortot said, "the field, here, is wide open to the imagination of the performer."[17]

PLAYING FAUST

The great orchestral conductor Carlos Kleiber, we are told, had a transcendent ability "to transform the human and emotional side into sound."[18] This is especially fascinating in the current context because it implies that for Kleiber the human and emotional were already out there, beyond the music, waiting to be summoned *into* the music he was bringing into being. So it is not only the composer who does the transforming, but the conductor too. The imagination of the conductor (performer) already exists, which is then brought to bear on the music that he or she is recreating. This is the same process experienced by an actor.

There is an easy association to be made between the words *play* and *playing*; between players (actors and pianists) and the make-believe they are playing (enacting) on stage. And it is but a short step to associate playing the piano and the play of a child—or indeed an adult. "Dream dreams, see visions," advised the pianist Edwin Fischer (along with Arrau one of the great pianists taught by Liszt's pupil Martin Krause).[19] Is this not what we do when playing the master works of the piano repertoire? This is what we learn to do from childhood in the games we play, the stories we enact, the make-believe that for a child becomes a more intense experience than reality.

The field of psychology has demonstrated the essential place of "play" in human development. But the danger of bringing our visions into the open— examining them through language rather than responding to them through music (or through play)—is that it can lead to an inhibiting self-consciousness that prevents, rather than promotes, the workings of the imagination.[20] This is the thin ice I am skating on in this book, but it is a hazard that needs be handled or there would be no talking about music at all. It is no doubt for similar reasons that Brendel once talked of *Faust* as his "private indulgence," and it is for this reason too that I hesitate to articulate my own relationship with *Faust* other than as literature. Brendel's account of the sonata is clear-eyed and wholly illuminating, and like Hamilton's (and Cortot's) concentrates almost entirely on the nature of the work as music. Even in a recent master-class in London (in 2016), Brendel concentrated on issues of orchestral color and voicing, and mentioned Faust and Mephistopheles rarely.

I will nevertheless offer some suggestions as to how a pianist might use Goethe as a way in to the demands of the B minor Sonata, and I will take my cue from Brendel's remarks about the opening motif: "Musically, the theme is representative not of speech or singing, but of thinking."[21] (figure 5.1, bars 1–7.) Despite eliminating two out of three possibilities, this illuminates a world of characterization. Liszt ascribed to the idea of music as analogous to thought, and it is an idea that can be argued, as the novelist J. M. Coetzee does, even in the case of music at its most absolute: "Bach thinks in music. Music thinks itself in Bach."[22] At the opening of the sonata we might see the music as thinking in process (a modification of Hamilton's idea of a "womb," of a coming into being); or we might see the music pro-

Figure 5.1.   B minor Sonata, mm. 1–17: themes 1–3.
Breitkopf & Härtel, 1924. Reprinted Dover Publications, 1989.

grammatically as enacting the process of thinking—related to the opening of scene 1 of *Faust* where we find Faust thinking. We should also take into account that we the pianists are thinking. All these attitudes to what we are making happen are simultaneously valid.

A considerable part of Goethe's play is thought as well as action—we are party to what goes on inside Faust's head (as we are in *Hamlet*, a play that dominated Goethe's own thinking). Imagining the sonata in terms of a drama on stage, the first sounds are not only representative of thinking but of silence (thinking can only be silent). In the music, silence is enacted through sound. In this (imagined) silence Faust is seen (imagined) "sitting restlessly at his desk." We don't know what thoughts are causing his restlessness (and we don't know what key we are in). What we sense from the music is deep unease. In the drama inside our heads (what Byron called "mental theatre," as we shall see in chapter 7), we witness a man thinking dark thoughts. He is restless in the silence, but he barely moves.

One feature of programmatic interpretations, in the absence of the specific guidance of a title, is that so many opinions proliferate they tend to cancel each other out. Even among those who favor a Faustian narrative there are disagreements. The second theme (figure 5.1, bar 8) for Arrau "is definitely Mephisto," whereas for Brendel "the actor makes his grand entrance on stage. . . . May I call him Faust?" Arrau sees the celebrated *Grandioso* theme 4 (figure 5.2) as "of course the majesty of the Almighty."

Figure 5.2.   B minor Sonata, mm. 105–118, theme 4.
Universal Edition, 1917.

Brendel will have none of it. For him the theme "is ruled out as a theme of religious character by the imperious gesture of its ending, which suggests, to a psychologically inclined listener, megalomania rather than omnipotence."[23]

My own inner narrative for the sonata aligns with Brendel's, whereas I find Arrau's too detailed (though I am bound to ask why my own might not be equally over-detailed). "To name an object is to destroy three-quarters of the pleasure of a poem," wrote the symbolist poet Stéphane Mallarmé.[24] Such detailed stories as Arrau's ask us to believe that Liszt composed his music with the play constantly to hand and matched his musical ideas to points in the narrative. That, surely, is not how instrumental composition works. When we listen to music, read poetry or a novel, or see a film, drama, or art exhibition, the meaning takes us beyond words. Liszt's response to Goethe is beyond words. But when we want to identify his response, talk about it, words are all we have. Brendel talks about it by adducing *Faust* as a way of "enlivening the terminology and simplifying description." But the play surely does more than enable us to talk.

Music has the capacity to grasp the life of things. It expresses this in a medium that opens up multiple interpretations because it is able to grasp nuances, states of mind, apprehensions, senses, competing desires, not only as changing states but even as simultaneous events. For Liszt the meaning of *Faust* in all its psychological complexity is grasped as an instantaneous experience—after long acquaintance, re-readings, mediations, questionings—just as a pianist, with long preparation, might grasp it at the outset of the sonata: what is about to unfold is what we already know. The art, as for an actor, is to present what we know as if it is happening for the first time.

FAUSTIAN THEMES

So let us return to the opening of the sonata and what the pianist is bringing into being (figure 5.1). We have already experienced Faust as restless thinker, and in the second theme, bar 8, we have been introduced to the suddenly uncompromising strength of his presence. (So from the outset, in themes 1 and 2, we confront Goethe's twin themes of thought and action.) The third motif, which begins with the triplet in bar 13, Liszt spoke of as "hammer blows," an entirely appropriate description of its repeated percussive bass notes (*f marcato*). This for Brendel is the Mephistopheles theme, and it has all the characteristics that we might associate with negativity, scorn, sarcasm.

The purely structural processes in operation from the outset are absolutely clear: for example, the repeated Gs (*p sotto voce*) of theme 1 are integrated into the first bars of theme 2; each of the second two themes takes off from the last note of the previous theme; the repeated notes of theme 3 are a transformation of the repeated Gs of the first theme; the triplet upbeat of theme 3 precisely mirrors the rising eighth notes of Faust's theme. We see this clearly on paper (figure 5.1), but we can also hear it. The performer's task is to enable the listener to hear it. All we are doing with our narrative reference ("thinking" "Faust" "Mephistopheles") is taking the musical process onto a different plane of understanding by way of analogy and metaphor. But the idea of "musical process" has two components, because "musical" also means an experience of feeling (we praise a performance for being "musical"). Our narrative also references feeling, and hence character.

Brendel's "private indulgence" is really a confession of the methodology by which he controls his performing process. (He has also divulged that he gives titles to each of Beethoven's Thirty-Three Diabelli Variations.)[25] In many respects it is an intellectual game, with essential emotional reference points. We know the fundamental place of games in a healthy human psyche. The game we play here is to pretend there are three characters present throughout our performance of the sonata; and we find plausible correspondences in the music for their interaction. Our games and stories, as for a child, are metaphors for the experiences of life. As adults we find a delight, indeed a deep emotional satisfaction, in observing how these metaphors work.

The motivic connections of the opening material allow a reading that embeds Mephistopheles within Faust—we have already seen in the play that these two characters are not only deeply intertwined but actually two sides of a single entity comprising light and dark. Mephistopheles says,

> *I am part of that part which once, when all began,*
> *Was all there was; part of the Darkness before man*
> *Whence light was born.*[26]

This might explain Arrau's insistence that the second theme is Mephistopheles—the ambiguity of Faust's character is manifest. But if we return to Liszt's own characterization of the theme as Coriolanus (via Beethoven) then we will recognize the heroic grandeur of this moment, of this actor on stage who displays positive attributes unattainable by the devil. Brendel writes of Faust's "argument with fate,"[27] which captures both Faust and Beethoven in one entirely appropriate image. (Fate, in musical iconography, is indelibly associated with the opening theme of Beethoven's Fifth Symphony in C minor—of which the Coriolan Overture in C minor is a precursor—and Beethoven's claim that he "will seize fate by the throat."[28]) Brendel goes on to say that the performer should not allow this argument "to degenerate into hysterical or whimpering self-pity." He has in mind the *appassionata* "Recitativo" beginning at bar 301

Figure 5.3. B minor Sonata, mm. 297–311.
Breitkopf & Härtel, 1924. Reprinted Dover Publications, 1989.

(figure 5.3), with its clear declamation, in a high register, of the Faust motif in inversion, followed at once by the Mephistopheles theme in a high register. The agony of suffering expressed here is framed by the thunderous reiteration of the *grandioso* theme, whose grandeur is now replaced by terror. For me this is not the terror inspired by the Old Testament's God (Goethe's Lord at the opening of *Faust* is not at all terrifying), but the terror of Faust's conscience. This music is wholly human.

We have isolated three themes in the "thematic womb" of the opening. Another theme (figure 5.4) is present too, which we will come to recognize as the Gretchen theme 5. It is embedded within the repeated notes of the "thinking" theme, and visibly (audibly) within the Mephistopheles theme. In fact the Gretchen theme *is* the Mephistopheles theme. In *Faust* Mephistopheles utters the central paradox of the play when he describes himself as "Part of that Power which would / Do evil constantly, and constantly does good." Theme 3 becoming theme 5 is a musical metaphor for evil becoming good. The character of theme 5, in all its self-contained musical identity within a highly structured sonata structure, can also be experienced as Mephisto

Figure 5.4. B minor Sonata, mm. 153–155, Gretchen theme 5.
Universal Edition, 1917.

literally transformed into Gretchen. In musical terms, the horror that subsequently happens to her is all contained within Mephistopheles (and Faust). The music does not flinch from her tragedy, but Gretchen, for Liszt, and in his music, remains innocent—she is unassailable.

If we look at the Gretchen theme again, we will see what a listener might miss: the presence of the shape of theme 1 in the bass, complete with the rising 7th of the lower parts—listeners do not habitually listen to the bass lines of songs. But the pianist knows it is there and this knowledge has a profound effect on our emotional relationship with this music. At the very opening of the sonata—the moment that is the silence of the quarter-note rest, and which then proceeds to articulate a process of thinking—the performer can imagine Faust thinking of a Gretchen as yet unborn. Gretchen is an inchoate thought. Later, when she appears as theme 5, she carries Faust with her.

The way such musical symbolism works for the performer can be intensely moving. It is also a controlling methodology, it maps our journey, it tells us where we are and where we are going. This is not to say that the process during performance is fully conscious—like actors on stage we become what we have prepared ourselves to embody. What is conscious is our control of the material—for the pianist our ears, fingers, and feet take over and we make music. We are not singing, we are not speaking, we are thinking (and we are playing the piano).

The path from the preparation of the *grandioso* theme 4 (from the second half of bar 81) to its completion, and then on to the Gretchen theme 5 (beginning bar 153), takes us by way of an almost insupportable intensity through a *dolce con grazia* of translucent lyricism. The drama throughout this passage is breathtaking. We hear wave upon rising wave of theme 1, the *crescendo* reaching *ff* as the music proclaims the omnipotence of D major, to be followed by the resplendence of *fff* as D slips sideways to C (bar 109). The tonality now shifts through various keys, without settling; a movement toward F sharp fails to materialize—everything, as it were, stops and thinks (118–120). The Faust theme is heard in its entirety, at pitch (figure 5.5, bars 120–124), but softly, shorn of all heroism and energy. Then it is heard again, *dolce con grazia*, but so divested of anxiety (7ths becoming 6ths, and the suggestion of a plagal cadence) that we might at first miss the connection—but its shape is fully

Figure 5.5.   B minor Sonata, mm. 114–128.
Universal Edition, 1917.

discernible (bars 124–128). This is the Faust theme transformed. As beautiful as this moment is, the transformation is painful—a musical rendering of the pain of loneliness, a yearning for solace. (Faustian man "is constantly and painfully reminded of his solitude."[29]) The harmonic structure here conveys a sense of exploration, not restless so much as expectant. In sonata terms this is a bridging passage. We cannot linger. What is about to happen is one of those many events in this masterwork that repays constant revisiting, never to be forgotten. (I only single out this moment as an illustration—the whole work rests on a continuous play of such musical events, while the pianist's art is to discover the entire work as a single event, a whole.) The path away from the *grandioso* D major turns out to be circular, and by way of a soft reiteration and disintegration of theme 3 (Mephistopheles) we approach a reborn D major and the birth of Gretchen.[30] Faust's transformation turns out to be a move toward Gretchen by way of the total subjugation of Mephisto. But we know it is only Gretchen who achieves this, not Faust. In *Faust* Part 2 he will find redemption, but that is another story.

CODA

My purpose has been to review Goethe's *Faust* and its central place in Liszt's creative imagination, and to suggest ways in which a knowledge of the play and Liszt's reaction to it might lead to a methodology for performing the B minor sonata. I have aimed to show how music can provide a metaphor for the experience of human feeling and interaction, as well as storytelling, and how we can requisition literary texts as a means of "enlivening the terminology," in Brendel's words, when we need to talk about music. I also wanted to demonstrate that *Faust* provides, as indeed it does for Alfred Brendel, a far deeper experience for a pianist and listener than the term "enlivening the terminology" provides. My commentary has only focused on a small portion of the work, the introduction of the principal themes. Considerably more remains; and considerably more interpretations can be found.

So I will end by adducing another commentary on the B minor by Charles Rosen, who changes the metaphor and does not mention *Faust* at all (though he does mention Lucifer, a version of Mephisto). Rosen's commentary is critical and contrarian, yet it is woven with threads of the deepest admiration. He writes,

> The source of Liszt's Sonata is not only Beethoven and Schubert but Byron (above all the Byron of Manfred and Childe Harold), the popular Gothic novel, and the sentimental religious poetry of Lamartine. Even the saccharine religious art of the style known as Sainte-Sulpice plays a role in some of the most remarkable pages of the sonata.[31]

Without quite saying so, the implications of "saccharine" and "sentimental" are applied to Liszt. It is a curious compliment to yoke Liszt to the glutinous aspects of nineteenth-century art and religion. Certainly many performances of the sonata can easily degenerate into bombast and sentimentality, just as performances of Chopin can, but this is precisely the problem to be overcome—not the problem of Liszt's sentimentality but the sentimentality we bring to Liszt. The open-hearted, intensely emotional sensibility of the B minor Sonata, its thrilling emotional scope that at times suggests the uncontainable, seems to be an embarrassment to Rosen. Yet equally his admiration can be fulsome. Here is his commentary on the final two pages:

> In a magnificent revision [of the ending] Liszt returned to the religious mode with its erotic overtones. The most remarkable inspiration is a surprise cadential movement into a mournful grey despair with no brilliance ... Liszt follows it with an effect of religious absolution and a brief glimpse of heaven.[32]

Rosen analyzes the work with characteristic insight, but here the only reference to musical procedures is to a "surprise cadential movement"—otherwise the commentary is replete with metaphors. I am surprised Rosen finds eroticism here (for me all the eroticism of the Faust story is to be found in the Mephisto Waltz), but his reaction to the closing pages seems otherwise to be a wholly legitimate way of bringing this visionary music before us in the absence of the music itself. He then concludes that "a literal and naïve interpretation [of the sonata] is inescapable," adducing the gothic and the sentimental. It is of course Rosen's interpretation that is literal and naive. For me Hamilton captures better the experience of the final cadence—Rosen's "brief glimpse of heaven"—simply by describing it as "one of the most inspired final cadences in the entire keyboard literature."[33]

In the summer of 1854 Mary Ann Evans (soon to be known as the novelist George Eliot), and her partner George Henry Lewes, spent several weeks in Weimar with Liszt. She described him as "the first really inspired man I ever saw."[34] Lewes was gathering material for his book *The Life and Works of Goethe*. Of *Faust* he wrote that it "has every element: wit, pathos, wisdom, farce, mystery, melody, reverence, doubt, magic, and irony; not a chord of the lyre is unstrung, not a fibre of the heart untouched."[35] A case can be made for every one of these elements in Liszt's B minor Sonata (stretching a point with farce perhaps, although we might see a flicker of farce in the hair-raising dance of the fugue—Mephistopheles and Faust—and its denouement). A view that takes Goethe's *Faust* as a reference point aligns Liszt's greatest piano work with one of the greatest master works of European literature. That is the sonata's stature. That is justification enough for *Faust*.

· *6* ·

The Romantic Image

"Vallée d'Obermann"

One was mad with lyricism and art. One felt one was about to discover the lost secret, and it was true, one had rediscovered poetry.[1]

—Théophile Gautier

If to live is only to exist, what do we need to live for?[2]

—Etienne de Sénancour

*W*hat is Romanticism, other than a familiar word that is defined in relation to its companion Classicism? Looking back on the Paris of the 1830s, the great champion of French Romanticism, Théophile Gautier, quoted above—poet, literary critic, writer on dance, painting, and theater—provides us with a small clue, the beginning of an answer that seems to fit with what we know. At the least Gautier seems to capture the intoxicating atmosphere of Liszt's milieu at this time. Liszt and Gautier were exact contemporaries.

My other quotation comes from one of the cult novels of the period, *Obermann*, avidly read by the young Franz Liszt, and it provides another clue, in a more serious vein, in the form of another question. Liszt knew Sénancour personally, as he did so many of the writers of the time whom he sought out in his quest for literary insights.

The Romantics may well have been delighted, if not astounded, by the diagnosis of Romanticism from the later vantage point of the twentieth century, by the humanist historian and philosopher Isaiah Berlin (1909–1997). For Berlin, Romanticism was "the most recent movement to transform the lives and the thought of the Western world . . . the greatest single shift in the consciousness of the West that has occurred. . . . All the other shifts which have occurred in the course of the nineteenth and twentieth centuries appear in comparison less important, and at any rate deeply influenced by it."[3] This does not provide an answer, but it does make us sit up.

Before I turn to where Franz Liszt fits into such a phenomenon, I will quote a passage from a recent novel by the Nobel-Prize-winning novelist Kazuo Ishiguro, *Never Let Me Go*. Echoes of Romanticism persist into the twenty-first century. In Ishiguro's nightmarish but deeply compassionate world, cloned children, supposedly lacking souls, are encouraged by their teachers to make art. One of them is speaking excitedly about why this might be: "She told [us] that things like pictures, poetry, all that kind of stuff, she said *revealed what you were like inside*. She said *they revealed your soul*."[4] The possession of a soul would be used as an argument to treat the clones humanely. The possession of a soul, we might say, is another clue to the nature of Romanticism.

In this chapter I will discuss these questions in relation to one of Liszt's greatest piano compositions, the longest and most ambitious piece of the Swiss volume of the *Années de pèlerinage*, "Vallée d'Obermann"—inspired by Sénancour's *Obermann* and (in its first version) dedicated to him.

LISZT AND ROMANTICISM

A definition of Romanticism is a perilous undertaking, but all pianists will have in varying degrees some sense of it, probably more in line with Gautier's conception—"One was mad with lyricism and art"—than Berlin's. (In piano circles Gautier will be known as author of the six poems set by Berlioz for his song cycle *Les nuits d'été*.) Liszt was one of Romanticism's leading figures. Indeed he represents, along with Berlioz, what we sense Romanticism to be; they propagated it, lived it. Liszt's extraordinary fame and notoriety, his public persona, his endless travels, even his flowing hair and elegant clothes, were all aspects of Romanticism before we even begin a discussion of his music. But the music and the man cannot be separated, and that too is an aspect of the Romantic phenomenon. Schumann noted this of Liszt at the outset. Always an acute observer of the contemporary scene, Schumann wrote, "There can be no doubt . . . that we have here to deal with an extraordinary, multiply moved mind as well as with a mind influencing others. His own life is to be found in his music."[5] By "life," he means the life of the mind, the "multiply moved mind," moved by art, by literature and ideas. Art for the Romantics was made from life, from the psyche of the individual, from the artist's subjective response to the world and to Nature. Such was the Romantic ideal, which Liszt seemed to embody effortlessly; such was the transformation in perception the Romantic generation brought about. To generalize, Romanticism is subjective, Classicism objective.

However, the trap awaiting such a formulation is the belief that for the Romantic artist anything goes, that art relies on freedom from constraint. The fecundity of Liszt's artistic imagination, the panache and extravagance of his public performances, the colossal ambition of his creative project, might lead one to that conclusion. Indeed for the Liszt pianist, an uninhibited embrace of the music's emotional strength is paramount. But Liszt's constant search for a new musical art, for a sincerity of expression that would fuse the multiple aspects of his experience into a coherent whole—long preceding Wagner's concept of *gesamtkunstwerk* (total work of art)—is almost always accompanied by processes of revision that are unerring in their self-discipline. And Liszt of all artists knew the need for self-discipline because of the tremendous allure of its opposite. We might say that one of his greatest characteristics was his ability to bring discipline and structure to a compelling lack of restraint—the B minor Sonata is one of the greatest examples, and so is "Vallée d'Obermann."

Much can be learned about the nature of a phenomenon from the way it is satirized. In a French novel from the 1830s by Alfred de Musset, we get a glimpse of Liszt's milieu and how easily it invited mockery. Two excited observers are seen trying to keep up with the latest Romantic manifestations as they unfold year by year. "It was in 1828," one of them writes eagerly to a friend, "that [we] at last learned the difference between Romantic and Classical poetry":

> A single line of poetry, dear sir, one single line, can be either romantic or classical, according to the way it feels. When we heard this news we couldn't sleep all night. Then we heard that in the provinces "romantic" is a synonym for "absurd," and they make no fuss about it. Oh but the next year we learned that romanticism was nothing other than the alliance of the mad and the serious, the grotesque and the terrible, the farcical and the horrible. From 1833 to 1834 we thought that romanticism consisted in not shaving and in wearing vests with large heavily starched lapels. The next year we didn't think anything, as my friend had to make a short trip south for an inheritance and I was busy repairing a barn damaged by heavy rain.[6]

"According to the way it feels"—this is the kernel of the critique. But there are other grains of truth here too, along with a warning about the dangers of taking oneself over seriously. Liszt himself was constantly lampooned, for his vanity, his flowing locks, his piercing glances, even for his fingers that seemed a foot long; and for his eager, deeply serious association with what would later be called progressive thinking, in art, religion, and politics. But the high seriousness of the Romantic movement was its defining feature; it was all or nothing. For the Romantics, wrote Isaiah Berlin, "to stop expressing is to stop living":

For these romantics, to live is to do something, to do is to express your nature. To express your nature is to express your relation to the universe. Your relation to the universe is inexpressible, yet you must nevertheless express it. This is the agony, this is the problem. This is the unending Sehnsucht [longing], this is the yearning, this is the reason why we must go to distant countries, this is why we seek exotic examples, this is why we travel to the East and write novels about the past, this is why we indulge in all manner of fantasies. This is the typical romantic nostalgia.[7]

Even Berlin's voice sounds a note of irony, for all his deep respect for the Romantic movement and its consequences. With only slight adjustment his commentary might fit comfortably with the catalogue of words offered by de Musset's excitable duo (which culminate in grotesque, farcical, horrible, and unshaven).

Romanticism, before it was the music of Liszt and Berlioz, or the paintings of Delacroix and the poetry of Byron, and certainly before it became the province of poseurs and dilettantes, was a transformation of ideas, emanating from Germany at the end of the eighteenth century, from which the Romantic artists drew their raison d'être. Its leaders and adherents were writers and philosophers, and they largely remained so. Liszt was deeply entwined in this wider literary movement, of Goethe and Schiller in Germany, Byron in England, Rousseau in Geneva, Hugo, Chateaubriand, Sand, and Heine in France. And all these writers crossed borders, as did Liszt. Romanticism was pan European. By the time Liszt arrived in Paris as a young man, and exactly at the point when he was becoming the talk of the salons in the 1830s, the poets, novelists, and essayists of French Romanticism were engaging with the very transformation to which Berlin refers. The way this literary milieu affected Liszt's mind and imagination cannot be underestimated. He was a Romantic not just because of the music he wrote, but because of the ideas he imbibed from contemporaries who valued words, polemic, argument, philosophizing— in a word, literature—above everything. This was the air Liszt breathed and to which his temperament ardently responded.

One of his earliest biographers, writing when Liszt was only twenty-eight, pinpoints this phenomenon:

Casting his eye around, he saw celebrities, major intellectual figures poets, journalists, philosophers; he took their works, devoured them, reading with an acute sensibility, laying bare the heart of the writer. With this insatiable, nervous curiosity he read dictionaries with the same application as a poet, studying Boiste and Lamartine for four uninterrupted hours with the same investigative spirit and the same interpretive effort. Then once he had penetrated the thought of the writer he would call on him, asking him to explain his thoughts face to face. . . . He has assimilated their feelings and ideas, and every day he draws from their inspiration all he can transfer into his art. These relationships have made him discover in himself innumerable points of contact with other destinies.[8]

One of the many writers whom Liszt visited was the aging Etienne de Sénancour (1770–1846), the author of the "strange and painful poem" (George Sand's formulation[9]) *Obermann*. Liszt first knew of the book just before his deep engagement with the poetry of Byron, and it was one of the works with which he wooed Marie d'Agoult soon after their first meeting in December 1832. In his early letters to her, we witness how the twenty-two-year-old was at pains to impress her not only with the aristocratic circles he frequented but with his reading, and the writers whom he knew as friends—he quotes Petrarch, he brings up Montaigne, he mentions his acquaintance with Chateaubriand and Madame Recamier (Chateaubriand's mistress), and his easy friendship with Victor Hugo; and he offers to introduce Marie to "our celebrated compatriot Heine . . . one of the most distinguished men in Germany."[10] He also writes to her of his intention to have his new friend Chopin pass on to her the second volume of *Obermann* just after its republication in 1833, "which I ask you to be so good as to accept, underline and annotate. When you get back I shall myself have the honor of handing you the first volume, which you know already."[11]

"A STRANGE AND PAINFUL POEM"

Sénancour's *Obermann* exemplifies Berlin's sense of Romanticism in every respect, the nostalgia, the exultant reaching for the universe, the yearning for the inexpressible; and Gautier's too, in its ecstatic "rediscovery" of poetry. When George Sand called *Obermann* a "strange and painful poem," she was using the word "poem" like Gautier and Liszt used the word "poetry," to connote a concentration of feeling, that central concept of Romanticism. *Obermann* is a series of letters, an epistolary novel—though in his opening "Observations" Sénancour insists that "these letters are not a novel,"[12] freely admitting that nothing really happens. His book is a kind of fictional diary, or even in many places a stream of consciousness, a form of free association that anticipates the novels of James Joyce and Virginia Woolf. *Obermann* articulates an almost terrifying dejection, allied to a strength of mind that succeeds, in the main, in getting the better of it—the letters contain episodes of compelling optimism and lyrical beauty.

"It will be seen that these letters are the expression of a man who feels and not of a man who acts."[13] This is the first sentence Liszt would have read in the 1833 edition, from the preliminary "Observations" Sénancour offers in his pose as editor and compiler, at once allying himself with the priorities of the Romantic age. But *Obermann* was ignored for nearly three decades—first published in 1804, it was at once forgotten. The casual, meandering drift of the writing, with little tension and almost no dramatic arc, was not to the taste of a public already exposed to seminal novels of the age—to the emotional intensity of Rousseau's lovers (in *Héloise*), the exoticisms of Chateaubriand (*René*), and the obsessive passion of Goethe's hero in *The Sufferings of Young Werther*. The "feeling" of these novels leads to the kind of compelling action of which Obermann is incapable.

Then in the 1830s, in the ferment of discovery among the literary voices of Paris, the quiet sincerity of Sénancour's voice—his hero's self-analysis, his merciless observation of his own psyche—suddenly found an eager response. The book was republished with an introduction by the brilliant critic Charles Augustin Sainte-Beuve. George Sand wrote a fulsome, extended essay in the influential *Revue de deux mondes* to coincide with the publication—she claimed for the novel "a clear individuality, an image whose well-defined features have no model and no copy anywhere."[14] For a time Sénancour was in the eye of the French Romantic storm.

Liszt bought this second edition of *Obermann* immediately when it came out in 1833. Two years later he and Marie d'Agoult took the volumes with them on their Swiss travels. In Sand's essay we find quoted one of the long passages that Liszt chose as an epigraph to "Vallée d'Obermann" (see p. 89 below)[15]—she had an immense influence on him at this period. Liszt also knew and admired Sainte-Beuve and counted him among his friends. Sainte-Beuve went on to become one of the greatest literary critics of the nineteenth century, promoting a methodology of criticism that survived well into the following century and which indeed is still prevalent today: the idea that the artist and his art cannot be separated was Sainte-Beuve's. Liszt chose his mentors and friends with keen perspicuity.

Sénancour was at pains to distance himself from his protagonist but to little avail—Sainte-Beuve's critical method had caught on. "Obermann has a small gathering at his place," Liszt writes to Marie d'Agoult in July 1834, about a visit to Sénancour. "Sainte-Beuve has written a few words in the ugly album you entrusted me with. . . . I am going to take it to Obermann." (For some reason it seems Liszt did not like the look of the autograph album that Marie was wanting to hand around—a fashionable pastime in the salons. She had wanted Chateaubriand's autograph too, in the same ugly album, but Liszt refused: "I dare not ask him for anything. I know that he doesn't like writing in albums."[16])

The fictional Obermann is a young man who lives as a recluse, mainly in the Jura mountains on the French-Swiss border. His letters are written to

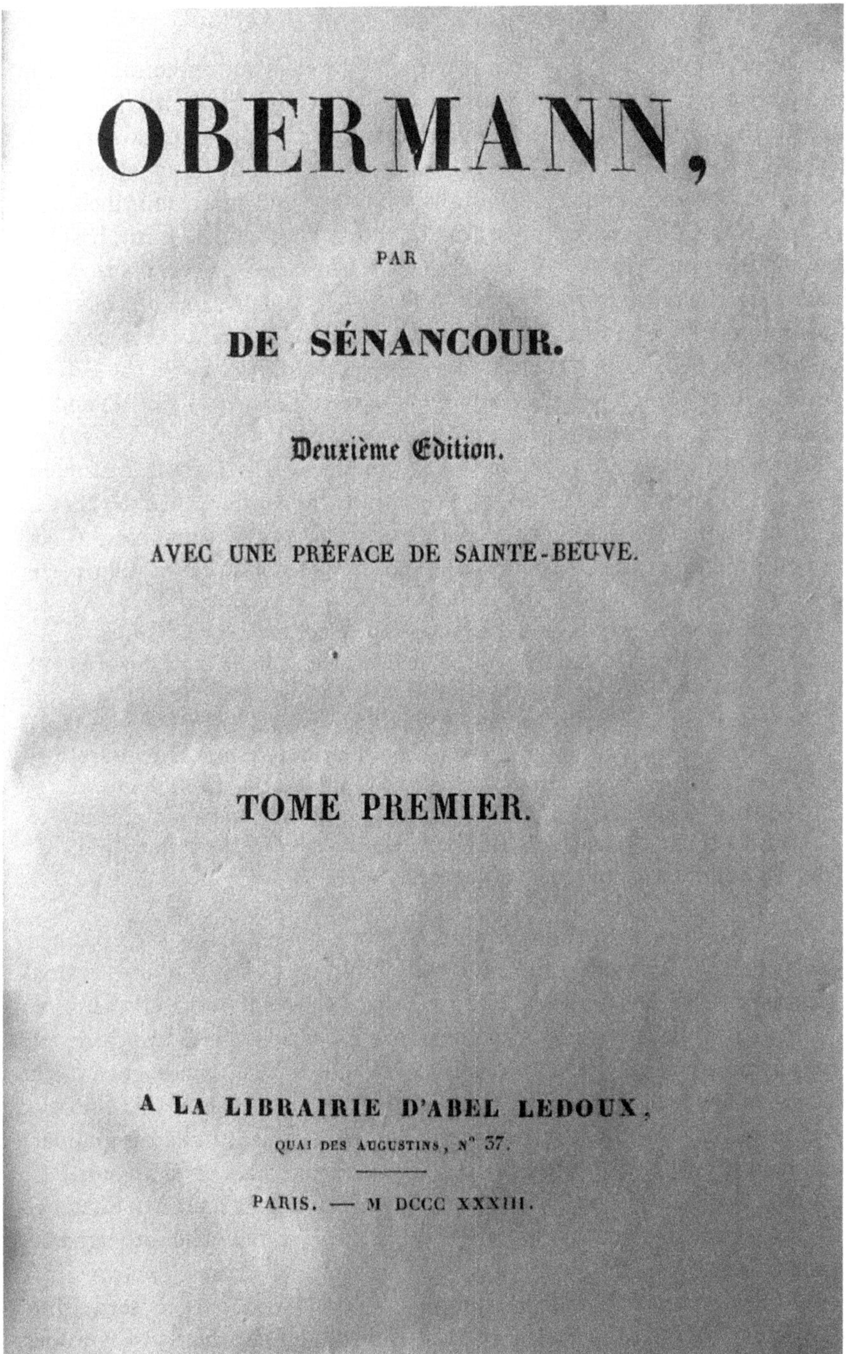
OBERMANN,

PAR

DE SÉNANCOUR.

Deuxième Edition.

AVEC UNE PRÉFACE DE SAINTE-BEUVE.

TOME PREMIER.

A LA LIBRAIRIE D'ABEL LEDOUX,

QUAI DES AUGUSTINS, N° 37.

PARIS. — M DCCC XXXIII.

Figure 6.1. Title page of the second edition (1833), Volume 1 of *Obermann* by Etienne de Sénancour. This was the edition Liszt read.

(Public Domain).

an unknown friend over a period of ten years (Sénancour wrote the book in less than two). He writes out of necessity: "all that runs through my head, all my stray thoughts . . . all that I think, all that I feel."[17] In the middle years he settles in Paris and lives for a time in the forest of Fontainebleau, returning to Switzerland in year eight. Each letter is carefully dated apart from the actual year, which is only given as "First Year," "Second Year," and so forth. It seems Liszt modeled his "Years" on Obermann's when he came to subtitle his *Années de pèlerinage* volumes. At the front of "Vallée d'Obermann," in addition to the quotation to which he was alerted by George Sand, Liszt adds another, and a dedication to Sénancour. (For the final version, in *Années Suisse*, the dedication was dropped, for reasons we will come to in chapters 7 and 8, and he added a long quotation from Byron.)

Toward the beginning of *Obermann*, Volume 1, Liszt would have come across the moment when Obermann first finds his dwelling in the valley of the River Rhone. We might notice, on the edge of Liszt's vision, that the path through Switzerland also leads to Italy, and to his second year of pilgrimage:

> At the sight of these gorges, fertile and inhabited, yet still wild, I turned aside from the road to Italy, which at this point takes a bend towards the town of Bex, and pressing on towards the bridge of the Rhone, I wandered through paths and across fields undreamed of by our painters. . . . The site is somewhat melancholy, but of a sadness that I love. The mountains are beautiful, the valley level; the rocks touch the town and seem to cover it; the muffled rumbling of the Rhone gives a note of melancholy to this land, which lies separated, as it were, from the world, hollowed out and shut in on all sides.[18]

My own interest in *Obermann* began when I came across such passages in an American translation from the beginning of the last century—a small selection of the letters from Volume 1 clearly designed to represent Sénacour as an epic poet of landscape. The gloom and dejection that I had been told were characteristic of the book were to my mind, then, outweighed by its descriptive beauty. I was alerted by the translator's view that Sénancour had "written pages more beautiful perhaps in their simplicity, charm, grandeur even, than have many of his better known contemporaries or successors."[19]

Obermann is a quasi-philosophical meditation on the nature of existence, and humankind's relationship with the natural world. The protagonist's constant self-awareness swings between ecstasy and depression (today we would call him bipolar), a depression which in the middle years settles into an utter dejection that is painful to read. But throughout the Swiss episodes, which clearly are Liszt's point of departure—the "valley" in which his musical imagination dwells—the writing is brought alive, the gloom banished (paralleled in Liszt's composition) by vivid evocations of landscape that have an almost cinematic actuality: the sublime vistas of the alps, the pastoral beauty of the valleys, the heat of the sun, the weariness of the traveler, the comfort of wayside inns. In the unadorned simplicity of the prose, its effortless musical rhythms and phrasing, Sénancour achieved some of the finest nature writing of the early nineteenth century. In many respects *Obermann* is similar to the extended autobiographical poem by William Wordsworth, *The Prelude*, and could perhaps have been similarly subtitled "The Growth of a Poet's Mind."[20] The two works are almost contemporary. And for all Senancour's protests to the contrary, *Obermann* certainly reflects the author's own life.

One wonders by the end of the book, however, exactly what for Obermann/Sénancour the growth has amounted to, so devastating has been his experience of what he calls "the void" within him, and his sense of failure. (It seems Liszt is asking the same question in the final cadence of "Vallée d'Obermann.") George Sand in her essay unerringly places Obermann's debilitating dilemma, and she gives it a political dimension, diagnosing a state of mind induced by the deep pessimism following the French Revolution. Contemplating the state of the world into which he was born, Obermann's dejection she suggests is the result of a bitter clear-sightedness: "For him it is about knowing the illness (*la maladie*); later he will find the remedy," writes Sand.[21] But the only remedy we can detect in the book is his response to the immutable beauty of the natural world. Struggling to find a meaning in his surroundings, he comes to feel nothing other than a separation, a disconnection. "Later" doesn't come. Sénancour in a footnote writes, "Perhaps he reaches conclusions in the continuation of his letters, but up to the present time this second part is wholly missing."[22] We are left wondering if time really will heal him. Wordsworth's vision of the world was far more positive.

Reading *Obermann* today, despite the meandering *longueurs* and the repetitive philosophizing of an age when there was more time for reading, one can still be drawn in, as Liszt would have been, by the intimacy of the protagonist's soliloquy—of a mind laying bare its delights and disillusions, its aspirations and idealism, and its darkness. Obermann's self-analysis is akin to Hamlet's. Shakespeare, and especially *Hamlet*, was a touchstone for the Romantics, in which they found the model for the Romantic hero. The difference, however, between Obermann and Hamlet is that the latter (like Faust) is finally goaded into action. Obermann remains passive, wrapped in his own dejection, his debilitating *ennui*. "This word ennui," writes Sainte-Beuve in his introduction, "is Obermann's most distinguishing feature, and his malaise; it was partly the malaise of the century [*le mal du siècle*], and Obermann is thus one of the truest books of this century, one of the most sincere testimonies, in which many souls will recognize themselves."[23]

LISZT AS OBERMANN

In 1833, when he first read *Obermann*, Liszt was twenty-two, the age of Obermann when he begins his letters. There is a distinct sense in "Vallée d'Obermann"—begun around 1836—that the story Liszt is telling is in some sense his own. Having sought out the writer, a few years later he sought out Obermann's *mis en scène*. He was lit up by the experience of the Swiss Alps, both in his imagination and in reality, and recognized in himself the same dilemmas that Sénancour lays bare.

This is not to discount the profound differences in their experiences. Liszt was perfectly able to identify with Obermann without having to experience his crippling ennui. He was in love with Marie, he was discovering the landscapes of Switzerland and Italy, he was breathing in the sun of the south and its art and monuments, its composers, writers, and artists. Nothing further from Obermann's (or Senancour's) existence can be imagined. Obermann shunned society, Liszt courted it. Obermann extolled passivity and contemplation, Liszt engagement and activity.

But Liszt's fullest engagement with *Obermann*, while in Switzerland, was at a time when he had himself escaped the tumult of Parisian life, and his own self-questioning was acute. Certainly, we cannot discount the excitement the young man felt at mimicking his literary heroes, in adopting a Byronic pose, an Obermann agony. But Liszt in these years was also another kind of artist of profoundly serious intent, one seeking an identity beyond that of a virtuoso performer playing to the crowd. The young Liszt recognized in himself all the dilemmas of Obermann, and he paid the deepest attention to the questions Obermann asked. "What do I want? What am I? What do I ask of nature?" Liszt placed these questions at the front of "Vallée d'Obermann," and he continued the quotation:

> All causes are hidden, all ends mistaken. All form changes, all time slips away.... I do feel, I do exist, only to be consumed by unconquerable desires, to drink in the seductions of a fantastical world, to be overwhelmed by its voluptuous deception.[24]

Liszt would have exulted in the fundamental place Sénancour ascribes to feeling, but we can also imagine him reading this with a shudder of a different kind of recognition. Amid the excitement of his fame, Liszt had a keen awareness of its perils, a fear of his own void, and he took immense steps to avert it. He lived Obermann's agonies. In chapter 3, I quoted a passage from the joint diary Liszt wrote with Marie d'Agoult, and I suggested it was apposite to his reading of Petrarch. It is equally relevant to what he would have found in *Obermann*. Liszt wrote,

> Two opposing forces are fighting within me: one thrusts me towards the immensity of space, higher, even higher, beyond all suns, up to the heavens; the other pulls me down towards the lowest, the darkest regions of calm, of death, of nothingness.[25]

Liszt's second quotation on the score comes from one of the most lyrically descriptive letters in Sénancour's whole book, early in Volume 1. Sand too quotes from this letter in her essay to show what she calls Sénancour's "exquisite sentiment of poetry"[26]: Obermann is awakened "by the splendors of the dawn and the scent of new mown hay, cut in the fresh night air, by the light of the moon." She also quotes Obermann's debilitating dejection that follows this euphoria, and it is this passage Liszt chooses to focus on in his own quotation:

> A sensibility I cannot utter, the charm as well as the torment of wasted years, a profound realization of overwhelming nature everywhere and everywhere inscrutable; all-absorbing passion, deepened wisdom, rapturous self-abandonment, all that a human soul can experience of deep desire and world-weariness, I felt it all, I lived it all on that memorable night. I have taken a fatal step towards my decay; I devoured, this night, ten years of my life.[27]

"A sensibility I cannot utter" is the Romantic myth of the "inexpressible" diagnosed by Isaiah Berlin: "Your relation to the universe is inexpressible, yet you must nevertheless express it."[28] Obermann professes an inability to communicate, yet he finds all the words, and he is expecting the recipient of his letters to read his words. That the novel was virtually ignored when it was first published in 1804 is merely an irony of history. Those who avidly read the second edition of 1833 most certainly heard him.

When Liszt came to revise "Vallée d'Obermann," the many influences on his creative imagination during the 1830s were long in the past. The *Années de pèlerinage—Suisse* of 1855 present a clearer, wiser vision of youthful discovery, without any sacrifice of excitement or spontaneity (indeed several of the pieces remain almost identical to their originals). In the case of "Vallée d'Obermann," much changed, as we will see, not least the rejection of the Sénancour dedication and the addition of a stanza from Byron. Clearly Liszt came to see the Byronic dimension in the second passage from Sénancour, for for the long quotation he later added from Byron articulates the very dilemma at the heart of the *Obermann*: "[C]ould I wreak/My thoughts upon expression." This too is the artist lamenting an inability to express the vision within, saying in effect "I can't" at the very point when demonstrating "I can." We will look in detail at this Byron quotation in chapter 8.

"VALLÉE D'OBERMANN"

Liszt's "Vallée d'Obermann" captures the sensibility of *Obermann* in musical form, not as illustration but as an analogous work of art. We only have to consider that Sénacour's novel recounts a period of ten years to realize that Liszt's music, lasting twelve minutes, is not mere illustration. As in the Faust Symphony and the Petrarch Sonnets, Liszt feels his way into the psyche of his protagonist; his music is able to be a synopsis of the text, a distillation, and at the same time an expansion of its central psychological meaning. Yet musical illustration remains a component of Liszt's art, as a brief account of the main events of the music will show.

The opening (figure 6.2) enacts the deepest pessimism, dark E minor destabilized by constant chromatic modulation. The theme is built from a persistent and repeatedly falling scale. Whenever the melodic line reaches upward, it obsessively falls back—Obermann's agony is unerringly delineated. At bar 51, *dolcissimo*, the same theme briefly evokes a memory of solace, as if in a dream, only to sink back at the *dolente* into deeper despondency. The story Liszt is enacting through his music has the palpability of a novel. The reiterated E minor triads at the end of this long opening section, a kind of first movement, an opening chapter, suggest the darkness of a tomb. The silence instructed in the score (figure 6.3, bar 74) is the silence of despair.

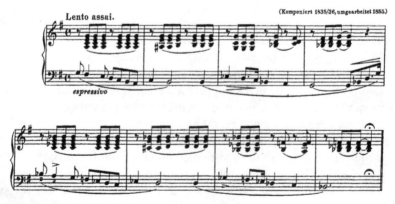

Figure 6.2. "Vallée d'Obermann," mm. 1–8.
Breitkopf & Härtel, 1916.

Figure 6.3. "Vallée d'Obermann," mm. 70–74.
Breitkopf & Härtel, 1916.

Analogous to the reiterated mood swings throughout *Obermann*, what now follows is an unexpected change of direction (a switch to C major *dolcissimo*, and a change of register). There is nothing abrupt about this shift, continuity is perfectly controlled, but now the repeated chord figurations of the accompaniment instead of dragging back, imposing weight and weariness, suggest an awakening (figure 6.4). The mood here has an exquisite sweetness; the pain remains (the first three notes of the opening theme are carried over into the new theme), but there is a sense that the deep gloom of the valley might not be forever—that perhaps we can breathe mountain air. But this mood cannot be sustained and gradually the full extent of the seven-note falling scale of the opening theme returns and we are once more in the dark registers of the bass. We have to begin again.

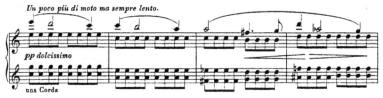

Figure 6.4. "Vallée d'Obermann," mm. 75–78.
Breitkopf & Härtel, 1916.

Section 3 (bars 119–160) is Liszt in full Shakespearian mode, or indeed Byronic dress. The quotation he later added from Byron describes the poet's response to a storm in the Alps. In "Vallée d'Obermann," Liszt uses the tropes of storm music—of which he was master in his public improvisations—to evoke the turmoil in Obermann's psyche (just as Shakespeare's storm in *King Lear* symbolizes the madness of Lear). At the end of this section the emotional narrative reaches its maximum dislocation—the noise and fury give way to bleak monody, the three-note motif is like a cry, reiterated as unadorned recitative followed by further silence (those concentrated silences that Liszt learned from Beethoven). Hope appears to have been abandoned.

A storm destroys, but it can also bring renewal. The emerging warmth of E major at the opening of the final section (bar 170, Lento) is one of the most transfixing moments in all of Liszt's piano music, the equal of his supreme mastery of such moods and material in the Dante Sonata, the B minor Sonata or "Bénédiction de Dieu dans la solitude." This seems to be a hymn to love, one of the many in Liszt's music; or a hymn of thanksgiving that turns into triumph. In Letter 4, from which Liszt takes his second quotation, Obermann writes of being "in harmony with the totality of things. . . . I love existing things, I love them as they are."[29] Liszt would come across the same sentiment in Byron—"I live not in myself, but I become / Portion of that around me"—the quotation he added, as we shall see in the next chapter, to the first version of "Les Cloches de Genève."

CODA

Liszt triumphantly asserted "I can" in "Vallée d'Obermann." His addition of an epigraph from Byron over ten years later was a sign of confidence, of his complete conviction in the art he was making in the *Années de pèlerinage*. He had not moved on from *Obermann*, so much as broadened his points of reference, embraced the plurality of the literature he was reading, all of which had liberated his creative imagination. No one I think would prefer the early version of "Vallée d'Obermann" to the later masterpiece in which Liszt recognized a kinship with Byron. Liszt's literary growth led to the growth of his music—through literature he was freed into music. All the pieces we are discussing in this book manifest this phenomenon. All are profoundly musical, of music, pure music. "Has anyone ever known a more musical composer than Franz Liszt?" asked Wagner toward the end of his life. And yet all these compositions arise from a response to literature without which one can confidently say the music would not have come into being.

We might say that "Vallée d'Obermann" is about the nature of creativity, an enactment of self-doubt and the ecstatic discovery, for Liszt if not Obermann, of creative power. (Liszt would follow this trajectory again in a later masterpiece, "Bénédiction de Dieu dans la solitude," inspired by a poem by Alphonse de Lamartine.) The writers Liszt drew on were those who expressed his own creative and personal struggle. They asked the questions he was asking, and the act of questioning itself provided a kind of answer. The artwork was the answer. When Liszt was in the midst of his own Obermann-like dejection toward the end of his life—what he called his "bitterness of heart"—he would have remembered the profound lessons of Sénancour and Byron, Petrarch and Goethe, Lamartine and Dante.

"Vallée d'Obermann" is not musical illustration in the sense that it is only about valleys and mountains and storms. It does not, and cannot, illustrate a place in the manner of a painting, or even a poem. In "Vallée d'Obermann," Liszt imagines himself into the psyche of a recluse, and by extension the psyche of an artist. For the duration he is Obermann, just as the pianist should be when performing. This great composition encapsulates the character of Romanticism, the inner workings of the human animal. The valley of the title is not a place; rather, it represents the Romantic conception of the soul—Ishiguro's soul, the all too human psyche, "what we are like inside."

· *7* ·

The Aura of Byron

Années de pèlerinage—Suisse

When I flatter myself, I tell myself that I shall perhaps one day be Byron's moon.

—Liszt[1]

*I*n a famous oil painting from 1840 of Liszt at the piano, a portrait of Lord Byron hangs center stage, but in shadow, just above Liszt's illuminated head. The full thrust of the scene focuses on the pianist gazing in a trance at a bust of Beethoven, surrounded by leading figures of his literary and musical circle: Alexandre Dumas (père), Victor Hugo, George Sand, Paganini, and Rossini. Swathed in gorgeous velvet at Liszt's feet, back turned toward us, is his lover Marie d'Agoult in a pose reminiscent of a portrait by Liszt's friend Dominique Ingres (figure 7.1).

The painter was Josef Danhauser, commissioned by the Viennese piano maker Conrad Graf to promote the finest of his instruments. An association with the most famous pianist of Europe was every piano maker's dream, but clearly a more ambitious form of propaganda was being commissioned. Not only does the painting avow that Graf's instrument is worthy of the greatest musicians past and present, it also proclaims an intimacy with the living tip of European literary culture. Playing a Graf piano, it is clearly implied, will lead one into the inner secrets of cultured discourse. Hugo has lowered his book, entranced by the music; Sand's hand reaches across to touch the book Dumas has just closed (or which perhaps she has closed for him) as if to say "words are no longer adequate." An air of transfixed listening pervades the entire scene.[2]

The piano here is an instrument not of mere virtuosity (one of the buzz words of the age and used with increasing pejorative intent), but of poetic insight and experience. (Such was the ideal, though the reality was sometimes different. Clara Schumann's father, Friedrich Wieck, records Liszt playing at Graf's Vienna showroom in 1838 with the piano maker "sweating as his piano did not survive the great duel." And another time how his playing

Figure 7.1. *Liszt at the Piano*, by Josef Danhauser, 1840, oil on panel. From right to left: Marie d'Agoult, Liszt, Rossini, Paganini, George Sand (seated), Hugo, Dumas.
Nationalgalerie der Staatlichen Museen zu Berlin–Preußischer Kulturbesitz. Photographer: Jörg P. Anders (CC BY-NC-SA).

"destroyed" two Grafs and an Erard, "but everything full of genius."[3]) We might see the painting as a visual representation of Liszt's avowed intention, just the year before, "to be the first to introduce poetry into piano music with sense of style"—by which he meant the feeling of poetry, the "poetical."[4] The literati themselves appear to consent, and the spirit of Beethoven gives its blessing. Piano music has achieved the status of the finest of the fine arts.

And Byron, the creator and personification of the "Byronic hero" whose influence resonated throughout the literature of the nineteenth century, hangs quietly above it all. But here his handsome profile, a copy of a portrait taken in 1816 by the English painter George Harlow, has no claim to heroic status. Instead the prestige of Byron has been subsumed by the figure of Franz Liszt, not only the greatest executant of the keyboard but also a comparably heroic "poet." The painter Danhauser knew precisely what he was doing. We might even wonder whether the figures in his imagined scene were chosen in consultation with Liszt himself, who held them all in enormous regard.

Since the publication of the first two parts of *Childe Harold's Pilgrimage* in 1812 (cantos 3 and 4 came in 1816), Lord Byron had become not just the most famous and courted English poet, but Europe's poet too. In 1816, mired in scandal, he had to leave Britain never to return. He became the embodiment of his own myth, the wandering Childe Harold of his invention who turns his pessimistic, skeptical gaze onto the world around him and sees the bitter truths of things. "Mad, bad and dangerous to know" was the famous verdict of Lady Caroline Lamb, briefly Byron's lover following the overnight success of *Childe Harold's Pilgrimage*. The notoriety was only partly justified, but perhaps more so than the notoriety of Liszt, who was later to suffer similar scandalized publicity. In neither case did it dampen the ardor of the public's response.

> I have dined with a handsome and charming young man, his face an eighteen-year-old's, even though he is twenty-eight, with the profile of an angel. . . . When he enters an English drawing room all the women leave at once. He is the greatest living poet, Lord Byron.[5]

Such was the fusion of man, myth, and poetry captured by the French novelist Stendhal, in a recollection of his first meeting with Byron in Milan in 1816. It could equally have applied to Liszt two decades later, with the difference that his own notoriety rarely compelled women to leave the drawing room.

In France the mania for Byron—the long, rhymed narrative poetry, the semi-fictional Byronic heroes, the life of the man himself—reached its peak in Liszt's literary milieu of the 1830s. Liszt's desire for literary knowledge, as we have seen, was formidable. Marie d'Agoult recalled in her memoirs that at the age of twenty-two, Liszt's insatiable intellectual "restiveness" led him to explore all "innovations in the arts and letters which threatened the old disciplines: *Childe Harold, Manfred* [Byron], *Werther* [Goethe], *Obermann* [Sénancour], all the proud or desperate revolutionaries of romantic poetry were the companions of his sleepless nights."[6] She has enumerated here the backbone of Liszt's literary inspiration over the next decade, which in musical terms gave birth to the Swiss volume of *Années de pèlerinage* (and if we add his reading of Petrarch and Dante, the Italian volume too). "He is conversant with French *belles-lettres* in an unusually comprehensive way," wrote the highly influential Berlin critic Ludwig Rellstab:

> The more recent works of Romanticism, especially Victor Hugo, have inspired him profoundly. He knows German literature less well, only a few things of Lessing and Goethe's Faust, and some recent works. . . . [But] he feels the strongest kinship with Lord Byron. He is the poet, as Liszt himself admits, whom he has embraced, to whom he has abandoned himself completely.[7]

The formidable Rellstab, one whom Liszt above all wanted to have on his side as he made his way, was a polymath in the field of literature and poetry as well as music criticism. A year earlier, in a review of one of Liszt's Berlin concerts, he had given public recognition to Liszt's self-image as a "poet" of the keyboard—that same image captured in Danhauser's painting. "His art is a poetic one, belonging to higher spiritual elements, and accordingly we too consider ourselves justified in attempting to *describe* it poetically rather than analyse it critically."[8]

We have already seen how Liszt identified with his literary heroes—with Petrarch as a lover, with Faust as a divided soul. We are who we read. In 1840, in anticipation of a visit to Byron's home, Newstead Abbey in Nottinghamshire, during his tour of Britain, Liszt wrote to Marie d'Agoult of his "feeling for—I could almost say affinity with—Lord Byron. . . . I know not what burning, whimsical desire comes over me from time to time to meet him in a world where we shall at last be strong and free." (Liszt's allusion is not only to the narrative works, but to Byron's active support for liberal causes.) Then the next day, "As I left, the moaning of the pine trees awakened corresponding harmonies within me, and hollow voiced I sang and mused out loud. I shall write all that down one day."[9]

What excites him is an identification with Byron, and the knowledge that he has it in him to create as great a poetry in his own medium. Indeed he had already published an early version of *Années de pèlerinage (Première année, Suisse)*, with Byron quotations attached, which revised and amplified would become the great set of pieces we now have, published some fifteen years later.

It is probable that Liszt would have known Byron's poem from 1803 "On Leaving Newstead Abbey," which perfectly captures his own dark communion with his hero:

> *Through thy battlements, Newstead, the hollow winds whistle;*
> *Thou, the hall of my fathers, art gone to decay;*
> *In the once smiling garden, the hemlock and thistle*
> *Have choked up the rose that once bloomed in the way.*

In the same vein he tells Marie, "[F]locks of ravens were cawing above my head and for a long time I listened to their funereal music."[10]

Liszt spent several years trying to write an opera after Byron. After many false starts he finally settled on Byron's play *Sardanapalus*, completing one act between 1845 and 1851 before abandoning the project.[11] But it is in the first book of the *Années de pèlerinage* that his engagement with Byron's poetry is the most clearly expressed: five of the nine pieces are preceded by quotations from *Childe Harold's Pilgrimage*. One commentator has even argued that "listening to Liszt [the *Années-Suisse*] becomes a musical analogue of reading Byron."[12] My emphasis is different, and it is to this question that I will now turn. Despite the association of Byron's title with Liszt's—in French, Byron's is translated as *Les années de pèlerinage de Childe Harold*—there are other echoes. Byron was by no means the only literary catalyst.

TRAVELER AND PILGRIM

Liszt's creative demon rarely stood still; second thoughts, spontaneous responses to ever-changing stimuli, were his habitual modes of operation. (On the concert stage he was one of the most masterful improvisers the piano world had ever known.) Even the overall title of what was to become one of his greatest masterpieces for the piano changed—and changed again. The pieces have a confusing publication history, appearing in various guises.[13] Early versions were published as both *Années de pèlerinage* (Years of Pilgrimage) and *Album d'un voyageur* (Album of a Traveler). It is an ambivalence that reveals the complexity of associations in Liszt's mind as he attempted to account for his cognitive experience, his fascination with his own creative responses to literature, landscape, and music; and as he defined and refined his sense of the union of music and poetry.

In 1842 Ludwig Rellstab heard Liszt perform the first versions of "Au lac de Wallenstadt" and "Au bord d'une source" in Berlin. He singled them out as a milestone in Liszt's formation—part of a collection, Rellstab claimed, "that he has not yet published nor even yet arranged and written down as a unit":

> He has nevertheless gathered part of them together in a large work in several volumes, to which . . . he has given the title *Années de pèlerinage*. It is above all from what he sends out into the world of this collection that his importance as a composer will be judged. The two samples he offered in his concert promise something extraordinarily beautiful.[14]

Although Liszt had in fact published some of the pieces, very soon after came another extended publication, with the new title *Album d'un voyageur*. Later he withdrew both publications, bought back the rights, and radically recast the overall idea. But Rellstab's prediction, on the slender evidence of two short pieces he had heard, was confirmed—although far from universally recognized—by the 1855 publication of *Années de pèlerinage–Suisse*.

What can be deduced from Liszt's indecision over the title? Why should it matter, especially considering both titles occupy the same ground?—after all, the traveler and the pilgrim can be seen as almost two of a kind. On one level the answer was simply practical: the original *Années* publication became one section (now called "Impressions et poésies") of the much larger *Album*, which comprised nineteen pieces divided into three books. But the answer also lies in the breadth of Liszt's literary references, in his eager embrace of literature that spoke to his own idealism and his search for identity. The question leads us into Liszt's thought processes as he developed his ideas on the unity of music and poetry; it is indeed at the heart of how the experimental piano pieces from the second half of the 1830s became the master work of 1855.

The title *Années de pèlerinage* would have had very strong associations for Liszt and his contemporaries not only with Byron but with Goethe's seminal *Wilhelm Meister* novels—*Wilhelm Meisters Lehrjahre* (Apprentice Years) and *Wilhelm Meisters Wanderjahre*, literally Wandering Years. The latter in French is known as *Les années de pèlerinage de Wilhelm Meister*. It is a quintessential coming-of-age novel, a story of self-discovery, relating the adventures of a young man who runs away to join a theatrical group. His relationship with the enigmatic child, Mignon, became one of the most ubiquitous stories in nineteenth-century literature, art, and music.[15] Goethe had died in 1832, so he was still very much alive, as it were, in Liszt's imagination throughout the remaining years of the decade. *Wilhelm Meisters Wanderjahre* had only been completed in its final form in 1829—like Liszt, Goethe was an inveterate reviser—and translated into French shortly after.

The second title, from 1842, *Album d'un voyageur*, would also have had strong literary connotations for Liszt's contemporaries. His allusion is to the travel diaries that were another feature of his age, those of Heine, Madame de Staël, and Goethe. But above all it associated Liszt with one of his most celebrated contemporaries, George Sand. In 1835 they exchanged long open letters in the leading Parisian literary journals, expounding their views on art and artists, politics, and people, each taking on the persona of a clear-eyed observer of the world, its problems and foibles. Sand's twelve *Lettres d'un voyageur*, collected into one volume in 1837, had an avid readership. Liszt followed suit: he replied to Sand in the *Gazette musicale* with his own travel pieces addressed to *Un poète voyageur*.

Liszt's title, *Album d'un voyageur*, indicated an experiment in a new genre of artmaking. It captured his conception of a travelogue in music: a collection of impressions of the Swiss landscape (and the music to be heard there), evoking the heady experience of mountains, streams, Alpine storms, and lake Leman at the foot of Mont Blanc, along with a running commentary, in the section titled "Impressions et Poésies," of literary quotations. Even the political dimensions of the literary travelogue were present, proclaiming the writer's (composer's) solidarity with oppressed peoples in this age of revolutions. The opening piece of the *Album*, "Lyon," was written in response to the uprising of the silk weavers of that city and bears a quotation from one of Liszt's early mentors, the social reformer Félicité de Lamennais: *Vivre en travaillant ou mourir en combattant* (Live working or Die fighting).

It seems the strength of this idea—the traveler as a curious, open-eyed tourist, recording first impressions, and displaying a social and historical awareness—was what initially turned Liszt away from the idea of a *pèlerinage*, a pilgrim seeking wisdom. When he came to rethink and revise the collection, the title of self-discovery, *Années de pèlerinage*—with its echoes of both Goethe and Byron—was appropriately reinstated. The final version combines the freshness of Liszt's earlier responses to landscape with a far superior skill in composing music. The pilgrim title discarded in 1840 suggested the composer he wanted to be. In the next decade it became the sign of the composer he had become.

"A TALENT OF LITTLE IMPORTANCE"

In 1843, while Liszt was in the full throes of his tours as a virtuoso, a curious comment appeared in a Belgian music journal:

> Liszt, they say, has just declared that he considers a pianist's talent a talent of such little importance that he would much prefer to be known as a good writer capable of handling musical matters than a celebrated performer on the piano.[16]

This can be greeted with a certain skepticism, but we should recall Liszt's lament that "there is nothing quite as ludicrous as the travelling musician" and that he often felt like "a useless clown, an ill-fated troubadour."[17] And we know too that a few years later he gave it all up.

Liszt's travel writing had as large a following as George Sand's; his *Letters of a Bachelor of Music* (those he wrote for the *Gazette musicale* in imitation of hers for the *Revue des deux mondes*) were widely disseminated in translations throughout Europe. It is one further sign of his huge ambitions beyond concert pianism, of his extraordinary ability to combine multiple interests, musical, literary, political—and after 1840, what is more, combine them with his strenuous life as a touring virtuoso.

A snapshot of his activities just at the time of the Belgian gossip piece includes four recitals in ten days in Berlin in January, immediately followed by ten concerts in Breslau (now Wroclaw in Western Poland), where he also conducted Mozart's *Magic Flute*; in February he was in Berlin again, conducting Beethoven's *Coriolan* Overture, Weber's *Oberon* Overture, and performing Mendelssohn's D minor Piano Concerto. In March and April, he was performing in Cracow, Warsaw, and then on to St. Petersburg and Moscow. This is not the itinerary of one who, on the surface at least, considered "a pianist's talent a talent of such little importance." And during these years of travel—his own years of pilgrimage—he was also composing his multiple transcriptions of popular operas, the crowd pleasers of his concerts. "He often performed these works in the concert hall only hours after noting them down in his hotel room or in the mail coach."[18]

In 1837 Liszt had written a preface to his projected collection of piano pieces (later published in both the *Album* and the first version of *Années*) in which he had articulated his ideas on how art is made. He touched eloquently on a central aspect of the Romantic artist's creative imagination:

> Having travelled of late through many new lands, many different places, many locations consecrated by history and poetry, having felt that the diverse sights nature afforded and the scenes related to them did not pass before my eyes in meaningless images, but that they stirred profound emotions within my soul, that there existed between them and me a vague but direct relation, an indefinite but real connection, an inexplicable but sure communication, I have attempted to render some of my strongest sensation, my livelier impressions in music.[19]

What is notable here is the almost mystical sense of rapport Liszt feels between his artist's identity and the scenes he witnesses. This we will see is closely aligned to Byron's manner in *Childe Harold's Pilgrimage*, but it also echoes George Sand. For Liszt music was essentially a subjective response to experience, above all emotional experience, that could not be put into words. His many long discussions with George Sand had borne fruit in his own enterprise. Sand had written in one of her *Lettres d'un voyageur*,

> You must never read my letters with the intention of understanding the least thing about external objects. I see everything through personal impressions. A trip is for me only a course of psychology and physiology of which I am the subject.[20]

In his preface, Liszt shows his total commitment to Sand's view. It is worth dwelling not just on the meaning of his words, but on their literary construction. His paragraph is a single sentence, self-consciously so, modeled on the kind of writing Liszt knew and revered.[21] Along with everything else he did, Liszt identified as a writer. (The suggestion, long disseminated, that Marie d'Agoult wrote Liszt's articles has been convincingly repudiated.[22])

THE BYRONIC HERO

In the early 1840s, Liszt was considering Byron's *The Corsair* for an opera setting, the narrative poem that even more than *Childe Harold's Pilgrimage* defined the parameters of the Byronic hero as the flawed, lonely genius (often a warrior, a bandit, or an excommunicant), beyond the pale of social conventions. Byron describes Conrad the "Corsair" thus:

> *He knew himself detested, but he knew*
> *The hearts that loathed him, crouched and dread too.*
> *Lone, wild, and strange, he stood alike exempt*
> *From all affection and from all contempt:*
> *His name could sadden, and his acts surprise;*
> *But they that feared him dared not to despise.*[23]

The Byronic hero was one of the central aspects of Byron's appeal, without which the Byron myth would not exist. The consequences of Byron's creation were game changing for European literature—he had drawn a psychological type that at once touched a nerve, one that became embedded in subsequent writing: Britain's Emily Brontë (Heathcliff) and Charlotte Brontë (Rochester), in Russia's Lermontov (Pechorin) and Pushkin (Onegin) and the novels of Dostoevesky, in the philosophy of Nietzsche, and on into the twentieth century's fascination with the anti-hero. Even the original James Bond in Ian Fleming's novels has the marks of the Byronic hero.

The *Corsair* plan came to nothing and for a while Liszt took up Byron's short four-act drama *Manfred*. For George Sand, Byron's *Manfred* was "perhaps the most magnificent example of his genius."[24] Yet again we see her influence on Liszt during these years of his literary discoveries. And, of the greatest significance to Liszt's later direction, the narrative of *Manfred* has marked similarities to Goethe's *Faust*. "In my youth," he recalled nearly two decades later, "I passionately admired Manfred, and valued him much more than Faust."[25]

The influence of Byron was colossal for the growing middle classes of Europe in the first half of the nineteenth century—for the literati and opinion formers, for aspiring artists, musicians, and painters, for general readers, and not least for those who espoused, either actively or tacitly, radical politics. The framing context for his reception in European countries across the English Channel was the political disruption and realignment left in the wake of Napoleon Bonaparte. Byron offered a safety valve for liberal opinion disenchanted by the failure of what they had originally believed to be Napoleonic salvation. Napoleon began as a liberator and ended up an emperor. But Napoleon vanquished, finally defeated at the Battle of Waterloo on June 8, 1815, resulted in even greater political repression. For the rulers of Europe, Richard Cardwell writes,

> Byron represented, clearly, a challenge on two fronts: the struggle for the liberty of oppressed peoples and the struggle to define a new artistic language for the expression of that desire for freedom, social and individual. The two, it seemed, were inseparable. . . . Byron, then, proved to many that a poet could be a man of action as well as a thinker. It was a view which held an extraordinary fascination for writers of his own and successive generations.[26]

It was a view that held an extraordinary fascination for the young Franz Liszt, too, whose aspirations as a pianist and composer were deeply interwoven with a burning social conscience. He too, as poet-pianist, aspired to be "a man of action as well as a thinker," proclaiming solidarity with the July Revolution of 1830 in Paris, with the oppressed silk weavers of Lyon in 1831, and the flood victims of Hungary in 1838.

The Napoleon cult lasted decades after his demise. In the gallery of major historical figures of the first half of the nineteenth century, it was Napoleon and Byron who were spoken of in the same breath—Napoleon as liberator rather than destroyer. In the late 1830s Liszt rapidly became one of this company.[27] It was not only that he was called "the Napoleon of the piano"—an easy enough conjunction for capturing celebrity—but that the metaphor commentators often employed to describe the astounding strength and spectacle of Liszt's performances was one drawn from the victories and triumph of the battlefield. Even in appearance he was compared to Napoleon. Liszt wrote in delight from London to Marie d'Agoult in 1840, "Lady Blessington affirms that I resemble Bonaparte and Lord Byron."[28]

Liszt as the Napoleon of the piano and the Byron of the piano—the triumvirate was complete, and Liszt's celebrity and notoriety was assured. He was caricatured in military dress on horseback; and in a lithograph from 1840 we see him looking Byronic in an embroidered traveling coat. Beneath the picture Liszt has handwritten the second stanza of Byron's poem addressed to Thomas Moore, Byron's friend and subsequent biographer:

Here's a sigh to those who love me,
And a smile to those who hate;
And, whatever sky's above me,
Here's a heart for every fate.

Liszt had almost no English when, in 1820, in his late teens, he first acquired his volumes of Byron—this was the edition of Amédée Pichot, pub-

Figure 7.2.   *Liszt in Travelling Coat*. Lithograph by Josef Kriehuber, 1840.
(Public Domain).

lished in France in 1821, two years before the poet's death. It was, to Moore's (and Byron's) disgust, a prose translation. So initially for Liszt, as for many French readers, it was the narratives, the exploits of the hero, that held sway. Byron might have been a poet, but for the French he was at first a storyteller in prose. The extra appeal of *Childe Harold* was that it combined the hero as misunderstood outcast (taken on compelling evidence to be Byron himself) with Byron's exhilarating sweep across contemporary European history and culture. His virtuosity as a commentator, his command of the zeitgeist, his irony and skepticism, his willingness to say the unsayable, was an intoxicating mix in a Europe ravaged physically and psychologically by war.

The belief that the hero was Byron in disguise was given extra support in France by the publication in 1830 of a translation of Moore's biography, *The Life of Lord Byron*. Subsequent French editions of Byron's poetry drew heavily on it, printing biography and poetry side by side. Central to the Byron aura was his death in Greece in 1823, where he had gone to support the country's fight against Ottoman oppression. He had died of fever and not in battle, but this befitted the myth of the hero who puts himself in harm's way, only to be cut down by mundane reality. In Britain such commentators as Sir Walter Scott and the historian Lord Macaulay added their prestige to the myth. Scott suggested that "in the features of Conrad those who have looked upon Lord Byron will recognize some likeness."[29] And Macaulay wrote, in a review of Moore's *Life of Lord Byron*, that the poet "was himself the beginning, the middle, and the end of all his own poetry, the hero of every tale, the chief object of every landscape."[30]

The fact that Liszt read Byron at first not only in French but in prose makes it all the more remarkable that when he came to quote Byron's poems in English in the *Années de pèlerinage*, he chose, as we shall see, some of the finest lines. At some point he came to read Byron very closely, in other translations than Pichot's, and certainly in English.[31] He must soon have sensed the strength of the original, through his natural affinity for literature and his astutely discerning ear.[32]

CHILDE HAROLD'S PILGRIMAGE

Reading Byron today, especially out loud, one soon picks up the virtuoso style that so captivated his first readers, the sheer brilliance of his versification and rhyme schemes, his deft mastery of language. In one's head, read silently, Byron needs attention; his lines need to be heard as music is heard, until their rhythms and rhymes become an effortless mode of cognition; the poetry needs to move swiftly and musically. Byron spoke of his plays as "mental theatre"—"no matter for the stage or not, which is not my object."[33] This is equally valid for his narrative poetry. *The Corsair, Mazeppa*, and *Manfred* still have the capacity to thrill, even though our comfortable embrace of the prose novel today means we no longer have the same taste for adventure stories in rhymed verse as Byron's readers had (and when the realist novel was in its infancy). But *Childe Harold's Pilgrimage* is more challenging on account of its cultural and political agenda. In ambition it was the precursor of

Byron's greatest work, *Don Juan*, a virtuosic *tour de force* of satirical writing, of epic dimensions, which one commentator has called "a conscious attempt to explain critically the meaning of the entire period in Europe stretching from 1789 to 1823."[34]

All the lines of Byron that Liszt quotes as epigraphs in the Swiss volume of the *Années* come from canto III of *Childe Harold's Pilgrimage*. Specifically, they come from the point in the narrative when Harold is in Switzerland. Byron was in Switzerland too when he wrote this canto, having just fled England. Like Goethe's Wilhelm Meister (and like Obermann), exiled Harold/Byron is yet another wanderer in search of anonymity, solace, and enlightenment. But the quotations Liszt employs throughout (with the exception of the epigraph to "Vallée d'Obermann," as we have seen) evoke not the wanderer, not the hero, so much as the landscape he is wandering through. Harold extolls the sublimity of the Swiss landscape, seeking refuge in the all-embracing power of Nature. The Swiss book of the *Années de pèlerinage* is geographical, or in terms of genre, pastoral. It is this characteristic of the original *Album d'un voyageur*, and of the pieces Liszt aptly titled "Impressions et poésies," that is carried over into the final *Années de pèlerinage*.

Nature, with a capital N, was at the center of Romantic literature—emanating from Rousseau in France and Wordsworth in England—but it was not always central to Byron. He was deeply influenced at exactly this point in his exile by another seminal Romantic poet, Percy Bysshe Shelley, whom he had met for the first time in Geneva. The two established a close friendship, but Byron complained that Shelley had "dosed" him with Wordsworth "even to nausea" just when he was writing the third canto of *Childe Harold*.[35] (Later he mercilessly satirized Wordsworth in *Don Juan*.) It was also during his stay in Switzerland that Byron first became acquainted with Goethe's *Faust* and its enactment of psychological exile (and where he conceived his Faust-inspired play, *Manfred*, admired by Liszt); at this time too Mary Shelley was writing, and reading aloud to Shelley and Byron, her gothic novel *Frankenstein*, a work equally concerned with the nature of the outcast and exile.

It is only Liszt's "Vallée d'Obermann" that expressed this aspect of Byronism, but it is a connection complicated by Sénancour's novel *Obermann*, from which Liszt also quoted long passages. *Années de pèlerinage—Suisse* is not exclusively a Byronic conception. ("Le mal du pays" too has a long epigraph from *Obermann*; "Au bord d'une source" bears a lovely quotation from a poem by Schiller.) It does seem, however, that when Liszt settled on the final form and ordering of the *Années Suisse* its associations with Byron strengthened. To the 1855 publication he now added the pastoral "Eglogue," with its Byron quotation (written in 1836 but not previously published); to "Orage," the only piece newly composed, he added another Byron quotation; and for the considerably redrafted "Vallée d'Obermann," he added in addition to the already existing epigraphs from Sénancour, a complete stanza.

IMAGES OF NATURE

After extolling "mountains, waves, and skies" as "part of me and of my soul," in true Wordsworthian fashion, Byron attempts to distance himself: "But this is not my theme; and I return / To that which is immediate." Yet some of the most vivid passages of canto 3, verging on pantheism, are eloquent evocations of the Swiss landscape and its effect on the poet's psyche:

> *The gush of springs,*
> *And fall of lofty fountains, and the bend*
> *Of stirring branches, and the bud which brings*
> *The swiftest thought of beauty, here extend,*
> *Mingling and made by Love, unto one mighty end.*[36]

It is specifically from this aspect of Byron's poetry that Liszt takes his quotations for *Années de pèlerinage—Suisse.* Curiously, when he came to revise "Les cloches de Genève," he suppressed his original epigraph, in which Byron captures in a mere line and a half the essence of the Romantic artist's attitude to Nature:

> *I live not in myself, but I become*
> *Portion of that around me*[37]

This is precisely the idea that Liszt articulated, as we have seen (p. 102), in his original preface to his *Album d'um voyageur*: "There existed between [these scenes] and me a vague but direct relation, an indefinite but real connection, an inexplicable but sure communication."

Dropping the Byron quotation runs counter to the strengthening of the Byronic associations elsewhere in the Swiss volume. It is possible that Liszt, as a devout Catholic, wanted to distance himself from suggestions of pantheism. But more likely there were complex personal reasons to do with the memory of the birth of his first child, Blandine, to whom the piece was originally dedicated. Significantly this dedication too was dropped in the final version. The first title of "Les cloches de Genève" was "Les cloches de G . . . ," suggestive of secretiveness, concealment of place, but also, for the initiated, concealment of sexual delight (concealed in plain sight in the dedication "To Blandine"). Liszt and Marie d'Agoult had gone to Geneva expressly, and discreetly, for

Marie to give birth to their first child away from the eager eyes of Parisian society. But by the time Liszt came to revise and reassemble his *Années de pèlerinage* his relationship with Marie had disintegrated and he had become the target of lies and recriminations. What is more, still unmarried, he was now settled in Weimar with Carolyne von Sayn-Wittgenstein, who for obvious reasons jealously guarded his reputation and who wanted nothing to do with his former lover. A Byron quotation and a dedication to a composition intimately related to his former life were clearly dispensable, notwithstanding their relevance to Liszt's circumstances at the time of composition—and indeed to Byron's circumstances too.

The birth of Blandine in Geneva in December 1835 drew Liszt even closer to the poet "whom he has embraced, to whom he has abandoned himself completely"—in Rellstab's appositely sexualized interpretation of Liszt's self-identification (see p. 97). Canto III of *Childe Harold* begins and ends with a lament for Byron's own baby daughter left in England. The quotation that Liszt takes—"I live not in myself"—comes immediately after the poet's evocation of a mother suckling her child. Extolling the wanderer alone within the eternity of nature, Byron writes,

> *Is it not better, then, to be alone,*
> *And love earth only for its earthy sake?*
> *By the blue rushing water of the arrowy Rhone,*
> *Or the pure bosom of its nursing lake,*
> *Which feeds it as a mother who does make*
> *A fair but froward infant her own care,*
> *Kissing its cries away as these awake;—*
> *Is it not better this our lives to wear,*
> *Than join the crushing crowd, doom'd to inflict or bear?*[238]

This is some of the most wholesome poetry that the arch-sceptic Lord Byron ever wrote. His image of plenitude compares a mother feeding her child in the way a lake (Lake Geneva) feeds a river (the Rhone, flowing down from the Alps into Lake Leman and through Geneva to the Mediterranean). It does Liszt's art no disservice, nor Byron's, to point out the irony that their actual experience of suckling children was nonexistent. (Blandine was at once accommodated with a wet nurse, as later were their children Daniel and Cosima. Their parents saw almost nothing of them as children. Byron never saw his own child at all.)

Both Liszt and Byron would have been deeply aware of the aura of Rousseau in Geneva, who was born there and lived there. (In addition to his extensive writings in almost all genres, including philosophy, biography, politics, and education, Rousseau was also a composer and the compiler of the first Dictionnaire de Musique.) His novel, *Julie, ou la nouvelle Héloïse*, originally title (in translation) *Letters of Two Lovers Living in a Small Town at the Foot of the Alps*, was one of the seminal literary works of the late eighteenth century. Its tale of an elicit love, in the context of rapturous descriptions of the Swiss landscape, had an enormous influence on the development of Romanticism, not least on Byron during the composition of *Childe Harold*. Liszt would have known that Byron's allusion to the unity of Nature and Love, "to one mighty end," was an allusion to Rousseau.

When Byron appears to turn his back on Nature, proclaiming, "This is not my theme," he is being disingenuous. What he wanted to be seen as and what he was were not at all the same. Nature, at this point at least, is most certainly Byron's theme, for he then immediately introduces Rousseau into his narrative, whom he continues to address, interspersed with rhapsodic evocations of landscape, for some thirty stanzas. In his extensive notes to canto III, Byron describes his voyage around Lake Geneva, and his "survey of all the scenes most celebrated by Rousseau in his 'Héloïse.'"[39] Again we can adduce Liszt's preface to *Album d'un voyageur*, where he associated himself with the "wanderer" of Romantic literature, seeking meaning from everything he witnesses: "Having travelled of late in many lands, many different places, many locations consecrated by history and poetry," he becomes convinced (like Byron) that he has something important to say, insights to impart. And then comes his simple article of faith, that from these insights art is born: "I have attempted to render some of my strongest sensations, my livelier impressions, in music."[40] Not only art is at stake here. In the background is Byron's conception of the unity of Nature and Love. This is the meaning of Liszt's "Les cloches de Genève," the philosophical and emotional context of *Années de pèlerinage—Suisse* which ends with Liszt's hymn to Love, and to which he had originally added a resonant quotation from Byron.

Not only the Byron quotations, but all nine of Liszt's titles allude to landscape. Even the opening piece, "Chapelle de Guillaume Tell" (see figure 8.1, p. 116); asks us to imagine the traveler-pilgrim coming upon a chapel beside a lake; while "Les cloches de Genève," subtitled "Nocturne," evokes bells heard across Lake Geneva at evening. The pastoral context of the remaining seven titles is self-explanatory.

In canto III of *Childe Harold*, we find the familiar confrontation enacted in pastoral poetry between the evils of urban life and the blessings of the countryside. "To fly from, need not be to hate, mankind," Byron writes (he who had certainly fled, as had Liszt and Marie d'Agoult). One cannot hate mankind in the life-giving setting of the Swiss landscape. City and countryside are specifically juxtaposed in the complete thought that frames the quotation at the front of "Les cloches de G . . ."—The poet's wish to escape the "crushing crowd" is followed by his ecstatic vision of nature:

> *I live not in myself, but I become*
> *Portion of that around me; and to me,*
> *High mountains are a feeling, but the hum*
> *Of human cities torture: I can see*
> *Nothing to loathe in nature, save to be*
> *A link reluctant in a fleshly chain,*
> *Class'd among creatures, when the soul can flee,*
> *And with the sky, the peak, the heaving plain*
> *Of ocean, or the stars, mingle, and not in vain.*[41]

The supreme skill of Byron's verse-making here, the apparently effortless virtuosity, is all part of the Byronic aura that so intoxicated his readers. Words, lines, and rhymes poured from his pen as would notes from Liszt's fingers some twenty years later, all the more arresting for being at the service of an intensity of expression, a descriptive strength that spoke directly to his readers—seductively and musically—in a voice that was simultaneously confidential and rhetorical. This stanza is teeming with complexity and yet it is in plain language, molded by a perfect control of phrasing, unforced rhyming, line breaks, commas, at once approachable and immediate. The aural texture of the language, heard in the mind or spoken aloud, is thrilling. "I despair of rivaling Lord Byron, as well I may," wrote Shelley, "and there is no other with whom it is worth contending."[42]

Throughout *Childe Harold*, Byron employs a rhyme scheme invented by one of the masters of Elizabethan poetry, Edmund Spenser, for his allegorical epic *The Faerie Queen*, in six books. The rhyming of the first four lines (ABAB) is mirrored in the second four lines (BCBC) with the longer ninth line (known as an Alexandrine, always of twelve syllables), rhyming with the penultimate line. The thrum of rhythm, the music of language, is a constant presence, by means of which Byron controls the pace and tone of his tale. His skill is breathtaking. He manipulates words into a coherent whole like a conductor on the podium, at once pressing forward, holding back, interjecting—Byron is a poet of verbal gestures, rhetorical flourishes, intimate whispers, the archetypal performer.

But there is more to Byron than skill, just as there is more to piano performance (and conducting) than technique. Byron has something to *say*; his greatness lies as much in *what* he says as in the form in which he says it. (In the case of Liszt's music, the performer has as big a role to play in terms of technique and meaning as the composer: technique alone will not bring the music alive; but without technique the music will remain inert.) But those two concepts—content and form (or meaning and technique)—cannot be separated, not in Byron's *Childe Harold*, not in Liszt's Sonata in B minor. The essence of Byron's and Liszt's art—which we might see as occupying the same ground as performance art—comes from the conjunction of insight and form, from the way in which the substance of what is said is contained within—totally reliant upon—the structure of the language, the means, used to say it.

In the quotation from Byron that Liszt chose for "Vallée d'Obermann," the poet articulates the fundamental problem of writing poetry: "[C]ould I wreak / My thoughts upon expression." (See p. 125.) He asks whether he has the ability—does language have the ability—to express his insights. Of course it does, though he suggests, in the pose of the struggling artist, that he is not up to it—just as Petrarch lamented his inability to write poetry, and Obermann his inability to communicate, in words that prove an exquisite ability. Liszt musicalizes Byron's idea in "Vallée d'Obermann." This great piece "wreaks" Liszt's "thoughts upon expression."

In literature the greatest examples of the pastoral genre (such as Virgil's *Eclogues*, and Ovid's *Metamorphoses*) present allegorical critiques of human behavior and institutions. Instrumental music cannot, by its very nature, replicate that aspect of the genre but Liszt aspired to it. *Années de pèlerinage* is not literary (as if music ever could be), but it does adduce the prestige of literature—in the Swiss volume Liszt is claiming the same meaning for his music as to be found in Byron and Sénancour; in the Italian volume he claims the meaning of Petrarch and Dante. For the new middle-class audiences of the nineteenth century, those whom Liszt cultivated as well as created, it seems this was how they wanted music to be. As Leon Botstein observes, for Liszt (for Schumann and Berlioz too), "the underlying ambition was to create an aural analogue to the experience of reading fiction."[43] In the same way as Byron conceived his plays and poems as "mental theatre," so listeners started to hear in music that same realism, that same emotional force that spoke to the private world of the mind, thrillingly meaningful and "real" as was their experience of fiction. The burgeoning art of the novel—highly extended and discursive prose fiction, giving the illusion of everyday life—was gradually replacing Byron's verse and Sénancour's and Goethe's epistolary narratives. Not only public performance but domestic music-making, writes Botstein, became a "Rousseau-like celebration of human capacity, imagination, sensitivity and empathy." I would add that through their experience of performing music in the home, on the instruments eagerly sought from the innumerable piano makers such as Conrad Graf, the new consumers learned how to listen to the large-scale instrumental works of the concert hall.

GOETHE'S BYRON

In France, for George Sand, Byron had been her "prophet"; in Germany, Goethe considered Byron to be the greatest poet of the age (as Shelley did in England). Byron dedicated *Sardanaplus* to Goethe, the play that Liszt long worked on for an opera. Goethe's clear-eyed view was that Byron "was destroyed by his own unbridled temperament," aligning him with his fictional Byronic heroes. We can be sure that Liszt was hugely drawn to Byron's "unbridled temperament," recognizing a kindred spirit. But we might wonder what he would have made of Goethe's further diagnosis:

> His revolutionary turn, and the constant negation and fault-finding is injurious even to his excellent works. For not only does the discontent of the poet infect the reader, but the end of all opposition is negation; and negation is nothing. If I call bad bad, what do I gain? But if I call good bad, I do a great deal of mischief. . . . The great point is, not to pull down, but to build up; in this humanity finds pure joy.[44]

Goethe had the extraordinary ability to convince his readers of an idea and its opposite simultaneously (fully on display in *Faust*). So when challenged that his view of Byron must therefore cast doubt on whether "pure human culture is to be derived from his writings," he at once turned about:

> The audacity and grandeur of Byron must certainly tend towards culture. We should take care not to be always looking for it in the decidedly pure and moral. Everything that is great promotes cultivation as soon as we are aware of it.[45]

Liszt and his generation would have felt the same about the audacity and grandeur of Byron. But it was more the wholesomeness on display in canto 3 of *Childe Harold*—in Liszt's quotations not a trace of a cynical "pulling down," but rather, in Botstein's formulation, a "Rousseau-like celebration of human capacity"—that provided the stimulus for *Années de pèlerinage—Suisse*.

We also know Byron is not the only literary presence. In the next chapter we will visit Byron again as he appears among other epigraphs as each piece takes its turn. How does our understanding of all these epigraphs affect our understanding of the music? How do we as listeners or performers convert the lines of poetry into a musical experience, or the musical experience into the lines of poetry? Put at its simplest, as we asked of the Petrarch Sonnets and Sénancour's *Obermann*, what do the epigraphs do, or what are they intended to do? If there is an answer that has any meaning for the way we respond to this music, then we have to look at the poetry first, and understand it as poetry. And this entails moving away from the proposition that the music simply "illustrates" the words, however evocative Liszt's pianistic tone-painting, like Schubert's in his songs, might be.

We also need to perceive *Années de pèlerinage—Suisse* as a whole, to find a unity of conception that must have been Liszt's own, despite his reordering of the pieces and their composition at different times. In the next chapter, in examining the context of each of the nine pieces, we will get a sense of how this might be achieved. The nature of a "travel album" suggests a disparate collection of pieces, a collection of pictures, disconnected fragments of poetry. "Years of Pilgrimage" suggests a purpose, a seeking, a quest for unity, of which Liszt was only partly aware in 1840. It was this unity that he achieved in the years of revision and rethinking, and it is this that the performer must sense—and create—in a performance of the complete book. It seems that the strengthening of the Byronic context was a strengthening of this purpose, enabling its achievement.

• 8 •

Mental Theater

Années de pèlerinage—Suisse

"High mountains are a feeling."

—Byron, *Childe Harold's Pilgrimage*[1]

It is one thing to establish the pastoral nature of *Années de pèlerinage—Suisse*, quite another to understand how the presence of Byron, and the other epigraphs in the score, affect how we receive and perform the music. What do we do, as performers, with this information? We might find a clue in Byron's line, quoted in the previous chapter, "High mountains are a feeling"—a statement that evokes a "feeling" but fails to describe it. What is this feeling? Definition is evaded by being assumed. All one can say is that Liszt was entranced by Byron's example, by his heroic attempt to capture in words a sense of his (and mankind's) place in a world so much bigger and older than himself. Liszt's music presents the same aspiration. Through Byron's language we sense not only the *frisson* of the natural world, the intoxication of the mountain air and the expanse of sky, but the sublimity of the experience that finally, paradoxically, cannot be put into words. The poet can only reach for the undefined "feeling," which is actually the undefined realm of music—not Byron's conclusion, but very much Liszt's. For the performer, the Swiss volume of *Années de pèlerinage* in its entirety is "a feeling." The journey it charts through named landscapes is a wholly musical journey, an experience in musical time, but one which, through the texts, asks us to reference (to feel) other modes of expression. The texts are there as a sign of both homage and solidarity; the music does not so much illustrate the texts as exist in parallel. We are directed to Byron in Switzerland, to William Tell, to Sénancour's self-analyzing Obermann, and to Schiller, but the music remains itself. *Années de pèlerinage—Suisse* enacts for the listener Byron's concept of "mental theatre," but in music not in words.

115

"CHAPELLE DE GUILLAUME TELL"

The title of the opening piece takes us to Switzerland's proud national identity via its celebrated folk hero Wilhelm Tell. The epigraph is the Swiss national motto *Einer für Alle/Alle für Einen*—"All for one / One for all."

Figure 8.1.   Illustration for Liszt's "Chapelle de Guillaume Tell" from the Schott edition of 1855.
(Public Domain).

Liszt had opened the original *Album d'un voyageur* with a tribute to the rebellious silk weavers of Lyon, prefaced with a quotation from Lamennais: *Vivre en travaillant ou mourir en combattant* (Live working or Die fighting). "Lyons" is dropped from the final Swiss volume, but the political gesture—solidarity with oppressed peoples in the age of revolutions—remains. Our pilgrim's imagination is alerted and enlivened when he comes across the chapel on the shores of Lake Lucerne dedicated to the Swiss hero. Liszt is taking on the mantle of Harold/Byron in the guise of Tell. The piece evokes heroism and the grandeur of mountain landscapes, the echoing of alpine horns, and the religious awe of the chapel's interior. The music is thrilling with a kind of pictorial splendor, almost cinematic in effect, requiring an unflinching confidence and boldness on the performer's part, a proud display of musical rhetoric and gesture. We will find this inimitable Lisztian manner again in "Orages" and "Vallée d'Obermann."

Editions today usually give the derivation of the epigraph as Schiller, an assumption which links it with Schiller's play *Wilhelm Tell*. The words were in fact well known in the 1830s in the context of Switzerland's identity and could have come from many sources.[2] The most likely was *Egmont*, Goethe's early *sturm und drang* tragedy, enamored by Beethoven. Schiller had criticized the play, in a now famous essay of 1788,[3] before he had met Goethe (so before they had begun their famous collaboration at the theater in Weimar). One of the first fruits of their work together was an adaption by Schiller, at Goethe's request, of *Egmont*. Liszt was reverentially aware of this history, and it was his ambition once he took up his work in Weimar as Kapellmeister to revive the spirit of Schiller and Goethe.

Both *Egmont* and *Wilhelm Tell* are tragic political dramas, Shakespearian in ambition, prefiguring quasi-Byronic heroes (a sign that Byron's heroes were all part of the zeitgeist of an age in which fiction and real life were blended in the examples of Napoleon and his challengers). Rossini had brought Tell to the attention of opera audiences with his *Guillaume Tell* of 1829, on a libretto based on a French translation of Schiller's play. In 1838 Liszt transcribed the famous overture for his ten fingers and made it one of the crowd-pleasing staple items on his concert programs. Even today performances can be a thrilling experience to witness.

Liszt's transcription—*Ouverture de l'opéra "Guillaume Tell"*—figures in a historical moment in the history of concert pianism. Liszt was the first to play without a supporting cast of other instrumentalists and singers. He described the occasion amusingly (and proudly) in a letter to his friend the Princess Belgiojoso:

> Imagine . . . I dared, for the sake of peace and quiet, to give a series of concerts entirely alone . . . saying cavalierly to the public, "Le Concert, c'est moi." For the curiosity of the thing here is the program of one of the soliloquies:

1. Overture to William Tell, performed by M. L. [Monsieur Liszt]
2. Rémniscences des Puritains [Bellini]: Fantasy composed and performed by the above mentioned!
3. Etudes and fragments, by the same to the same!
4. Improvisations on given themes—still by the same.

And that's all; neither more and no less, except for lively conversation during the intervals, and enthusiasm, if appropriate![4]

By the time Liszt came to rewrite his "Chapelle de Guillaume Tell" toward the end of the 1840s (almost none of the first version survives in the rewrite, apart from title and epigraph), he was no doubt aware that Alexandre Dumas (the Dumas in the painting by Danhauser that we saw in chapter 7, figure 7.1) had made the Swiss motto even more famous, in the mouth of D'Artagnan, in his novel *The Three Musketeers*. But even more significant for Liszt, Switzerland's own ancient struggle against Hapsburg oppression had become the touchstone and the overarching narrative of Hungary's own anti-Hapsburg revolution of 1848. The epigraph at the head of the opening piece of Liszt's newly conceived *Années de pèlerinage* took on a resonant contemporary relevance.

Pastoral simplicity is the pervading mood of the three pieces that follow "Chapelle de Guillaume Tell"—the cinematic sweep of history gives way to intimate lithographs.

"AU LAC DE WALLENSTADT"

This lovely composition, as small as it is, provides a perfect illustration of the kind of associations that can be made in the preparation and reception of a musical work. By itself it is a delightful exercise in Schubertian tone painting, but in the context of the whole collection it can be seen to face in many directions, connecting to the meaning of the whole *Années Suisse* and expanding into a wider understanding of Byron's poetry. "Au lac de Wallenstadt" provides a window onto Liszt's reactions to Byron; we begin to get a sense of how he read the whole of the third canto of *Childe Harold's Pilgrimage*.

> *Clear, placid Leman! thy contrasted lake,*
> *With the wild world I dwelt in, is a thing*
> *Which warns me, with its stillness, to forsake*
> *Earth's troubled waters for a purer spring.*[5]

Liszt misses out the first three words for the sole reason that he has transferred Byron's scene from Lake Leman (Lake Geneva) to Lake Walenstadt

Figure 8.2.   Illustration for Liszt's "Au lac de Wallenstadt" from the Schott edition of 1855.
(Public Domain).

(known as the Walensee), where he and Marie stayed for several days in June 1835 on their way to Geneva. Marie recalled,

> The shores of Lake Walenstadt detained us for some time. Franz wrote for me there a melancholy harmony, imitative of the sigh of the waves and the cadence of oars, which I have never been able to hear without weeping.[6]

There is little doubt that the piece was "Le lac de Wallenstadt" (Liszt's title and spelling for the piece as first published), though Marie's memory, long after the event, has replaced its masterful innocence with tears and melancholy.

A central motif in Byron's poetry is the opposition of light and dark, symbolizing the poet's struggle with positive and negative impulses, with creative forces and their opposite. The lines Liszt quotes, his first Byron epigraph in the Swiss volume, present the contrast as one between the worldly—the "wild world"—and the spiritual, "the purer spring" that feeds mountain lakes (and the poet's well-being). At this point for Byron, the forces of optimism, represented by the simple splendors of the natural world, win through; the human soul is purified. So it is fitting that for Liszt the heroic life of action represented by "Chapel de Guillaume Tell" gives way to pastoral simplicity: Liszt's own musical narrative "forsakes earth's troubled waters for a purer spring."

Byron's stanza continues by way of a delicate evocation of the senses at ease:

> *This quiet sail is as a noiseless wing*
> *To waft me from distraction; once I loved*
> *Torn ocean's roar, but thy soft murmuring*
> *Sounds sweet as if a sister's voice reproved,*
> *That I with stern delights should e'er have been so moved.*

What is remarkable in these lines is how Byron perfectly balances the oppositions without at all diluting the positive sensual ecstasy of his experience. We do not read the "torn ocean's roar" as a threat (and certainly not an evil) because it is associated with love ("once I loved"); the "soft murmuring" of the sail, which as in a dream is also "noiseless," morphs into the sounds of his sister's voice, sweet even though she is admonishing him; while the "stern delights" of his former life are also the stern tones of his sister's disapproval—yet she remains sweet and the ocean's roar remains delightful.

Would Liszt have picked up such nuances of meaning with the little English he had at this time? (In Liszt's notebooks the Byron quotations are written down in French.) Who can say, knowing his ear and his voracious intellect, that he would not have? But it barely matters. The epigraph is there at the head of the piece, in English, for us to read. Liszt's music leads us into the experience of Byron as much as Byron into Liszt. To change our analogy, to experience the poem and the music side by side is to find the same imaginative conjunction as we find in dance choreography. The way dance works on the imagination is almost impossible to put into words, though we try. But we know that in the greatest choreography—George

Balanchine, Kenneth MacMillan, Pina Bausch—the dancer does not dance *to* the music, but *with* it. Music and dance run side by side, independent entities, the one serving the other.

Repeatedly in *Childe Harold* there are images and lines apposite to Liszt's music, stanzas that he must have read but which he did not quote, which resonate with what we know of him. Having noted already that "we are what we read," it is inescapable that Liszt recognized a deep kinship with Byron that had a direct bearing on the music he conceived. This is not to say that his models were other than musical when he came to construct his music. Brendel directs us toward Bellini in the case of "Chapelle de Guillaume Tell."[7]

It cannot have escaped Liszt, reading *Childe Harold*, that he was experiencing on the Walensee what Byron experienced on Lake Leman. The self-identification would have been willed, acute, and thrilling for this twenty-four year old. And we can even notice that Byron's reference to his sister would have had undoubted, and amusing, resonance for the two lovers in their own small boat on the Walensee. Marie recalled that their own elicit union went unnoticed because "almost everywhere, seeing us so similar in colour of eyes and hair, in complexion and voice, people took us for brother and sister—which delighted both of us."[8] The scandal Byron was escaping from in his exile from England was an incestuous relationship with his half-sister. And in the stanza following the one from which Liszt quotes, we find this exquisite image of fecundity: "There breathes a living fragrance from the shore / Of flowers yet fresh with childhood." Marie, we recall, was pregnant. We will see such allusions and symbols further developed as *Années de pèlerinage—Suisse* unfolds. The work in its entirety is not only Byronic, but biographical. The music is born from the actual experience of the young Franz Liszt, subsumed into his imaginative experience via the literature he was reading.

"PASTORALE"

In the original *Album d'un Voyageur*, "Le lac de Wallenstadt" was followed by "Au bord d'une source"—Liszt even considered arranging the two pieces as a single unit, two titles but with the same number. The delightful "Pastorale" now inserted in between hardly disturbs this structure. The three pieces form a perfectly integrated experience in performance, three different views of the same Alpine scene. The lack of epigraph for "Pastorale" befits a piece that imitates the music of folk dancing and folk instruments—its "meaning," we might say, is already contained in the specific allusions of its style and its title.

"AU BORD D'UNE SOURCE"

The epigraph is from a poem by Schiller, *Der Flüchtling* (The Fugitive):

> *In säuselnder Kühle*
> *Beginnen die Spiele*
> *Der jungen Natur*[9]

"The games of young nature begin in murmuring coolness"—three short lines that imagine the birth of the natural world as the source of a mountain stream. The word *säuselnder* captures a meaning, and a sound, that is a combination of rustling, whispering, and murmuring—in translation we take our pick. The epigraph gives an extra dimension to the "purer spring" of "Au lac de Wallenstadt." Liszt, like his revered Schubert, was a master at finding keyboard figurations to evoke external sounds and moods. But as all pianists will know who have played this intricately challenging piece (in style a concert etude), it is not only the web of figurations, and the resulting dissonances, that produce the illusion, but the cross rhythms—the reiterative dancing and hopping, the "games."

Schubert set *Der Flüchtling* in 1816 as a song, the probable source for Liszt's knowledge of the poem. We can notice that Schiller's subject is a version of the wanderer theme, a version of the dark/light motif, which Schubert unerringly captures in his song. Images of innocent nature are placed as the painful recollections of a fugitive shut out from society. Not a shadow of the fugitive falls across Liszt's "Au bord d'une source"—the intoxication of birth and youth is everything. But in the imaginative context of the complete Swiss volume other considerations are held in the mind of the performer, intimations caught on "a noiseless wing," not invoked during the piece itself, but a vital element informing our understanding of the whole.

"ORAGE"

Liszt's "Storm" is the perfect foil for the pieces that have preceded it. It was a late addition, not in the original *Album*, and here creates an uncompromising change of direction in the narrative dynamic:

> *But where of ye, oh tempests! is the goal?*
> *Are ye like those within the human breast?*
> *Or do ye find, at length, like eagles, some high nest?*[10]

Figure 8.3.   Illustration for Liszt's "Orage" from the Schott edition of 1855.
(Public Domain).

The opening bars shatter the pastorale terrain, indeed like lightning. This is furious storm music *par excellence*, and it reminds us that the evocation of storms was one of the staple components of Liszt's public improvisations (no doubt included under the heading "Improvisations on given themes," in his proud letter to Princess Belgiojoso [see p. 118]). The virtuosity of the performer is foregrounded. Where in "Au bord d'une source" the intricacy of the pianism is mostly concealed behind the delights of the figurations—as in a Chopin étude—in "Orage" piano technique becomes integral to the imaginative effect. This is music theater, it requires performance. (I am reminded of Alfred Brendel's 1986 DVD presentation of *Années de pèlerinage,* where the camera angle from above the keyboard during "Orage" draws us into an arresting choreographic display of hands and fingers.) Storms are marvels of nature; Liszt's storms were marvels of a new kind of pianism. "Orage" is an act, just as Byron's poetry is an act, a virtuosic display that leaves us, as witnesses, breathless at the audacity. But it is this very audacity that carries the meaning—we are overwhelmed not only by the act itself but by what it is required to do, by what only virtuosity can do.

Byron spends several stanzas in canto III describing the storms he witnessed in the Alps. He employs the familiar literary device that finds symbols for human emotion in natural phenomena. It is an easy equation, though Byron exploits it with great skill, drawing attention to himself—his inner torments and ecstasies—at the same time as painting a word picture of considerable imaginative power. Again we see the poet drawing his readers into scenes they themselves can imagine, wish to have witnessed, while at the same time eliciting thrilled solidarity with his plight as he exposes his soul.

> *Now, where the swift Rhone cleaves his way between*
> *Heights which appear as lovers who have parted*
> *In hate, whose mining depths so intervene,*
> *That they can meet no more, though broken hearted*[11]

The reader is not only among the peaks with him but witness to his confessions. It was by such immediacy, and audacity, that Byron became the best seller of his age.

In his notes to canto III, he gives the precise date and time (midnight) of the storms, of which he has "seen several more terrible, but none more beautiful."[12] In stanza 93 he asks that he should be "a sharer in thy fierce and far delight / a portion of the tempest," so picking up a central motif of the whole canto. The stanza develops a similar image of birth to the Schiller quotation at the head of "Au bord d'une source." In "Orage," however, it is the birth of an earthquake rather than mankind. Both images suggest the gods of Greek mythology:

> *How the lit lake shines, a phosphoric sea,*
> *And the big rain comes dancing to the earth!*
> *And now again 'tis black,—and now, the glee*

Of the loud hills shakes with its mountain-mirth,
As if they did rejoice o'er a young earthquakes birth.[13]

Byron's "Big rain" and "loud hills" might be seen as the same order of audacity as Liszt's bagpipes in "Pastorale" and alpine horns in "Guillaume Tell"—both composer and poet effortlessly introduce into their highly sophisticated art down-to-earth elements that avoid any sense of bathos. (Liszt's model was not only Byron, but also Beethoven.) Both of them, and Beethoven, were indebted to Rousseau's concept of the nobility of primitive phenomena.

Liszt's change of direction at this point in his musical narrative, his inclusion of a new composition, and a new quotation, prepares the way for "Vallée d'Obermann." We can see in operation here a sign of the careful planning by which the whole volume emerged from the fragments of *Album d'un voyageur*, revised, pruned, reassembled. The narrative darkens even further in what follows.

"VALLÉE D'OBERMANN"

Liszt adds a new Byron quotation—stanza 97, quoted in full—at the front of the revised "Vallée d'Obermann." The stanza follows on directly from the previous lines at the head of "Orage," and it is where we reach the climax and purpose of Byron's storm image. The stanza also exemplifies his style at its finest. In the quotation Liszt placed before "Orage" the poet had asked a rhetorical question of the cosmos: what is the purpose of storms, what do they teach us apart from awe and magnificence? He watches, restless, troubled, hearing the "departing voices" of the thunder. "But where of ye, oh tempests! is the goal?" Then comes a stanza in which he dramatizes in one long passionate sentence, replete with the breath of spontaneous utterance, the culmination of his thought, the realization that in the face of a storm his expressive powers, by comparison, are impotent. This is the stanza Liszt quotes:

Could I embody and unbosom now
That which is most within me,—could I wreak
My thoughts upon expression, and thus throw
Soul, heart, mind, passions, feelings, strong or weak,
All that I would have sought, and all I seek,
Bear, know, feel, and yet breathe—into one word,
And that word were Lightning, I would speak;
But as it is, I live and die unheard,
With a most voiceless thought, sheathing it as a sword.[14]

It is of course a magnificent pose, for all its sincerity. He does indeed "wreak [his] thoughts upon expression," we do indeed feel the force of "that one word . . . Lightning." The poet laments that within himself there is the same potential as the forked lightning that illuminates and shatters the cliffs of the Rhone valley, even though he cannot match the same cosmic splendor. But notwithstanding his speechless humility (all the same, uttered in speech), he gains by comparison.

It is but a small step sideways to Liszt, who had the same passionate belief in the expressive power of art, and which in *Années de pèlerinage* reached its apotheosis, its most dramatic expression, in "Orage" and "Valleé d'Obermann." In these two pieces we can sense the presence of the Byronic hero, of man pitting himself against the elements, analogous as much to the paintings of Delacroix and Caspar David Friedrich as to Byron. Liszt by no means rejected the original conception arising from Sénancour. But as his reading of Byron developed, and his ambition as a composer became more focused, clearly he saw a wider context for "Valleé d'Obermann" as well as for the *Années* as a whole. Gradually (or maybe suddenly) Liszt saw Byron's stanza as wholly appropriate to the deeper origins of "Vallée d'Obermann," as a parallel commentary on the music as well as an expansion, and a confirmation, of the meaning of Sénancour. But the revision no more "illustrates" Byron than it does Sénancour. Rather the music now includes two writers within its orbit, a recognition of a parallel universe in literature, a shared experience, a common concern with meaning.

The question of illustration however is complex. Just as the sound of poetry can itself convey meaning—the sensuous "musicality" of language that seeps into our consciousness—so music can suggest aural phenomena (it can for example imitate thunder and birdsong). With the help of titles, it can evoke visual images too. The music of the nineteenth century, and on into French impressionism, is full of such aural and visual tone painting. But if this is all that Liszt is doing, he is not doing much, notwithstanding the skill with which he illustrates. There is another magnificent storm evoked at the center of "Vallée d'Obermann" (bars 119–156), but it is not the storm that transfixes us but the sound of a piano at full stretch, and the tension created by a tautly constructed musical composition. The passage is an extended transition between two key centers: C and E. The beatific calm at the onset of the E major section is a direct result of this transition. Before anything else it is a musical experience. That it also parallels the calm after a storm, or thanksgiving after a crisis overcome, is a separate issue, an analogous experience.

We see something similar operating in the Byron stanza. It articulates a thought at the same time as dramatizing the act of thinking; and it evokes an image of a lightning strike. The sudden illumination of lightning is a symbol of inspiration. The experience of lightning is evoked as the act of thinking and writing—the thought becomes the poem, the language of the poem enacts the strike. Byron arrives at the word, with a capital L, via a series of single-syllable words that increase the tempo and build tension as his breathless sentence charges forward, to be released with extreme suddenness in the middle of his line. In the poem we know this is language, not lightning (in this instance the lightning is not even described), in the same way as in the music we know Liszt's transition (and "Orage") is not a storm.

Despite the deep gloom of the opening pages of "Vallée d'Obermann," the final E major section is a hymn of triumph. (Liszt has indeed, as has Byron, wrought "his thoughts upon expression.") One wonders, however, in the sudden dissonant switch of the closing cadence, whether the relief has not been an illusion. But the Swiss volume taken as a whole tells us otherwise and the reader/listener is reassured: turn the page and the story continues. What follows is a cloudless sky and a return to pastoral bliss. After "Vallée d'Obermann" Liszt quotes at the front of "Eglogue" the first four lines of Byron's next stanza.

"EGLOGUE"

The morn is up again, the dewy morn,
With breath all incense, and with cheek all bloom,
Laughing the clouds away with playful scorn,
And living as if earth contained no tomb![15]

The match between the mood of the music and the words is perfect—innocence expressed by pentatonicism and skipping rhythms. This music never cloys, never falters in its mastery of the pastoral genre and its effortless expression of delight. One realizes again that Liszt is not providing a simple illustration of poetic images so much as a musical critique of poetry. We come to understand Byron in his stylized pastoral pose through Liszt's music in pastoral mode; our experience of the poetry is deepened.

"Eglogue" was not in Liszt's original plan, although the piece was written in the mid 1830s. He now adds it to the *Années* to strengthen the narrative, to clear the air after "Vallée d'Obermann," just as Byron evokes the clear air of the morning after a storm, "laughing the clouds away." The piece provides a buffer between the extended drama of "Vallée d'Obermann" and the heartache of the smaller "Le mal du pays." The ecstatic love song of "Les cloches de Genève," the denoument of *Années de pèlerinage—Suisse,* is in sight; but first there comes a meditation on the nature of Romantic expression, and a long prose poem by Sénancour.

"LE MAL DU PAYS"

The quotation Liszt adds here from Sénancour's *Obermann* is a discourse on the nature of Romanticism in the context of humankind's relationship to Nature. Sénancour's essay "De l'expression romantique et du ranz-des-vaches"—which follows Letter 38 in Volume 1 of *Obermann*—touches on the meaning of the Swiss *ranz-des-vaches*.[16] These were melodies played on the alpine horn by Swiss herdsmen as an expression of their love and longing for home, for their corner of the world (of the same significance as the blues or flamenco). The quotation is often lost (or ignored) among the pages of the *Années Suisse* because it seems over weighted, coming as it does before one of the shortest pieces. Yet Sénancour's poem-essay, which is quoted in full (some one thousand words), is in fact a central element of Liszt's ambition to create a union of words and piano music. The quoted text culminates in the writer's (and composer's) central artistic conviction about the hierarchy of the senses, with the ear as paramount. Sénancour even argues that Romanticism itself is an aural consciousness, that Nature demonstrates that the strongest impulses of the soul come through the sense of hearing: "The voice of a loved woman will be even more beautiful than her features; the sounds of sublime places will make a deeper and more lasting impression than their shapes."[17] This is the essence of Liszt's *Années de pèlerinage*. It connects with what is to follow in "Les cloches de Genève," where we hear in the central aria "the voice of a loved woman," and at the opening and close the bells of Geneva, "the sounds of sublime places."

Rousseau knew all about the *ranz-des-vaches* and first identified them in his *Dictionnaire de Musique* of 1768. He wrote that the melodies come from "custom and memories, and a thousand circumstances, which, retraced by those who hear them, and reminding them of their country, the pleasures of the past, their youth, and all the joys of life, excite in them a bitter sorrow for their loss. The music does not act precisely as music, but as a memorative sign."[18] Rousseau's observation developed from his influential views on what music could be, and indeed became.

Liszt quotes the *ranz-des-vaches* known as the "Appenzell," with its typical *accelerando* development. This he intersperses with a repeated melodic lament, moving from a folk genre to operatic arioso and back again. Where "Eglogue" made its point musically, with allusions to dance, the structure of

"Le mal du pays"—the interruptions and interjections—again suggests music theater. The piece becomes a declamatory meditation of immense dramatic power, "a memorative sign," in which Liszt identifies with the pain of longing, the strength of feeling that inspires the herdsmen's music. In the narrative that Liszt is creating in his wider commemoration of his own life in Switzerland, "Le mal du pays" is the obverse of "Eglogue," another view of the pastorale but a darker vision. The scene is finally set for the close.

"LES CLOCHES DE GENÈVE"

The final piece of *Années de pèlerinage—Suisse* provides catharsis and in today's language, closure. The volume begins with revolution and ends in peace. If the pastoral journey has been broadly benign it has also touched despair and desolation, frenzy, and heartache.

I have referred several times in this chapter to "Les cloches de Genève." It holds a significant place in Liszt's overall conception. I have suggested that it is a hymn to love and that it encapsulates the core philosophical meaning of the whole volume. It is the final statement with which the unity of the whole falls into place. And I have suggested why Liszt discarded the original quotation from Byron and the dedication "To Blandine," his daughter (see pp. 108–109). The music, nevertheless, breathes the rhapsodic air of Byron and Rousseau, and its placement at the end of the volume is a master stroke.

> *I live not in myself, but I become*
> *Portion of that around me.*[19]

These lines, discarded by Liszt, condense Byron's more detailed presentation of the same idea later in the poem:

> *The gush of springs,*
> *And fall of lofty fountains, and the bend*
> *Of stirring branches, and the bud which brings*
> *The swiftest thought of beauty, here extend,*
> *Mingling and made by Love, unto one mighty end.*[20]

In the rhymes and rhythms of his language, in the meanings of his words and images, Byron presents Rousseau's philosophy of the oneness of Nature, which crucially involves a concept of Love. The relevance of this to Liszt at the time of the birth of his first child cannot be overestimated. Blandine was a portion of himself as well as the world around him, of Marie d'Agoult, of the Swiss Alps through which they had traveled, and which they experience as a deeply personal revelation, reflected in the literature they were reading. Life, landscape, and literature had become one—"Mingling and made by Love, unto one mighty end." In December 1835 the creation of *Années de pèlerinage—Suisse* was envisioned.

The music begins by evoking bells heard from afar (the opening of Debussy's Prelude "Les Collins d'Anacapri" comes directly from the opening of "Les cloches de Genève"). The central section is among the most beautiful hymns to love that Liszt ever wrote (and there are many contenders), and such an outpouring would seem at once appropriate to his state of mind in Geneva in December 1835.

In fact this central section did not exist in the original "Les Cloches de G. . . ." Was Liszt recalling a past love or experiencing a new? We are reminded again of the biographical fallacy. In the final assemblage of the whole 1855 publication, Liszt discards Byron at this point, he even discards his daughter and by implication Marie d'Agoult. He proclaims the right to ask that his music be taken at face value. We can read Byron, Rousseau, and Sénancour as he did, we can remind ourselves of the birth of his daughter; but in the final issue we experience "Les cloches de Genève," and *Années de pèlerinage—Suisse*, as the sublime music it is. As Sénancour tells us in his essay "De l'expression romantique," the ear reigns supreme.

• *9* •

Music and Poetry

The Dante Sonata

The task of the poet, in making people comprehend the incomprehensible, demands immense resources of language.[1]

—T. S. Eliot on Dante

We touched on Dante, and Liszt's reverence for *The Divine Comedy*, in chapter 4, and how he had said "when traveling he always took Goethe's *Faust* and [Dante's] *Divina Commedia* with him, and that without these two masterworks, which he read again and again, he could not live."[2] It was Goethe and Dante who inspired Liszt's two great symphonies and his two great piano sonatas.

Dante, like Petrarch, was revered by Romantic artists. Indeed it was the Romantic generation who rediscovered Dante after a long period of neglect. In England, Coleridge lectured on Dante in his famous series of lectures in 1818. Dante became a touchstone for British poets—Keats, Coleridge, and above all, Shelley—as he did for the French. Byron translated the first five cantos of "Inferno," the first book of the *The Divine Comedy*. Dante became a fashion, as did Romanticism itself. In Thomas Love Peacock's novel *Nightmare Abbey*, in which the foibles of Romanticism are satirized, a character aptly named Mr. Listless announces, "I don't know how it is, but Dante never came in my way till lately. I never had him in my collection, and if I had had him I should not have read him. But I find he is growing fashionable, and I am afraid I must read him some wet morning."[3]

In France, Stendhal considered Dante the Romantic poet *par excellence*. For Liszt, Dante could not have been avoided. He was reading "Inferno" in his early twenties, even before his relationship with Marie d'Agoult, who was an ardent Dante reader (as was George Sand). Sand often referred to Liszt as "Dantesque" (another resemblance to add to those of Byron and Napoleon).[4]

In what way was the thirteenth-century Dante (1265–1321) perceived as Romantic? It seems his theology could be easily interpreted in terms of

Figure 9.1. Eugène Delacroix: *Dante and Virgil in Hell,* also known as *The Barque of Dante,* oil, 1822. The painting illustrates the first part of "Inferno" Canto 8.

© 1993 RMN-Grand Palais (musée du Louvre). Photographe inconnu. (https://collections.louvre.fr/en/ark:/53 355/cl010065871).

cosmic aspiration of the Obermann kind; but many Romantics had little trouble in accepting a religious view of the world, a belief in the essential viability of the spirit, even if this did not necessarily coincide with Christian theology. For Liszt of course, a devout Roman Catholic, Dante's world view would have deeply resonated.

But far more central to the Romantic sensibility was the imaginative power of Dante's colossal poem, his journey through a fantastical, parallel world of dream and nightmare, his vision of a hell and a heaven that could only have been conceived through the art of poetry. Dante as pilgrim was the compelling image for the composer of the "Years of Pilgrimage." It was inevitable that Liszt would aspire to turn such art into music, and entirely fitting that it should be Dante who provided the climax, the final piece, of Liszt's own Italian journey.

For T. S. Eliot, a century later, one of the signs of great poetry was its "width of emotional range," which he found supremely in Dante just as Liszt would have. "The Divine Comedy," wrote Eliot, "expresses everything in the way of emotion, between depravity's despair and the beatific vision, that man is capable of experiencing."[5] For the Romantics, Dante's journey into the gothic depths of hell, and upward through purgatory toward the dazzling vision of paradise, was their own journey, their own struggle to express the inexpressible, the interior darkness of the soul (Obermann's, Childe Harold's, Faust's) coexisting with the desire for love and spiritual transcendence. Victor Hugo's poem "After a Reading of Dante," from where Liszt found his final title for his Dante Sonata, begins, "The poet who paints hell, paints his own life." This is a high-flown pose on Hugo's part (worthy of Byron), and it is doubtful that he actually experienced his life as hell. But he could imagine it, and it was Dante who gave him, and the artists of his generation, the means with which to do so—the language, the sharp visual imagery, the agonizing narratives told by the innumerable lost souls of Dante's creation.

Dante's poem envisions as its central paradox the lives of the dead—their lives after death and the lives they recall they had lived. It is the story of an imagined journey through horror that is anchored in a fundamental belief in love, compassion, and hope. (Byron detected an extraordinary "gentleness" in the tumult of "Inferno." "Who *but* Dante," he wrote, "could have introduced any gentleness at all into *Hell*?"[6]) *The Divine Comedy* is one overarching metaphor for the experience of life, a narrative that attempts to encompass the history of the world and which journeys back to the beginning of time; it is peopled by a vivid array of characters who, through Dante's mastery of dialogue, have a palpable reality for us, as if they are people we know (and indeed many of them were people Dante himself knew).

Liszt started on what would eventually become what we now term the Dante Sonata in 1839, in Italy. It went through several stages of composition and alterations of title—in 1840 he performed, or more likely improvised, an early version that he called his *Fragment Dantesque*—and it was eventually published as the final piece of the Italian book of the *Années de pèlerinage* in 1858.[7]

There has been much debate about the title "Après une lecture du Dante," Hugo's title apart from what might seem an insignificant change of article from *de* to the ungrammatical *du*. Considering Liszt's perfect French, this can only have been deliberate, but it is still ungrammatical (and many editions of the Dante Sonata quietly change the *du* back to *de*). Clearly he was trying to convey the meaning "of *the* Dante," by which he meant *The Divine Comedy*[8] (or perhaps "the great poet Dante"), which is grammatically possible in German but not French.

For me the Dante Sonata is about Dante, not Hugo—Liszt could easily have quoted the Hugo poem at the front, a mere eighteen lines, had he wanted to make the connection. And surely the replacement of *de* with *du* places the emphasis incontrovertibly on Dante. Liszt would of course have known the Hugo poem (from the collection *Les voix interieures*), but the most likely explanation for his allusion is that he saw how perfectly Hugo's title fitted his own purposes, how it indicated an immediate response to the power of *The Divine Comedy* after a specific reading—but it would be Liszt's reading, not Hugo's. That the response was not actually immediate—that the Sonata took shape over time—does not weaken this argument. What Liszt achieved in the Sonata—which he also took care to indicate was a "Fantasia quasi Sonata"—was a palpable *sense* of immediacy, music that has the air of an improvisation, of living in the moment (the term *quasi improvisato* appears twice in the score).[9]

Liszt's composition captures the Romantic generation's response to Dante—the imaginative sweep, the terrifying journey through the nine circles of hell, and the experience of paradise. The music is compellingly theatrical and startlingly visual. Just at the point Liszt was devising his *Fragment Dantesque*, he had written to Berlioz: "Dante has found his pictorial expression in Orcagna and Michelangelo, and someday perhaps he will find his musical expression in the Beethoven of the future."[10] Later he became this Beethoven—the Dante Sonata's subtitled *Fantasia quasi Sonata* is a reversal of the formula Beethoven used for both his sonatas Op. 27 (*Sonata quasi una Fantasia*) that is too close not to be deliberate.

It seems Liszt responded to exactly that characteristic of *The Divine Comedy* that T. S. Eliot identified nearly one hundred years later: "Dante's is a visual imagination[;] . . . it is visual in the sense that he lived in an age in which men still saw visions."[11] During its fifteen minutes real time is suspended, imagined time prevails. As listeners we become transfixed by the story as it is being told, aural and visual narrative combine in our minds in a Byronesque "mental theatre," and at the end we have to shake ourselves from our reverie. Afterward, as Wallace Stevens observed (see chapter 3), we become "aware that we have had an experience very much like the story, just as if we had participated in what took place."

For the pianist this air of improvised story telling is the most vital performing skill of all. For of course we can no longer improvise the *Fragment Dantesque* as Liszt did—the score, the notes, were finally set, and took on the form we now have, "Après une lecture du Dante." The pianist's art, we see again, becomes that of the actor's. When Hamlet advises the acting troupe, who will perform before the king at Elsinore, to speak their words "trippingly on the tongue," he did not only mean with speed and fluency. He meant speak as if in the moment, as if the words are coming to you as they would in real life, as if you had just thought of them (this in itself was a bold new concept of the realist theater Shakespeare was inventing in the 1590s, three hundred years after Dante). And for Hamlet this was a matter of life and death, acting becoming reality. The king would see, in the moment, the very crime he had committed against Hamlet's father. The story was the truth; "then" becomes "now." Pianists might take this play-within-a-play in *Hamlet* as analogous to our own art: one play is Liszt's music, within which another play takes place, Dante's. And as we saw in chapter 5, the fact we are "playing" the piano is by no means an accident of language.

THE ROMANTIC FRAGMENT

At the beginning of this journey through Liszt's piano music, I recalled a celebrated piano teacher who was skeptical about Liszt's literary quotations. I recall now, at the end, another seminal moment for me in my early fascination for Liszt, my first acquaintance as a student with Alfred Brendel's essays in his book *Musical Thoughts & Afterthoughts* (published in 1976). He wrote there some sentences I've never forgotten, and at the time didn't fully understand:

> There is something fragmentary about Liszt's work; its musical argument, perhaps by its nature, is often not brought to a conclusion. But is the fragment not the purest, the most legitimate form of Romanticism? . . . This is a magical art. By some process incomprehensible to the intellect, organic unity becomes established, the "open form" reaches its conclusion in the infinite.
> Anyone who does not know the allure of the fragmentary will remain a stranger to much of Liszt's music, and perhaps to Romanticism in general.[12]

What did he mean by the Romantic fragment, and the open form reaching "its conclusion in the infinite"? What indeed did he mean by "magical"?

In chapter 6, on *Obermann*, we saw how Sénancour was at pains to discount his book as a novel. If it was not a novel, it did not have a form, or at least not a formal cohesion with an end point. It was essentially a fragment because it was awaiting completion. We will recall that Sénancour, in his fictitious role as editor, writes, "Possibly Obermann is more decisive in the continuation of his letters, but up to the present time this second part is wholly missing." For the Romantics the ideal work of art was one that was incomplete, because life itself was illimitable, not possible to contain. The fragment was the sign of this, and the idea of the fragment pervaded Romantic literature. The fragment did not have to be short—*Obermann* could be seen as a collection of fragments, but in all it runs for ninety-one letters spread over two volumes; Wordsworth's *Prelude*, as the title implies, was awaiting the main course, but it already contained thirteen cantos. Byron's *The Giaour*, which Liszt knew well, contains over thirteen hundred lines and copious notes. It is subtitled *A Fragment of a Turkish Tale.*

The Romantic fragment, in Brendel's formulation, could only reach its conclusion "in the infinite"—in other words it could not reach a conclusion at all. In Obermann's ninety-first letter, he is still asking the question "Que veux-je?" (What do I want?). The allure of the fragment is this very uncertainty, this remaining question. The "open form" nevertheless achieves a coherence, an "organic unity," which should not seem possible. This is its magic. We can recall Isaiah Berlin's picture of the Romantic artist: "Your relation to the universe is inexpressible, yet you must nevertheless express it. This is the agony, this is the problem. . . . This is why we indulge in all manner of fantasies" (see p. 82).

Liszt's Dante Sonata, his "Fantasie quasi Sonata," began as a fragment, and proudly so—a *Fragment Dantesque*. It ended up with a title that itself contained the implication of incompletion. Alan Walker suggests that "After a Reading of Dante" is "a phrase which can mean all things to all men," and he asks, "*Which* reading of Dante?"[13] But this misses the point. The title does not (at first) proclaim "this is a reading of Dante" in the sense of an "interpretation." It means "after having read Dante." Then comes the secondary meaning, the play on the word "reading": this is one reading for now, this is not the whole story (it could not possibly be), many other possibilities remain, other readings, other reactions. The title leaves open the possibility of an infinite number of other occasions, other readings, before this one and after it, because Dante's poem is inexhaustible. It was this realization that I believe Liszt took from the Hugo poem and why he saw it as so appropriate to what he had achieved. The title is quintessentially of Romanticism—of the Romantic fragment.

READING DANTE

Seen in this light, it remains for pianist and listener to provide the reading of Liszt's Dante Sonata in terms of the Dante poem, just as Dante exhorted his readers to find the meaning of his poem from within themselves. In "Paradiso," in which the poet envisions the radiance of another world, a blessedness beyond time and reason—indeed, paradoxically, beyond imagining—he repeatedly tells us, the readers, that his task can only be accomplished, if at all, through us: "Passing beyond the human cannot be worded . . . until grace grant you the experience."[14] Cannot be worded—we are reminded yet again of Byron's cry, "Could I wreak my thoughts upon expression" (which he knows full well he can without our help—Byron did not have the humility of Dante); but there is no doubt this paradox derives from *The Divine Comedy*. As with Byron and Obermann, Dante's "I can't" is repeatedly overwhelmed by the experience "I can." In Dante's case he is brought to this realization, that he *can* describe Paradise, through Beatrice, who symbolizes love, beauty, grace, all knowledge, all blessedness, and who in "Paradiso" leads him toward the shining vision of heaven and the music of the spheres. The presence of idealized femininity in *The Divine Comedy* was another reason the Romantics were so drawn to it.

The question we can ask, as we feel our way into the imagined world of the Dante Sonata, is whether the music alludes to the presence of Beatrice or indeed even to Paradise? It can be credibly argued that the composition is a response to "Inferno" alone, where Beatrice appears only very briefly as one of three "ladies of heaven" who are to guide the pilgrim on his journey. All we know at this point, of Beatrice, is that "[h]er eyes surpassed the splendor of the star's"[15] (an image that would be repeatedly echoed in Petrarch's poems addressed to Laura in the *Canzoniere* some thirty years later).

How do we read the tonal movement from minor to major in the sonata, that breath-taking opening-up that is so characteristic of Liszt in heroic mode? Is this to be sensed as a movement toward Paradise? For me these musical events seem too triumphant as a response to "Paradiso"; rather, they are more Liszt's exultant response to what he interprets as Dante's heroism. Liszt superbly and movingly imagines hell overcome. But Dante's paradise dazzles with light and love, it is not characterized by the blaring of trumpets and thunderous applause. The heavens and the stars that appear at the end of "Inferno" and continue into "Purgatorio" are images of an awaiting peace and serenity, after the noise and turmoil of Dante's hell. Emerging from hell at the beginning of "Purgatorio," he witnesses "the gentle hue of oriental sapphire / in which the skies serenity was steeped."[16] (Each of the three books of *The Divine Comedy* ends with an image of stars.)

But there is a fragment toward the end of the Dante Sonata in which it does seem that Liszt might be alluding to the beatific experience envisioned in "Paradiso." It comes after a move to the dominant, which is to establish the final tonic major. The music closes down; *piano* becomes *pianissimo* then *molto pianissimo*; the angularity of the tritone "hell" motif fades and becomes a perfect 5th and 4th; there is a long silence:

Figure 9.2.   Dante Sonata, mm. 283–289.
Editio Musica, 1974.

Then comes a vision of paradise:

Figure 9.3.   Dante Sonata, mm. 290–299.
Editio Musica, 1974.

In thinking himself into the experience of paradise—with ten fingers on the keyboard—Liszt would have had the shimmering image of Beatrice before him:

My mind enraptured, always longing for
my lady gallantly, was burning more
than ever for my eyes' return to her.

The sexual allure of Beatrice is manifest, but it is acceptable because the eyes are also a pathway to the immortal soul, and Beatrice's beauty is "godly." Dante muses on how art as well as nature—portraits as well as the human form itself—have always "fashioned lures to draw / the eye so as to grip the mind." But all these

would seem nothing if set beside the godly
beauty that shone upon me when I turned
to see the smiling face of Beatrice.[17]

A recent commentator on *The Divine Comedy* has interpreted Beatrice in a manner that we can be sure would have appealed to Liszt:

> Beatrice is Dante's instructor, guide and lure. Her beauty, and the emotions it generates, creates a powerful link between love and knowledge, an eroticization of knowledge that energizes the poet's enamored mind.[18]

Liszt's full engagement with Dante came, of course, in the Dante Symphony that he brought to fruition in Weimar in the mid 1850s. It is an irony that Wagner persuaded Liszt against a full treatment of "Paradiso" in this symphony. He wrote to him: "That *Inferno* and *Purgatorio* will succeed I do not call into question for a moment. . . . About this *Paradiso*, dear Franz, there is a considerable difficulty, and he who confirms this opinion is, curiously enough, Dante himself, the singer of Paradise." Wagner considered that not even Dante had succeeded in depicting Paradise (anymore, he tells Liszt, than Beethoven had in the final movement of the Ninth Symphony), notwithstanding his desire to throw himself "into the glow in order to sink my personality into the contemplation of Beatrice."[19]

NARRATIVE MEANINGS

The earliest sketches of the *Fragment Dantesque* show that the opening tritone motif was with Liszt from the beginning. Whatever it might "mean" in the precise terms of Dante's narrative is hardly the issue—it is the nature of music to mean, up to a point, what Walker calls "all things to all men." Liszt could be very precise with his programs, especially in his symphonic poems (and indeed in the Dante Symphony), but he was also fully aware, as we have seen, that a composer's language was "more arbitrary and less explicit than any other, lending itself to a multitude of different interpretations."[20] Often, as in the Dante Sonata, "the fundamental idea of his composition" was all he wished to convey, and in this case "After a Reading of Dante" was enough (and for Liszt's era the reference to Dante's *Divine Comedy* did not need spelling out). The opening tritone motif need refer to nothing other than a contemplation of hell. Is it necessary to identify precisely which part of "Inferno" is intended? Did Liszt actually know himself?

At the most obvious level his response throughout arises from the tur-moil, confusion, and agony of Dante's sequence of narratives as he travels downward into the noise and lamentations of the dead. In the opening lines the later image of "abandoned hope," inscribed on hell's gate, is foreseen:

> *When I had journeyed half of our life's way*
> *I found myself within a shadowed forest,*
> *For I had lost the path that does not stray.*[21]

Dante begins here, and so, surely, does Liszt. It would seem completely ap-propriate too that the famous inscription incised above the gate, staring out at the terrified pilgrim at the beginning of canto 3, plays at some level in Liszt's response, as does his immense compassion, and Dante's, for the hopeless souls of the damned:

> *Through me the way into the suffering city,*
> *Through me the way to the eternal pain,*
> *Through me the way that runs among the lost . . .*
> *Abandon every hope, who enter here.*[22]

This inscription was not only the backdrop to the whole first book of *The Divine Comedy*, but also to the nineteenth century's entire reading of the Gothic dimensions of Dante's poem. For Liszt and his contemporaries, the words proclaimed Romanticism's darkest soul, and symbolized their rejection of eighteenth-century rationalism.

It seems the sonata as a whole, not just its opening motif, is principally driven by the narrative's first book—with the exception of the possible allu-sion to "Paradiso" that we have seen. This has been taken as a vindication for the argument of Hugo's influence, for his poem is exclusively concerned with "Inferno." But such was the viewpoint of an age that saw "Inferno" as the principal (or at least the most exciting) achievement. Liszt's admiration for "Inferno" would not have needed any help from Hugo.

Just as Liszt unerringly captures the eroticism of Faust and the village girl in the "Mephisto Waltz" (see p. 152), so he does in the case of Fran-cesca and Paulo in the Dante Sonata. In the section beginning at bar 124 (Andante—*quasi improvisato*), he is surely responding to one of the most celebrated passages in "Inferno," the all-consuming desire and adulterous love of Francesca da Rimini and her brother-in-law Paulo Malatesta. Again and again, nineteenth-century artists reproduced, in painting, poetry, sculp-ture, and music, this short episode at the end of canto 5, interpreting the story through an idealized Romantic lens that was almost certainly contrary to Dante's more austere theological and moral intentions. The lovers were, after all, condemned to hell by Dante's god, in contrast to the heavenly place granted to Beatrice. But for the Romantics Francesca became a symbol of the power of spontaneity, of passion that is allowed to break the bonds of formal restraints and inhibiting codes of behavior. She was, in other words, despite her sin (or because of it), as revered as Beatrice, possibly more so because her sin was so fundamentally human. And her story is told in some of the most exquisite poetry in the whole poem. Whatever the austerity of Dante's implied admonition, his pity for the lover's plight is palpable; at the end of the scene, which is the end of the canto, he faints "as if I had met my death. / And then I fell as a dead body falls." Francesca died for love. Dante replicates her experience in his own swoon.[23]

Liszt in this section, which extends over several pages, even captures the theater of Dante. The scene begins with the pilgrim seeing from afar the two lovers who "seem so lightly carried by the wind." He gently summons them, and they approach. The wind is silenced, and he questions them. Liszt's response is at once visual and choreographic—we can imagine the scene as a ballet; the music is so tentative it hardly proceeds; the *quasi improvisato* peters out in pauses and then stops altogether—*lunga pausa*. The pilgrim, the spectators, the listeners—we all wait for Francesca to speak. (Paulo remains silent throughout.) I am not the first to connect the heart-breaking music which then follows at bar 136 (and the tears—*lagrimoso*—at bar 147), with Francesca's lament: "There is no greater sorrow / than thinking back upon a happy time / in misery."[24] Liszt's art here captures the ambiguity of this moment, the fusion of opposites, ecstasy and misery, life and death. This theme will later be transformed into what I have suggested is the "Paradiso" music, hell becoming heaven.

Following this, in Dante's narrative, is Francesca's highly eroticized recollection of Paulo's kiss, described by Dante as the point which "led them to the agonizing pass"—by which he means the moment when courtly love passed into forbidden passion. (Rodin's famous sculpture from 1882, *The Kiss*, now in the Musée Rodin in Paris, was originally titled "Francesca da Rimini." It was part of a series he titled "The Gates of Hell.") I will quote here from the recent translation by Clive James, because it takes the liberty (highly effectively for modern readers) of filling in many details that Dante elides and which would otherwise need explanation. Francesca is referencing the Arthurian tale of Lancelot and Guinevere, already well known in Dante's time:

> *Reading together one day for delight*
> *Of Lancelot, caught up in Love's sweet snare,*
> *We were alone, with no thought of what might*
> *Occur to us, although we stopped to stare*
> *Sometimes at what we read, and even paled.*

Figure 9.4.   Rodin, *The Kiss*, sculpture.
Credit: ARTINPL (CC0 1.0).

> *But then the moment came we turned a page*
> *And all our powers of resistance failed:*
> *When we read of that great knight in a rage*
> *To kiss the smile he so desired, Paolo,*
> *This one so quiet now, made my mouth still—*
> *Which loosened by those words, had trembled so—*
> *With his mouth. And right then we lost the will—*
> *For Love can will will's loss, as well you know—*
> *To read on.*[25]

The passage beginning at 157, *dolcissimo con amore* (with the added instruction *rubato quasi improvisato*) unmistakably references this moment, which is so much more than a moment because the lovers remain lovers for eternity, though eternally damned. The music effortlessly evokes grief, pity, and eroticism, and in the *accelerando* and *sempre accelerando* the "agonizing pass" from quiet restraint to intense passion.

The Dante Sonata dramatizes the experience of a journey. Its fragments are held together by a rhythmic momentum binding the different scenes upon which we cannot gaze for long. We are like the pilgrim himself, ever moving on. This is particularly apparent after the Francesca episode, when we are wrenched back once more on to the desperate pathway through hell (*Allegro moderato*, bar 181). Perhaps this is *all* that is happening in the last quarter of the piece—the performer is presented with the difficulty of keeping the drama going now that all the motifs are, as it were, used up. All we seem to have to hand is momentum and the noise around us. We cannot hold back on Liszt's demands here. Some listeners may even respond to his unique exploitation of pianistic sonority throughout the sonata by imagining not only the sounds of Dante's hell, but also its visual appearance. Liszt's art appears cinematic; harmonic color takes on an independent identity comparable to the visual framing of cinematography; the textures of piano sound conjure the circles and flames of hell. It was not only T. S. Eliot who identified the visual imagination of Dante. "Dante knows how to paint before the eyes what occurs in the depths of the soul," wrote Madame de Staël at the beginning of the nineteenth century (and at the beginning of Romanticism and the Dante revival), "and his imagination makes one really see and feel grief."[26] It seems certain that Liszt understood this too.

POETRY AND MUSIC

In the introduction to his translation of *The Divine Comedy*, Clive James makes a curious observation that for me articulates the paradox at the heart of the thesis presented in this book. He writes of "the onward surge of [Dante's] great story which was driven by its poetry; and [which] would be infinitely less great without its poetry, just as Wagner's *Ring* cycle would be infinitely less great without its music."[27]

It is not the "onward surge" that I want to draw attention to, though this is precisely one aspect of Dante's poem to which Liszt responds. It is, rather, the latent absurdity of the statement, James's willingness to separate two entities that cannot possibly be separated—other than in discussions of this kind. In order to grasp the nature of poetry and the nature of music, we are forced to isolate different components. We justly speak of the poetry of music and the music of poetry; we speak of the meaning of Dante's narrative and the sublime poetry of Dante. But we know at the same time, just as James knows, that *The Divine Comedy* is nothing but its poetry, that only by being poetry can it be what it is, can it enter into our consciousness replete with meaning. When James speaks of Dante's story "driven by its poetry" he is partly referring to its rhyme scheme, almost impossible to reproduce in translation (in Italian known as *terza rima*, a highly concentrated rhyming construction over three lines, echoed in the next three lines, which Dante invented). But he meant more than that; he meant something nearer to Eliot's comment, quoted at the head of this chapter, that the task of the poet is to help us "comprehend the incomprehensible." And for that, Eliot writes, poetry "demands immense resources of language."

For composers like Wagner and Liszt, music was the same. This is what James means in his comment on the *Ring Cycle*. Indeed there would be no *Ring* without its music—it would not just be less great, it would not exist. Yet the fact remains that our experience of the music is also intimately related to the story it is telling via Wagner's text. This is the paradox at the heart of this book.

In chapter 3, I quoted Charles Rosen: "Language must seek out poetic methods even to approach at a distance the subtlety and emotional resonance of music."[28] Liszt might have agreed with Rosen's estimation of music, for after all, despite his metaphors, Liszt was not actually a poet. We can recall again his passionate belief that "the musician thinks, feels, and speaks in music"; and I want to insist again that the meaning of Liszt lies in the music he wrote, not in the stories he told. But I don't agree that there is any distance separating poetry and music in terms of "subtlety and emotional resonance." There is only a difference in means. Liszt was equally passionate about the deepest resonances he experienced in poetry. That he saw it as his life's mission "to introduce poetry into piano music" is to our infinite benefit. Liszt's music helps us "comprehend the incomprehensible."

Appendix

LAMARTINE

Alphonse de Lamartine (1790–1869), charismatic French poet, sage, historian, and liberal politician, was another of the many remarkable people whom the young Liszt sought out in Paris the 1830s. He was from the French nobility, but his political leanings were republican. He became a leader of radical politics in France during the 1830s, and head of the government for a short time in the aftermath of the 1848 revolution. Lamartine can be seen as the first French Romantic poetic. In 1820, with his publication *Méditations poétiques*, he established a new lyrical voice for French poetry, which at once found an eager readership.

Initially the friendship between poet and composer, twenty years apart in age, was that of master and disciple. It seems that Lamartine's passion for the poetry of Petrarch and Byron—he even claimed lineage with Petrarch's Laura—fed Liszt's early literary education. In literary Paris Lamartine was closely identified with the Byron craze. In his poem from 1820, "L'Homme," dedicated to Byron, he proclaims how his love for Byron's poetry is the same as his love for "the thunderbolt's and the wind's noise / Mixing in the storm with the sound of the torrents."[1] In 1825, the year after Byron's death, Lamartine published a long narrative poem, *Le dernier chant du pèlerinage d'Harold*. Liszt's passion for Byron, a decade later, has unmistakable echoes of Lamartine's.

In 1830 Lamartine published the equally successful *Harmonies poétiques et religieuses*. One of Liszt's finest early piano compositions took its title from this collection. As an epigraph Liszt quoted Lamartine's preface, which begins, "There are meditative souls who are elevated ineluctably by solitude and contemplation towards infinite ideas." So began Liszt's life-long exploration of what he termed the union of poetry and music; and so too what Heine

145

called, not without a tinge of mockery, his "indefatigable thirst for divinity and enlightenment."[2]

Liszt's first *Harmonies* finally became "Pensées des morts" in his 1853 collection *Harmonies poétiques et religieuses*, which retained the overall title and preface from Lamartine. Three pieces bear epigraphs from the poems: "Invocation," "Bénédiction de dieu dans la solitude," and the "Andante lagrimoso." Liszt's symphonic poem *Les Préludes* also begins with an epigraph from Lamartine.

"BÉNÉDICTION DE DIEU DANS LA SOLITUDE"

The title comes from Lamartine's extended poem of the same name in his *Harmonies poétiques et religieuses*. Liszt quotes as his epigraph the first ten lines, which tell of a rediscovery of faith. The verse demonstrates an exquisite control of the twelve-syllable Alexandrine line, the staple of French classical poetry:

> *D'où me vient, ô mon Dieu, cette paix qui m'inonde?*
> *D' où me vient cette foi qui mon coeur surabonde,*
> *A moi qui tout à l'heure, incertain, agité,*
> *Et sur les flots du doute à tout vent ballotté,*
> *Cherchais le bien, le vrai, dans les rêves des sages,*
> *Et la paix dans des coeurs retentissant d'orages?*
> *A peine sur mon front quelques jours ont glissé,*
> *Il me semble qu'un siècle et qu'un monde ont passé,*
> *Et que, séparé d'eux par un abîme immense,*
> *Un nouvel homme en moi renaît et recommence.*

> From where, oh God, comes this peace which engulfs me?
> From where comes this faith overflowing my heart,
> To me, until now uncertain, troubled,
> Flooded with doubt, buffeted by every wind,
> To me who sought goodness and truth in the dreams of the wise,
> And peace in hearts ravaged by storms?
> Scarcely have those days passed before my eyes
> And it seems a century, a whole world, has passed away
> And that, separated now by an immense abyss,
> A new man begins again in me, reborn.

In four connected movements (the fourth a reorchestration of the first, plus coda), "Bénédiction" is music of extraordinary emotional power, reaching in the coda a spiritual repose that suggests late Beethoven. The style of the piano writing, Liszt's control of texture and sonority as components of the composition, as distinct from motif and harmonic structure (as in the Dante Sonata as we have seen), had far-reaching consequences, notably in the piano music of Messiaen.

Lamartine's poem expresses the immensity of passing time, and the visionary experience of time standing still. Liszt expresses the same paradox in musical time. His music demonstrates a total absorption of the text, which is treated not narratively—not as rediscovery of faith as a process in time—but rather as a single all-embracing experience of wonder and renewal, a unification of quiet intimacy and passionate ecstasy. The benediction is all around him and us. "A whole world has passed away . . . / A new man begins again."

* * *

TWO EPISODES FROM LENAU'S FAUST

Goethe's was by no means the only treatment of the Faust story in the nineteenth century. It is a sign of Liszt's abiding fascination for the Faust myth, and for great poetry, that not long after his major treatment of Goethe's play in his Faust Symphony he should turn to another *Faust* by the Austro-Hungarian writer Nikolaus Franz Niembsch von Strehlenau, who went by the pen name of Lenau. Lenau's poetry represented a characteristic of German Romanticism known as *weltschmerz*—literally world pain—the German equivalent, world weariness, of the French *ennui* suffered by Obermann.

Lenau's *Faust*, published in 1836, was markedly different from Goethe's, "more moving . . . more melting and much sadder," wrote Elizabeth Butler, in her compelling account of all the Fausts through the ages. "The greatness, the power and the glory, retreat before heart-ache and grief."[3] This aspect of Lenau's treatment is caught with immense insight by Liszt in one of his least known piano compositions, the first of the *Two Episodes from Lenau's Faust* (the second of which is the famous Mephisto Waltz). "Procession by Night" has until recently escaped the solo-piano catalogue because it was published first as an orchestral piece and also in a version for piano four-hands. The solo version was undertaken by a pupil of Liszt's, but it is clear that Liszt was fully involved at all stages.[4]

Liszt was not well served by his publishers: despite his insistence that the pieces should be published together, complete with full texts from Lenau, this never happened in his lifetime. "I am fairly indifferent as to whether the piano arrangement or the [orchestral] score appears first," he wrote, "but the two pieces must be published at the same time, with the 'Procession by Night' as no. 1 and Mephisto's Waltz as no. 2. True there is no thematic connection between the two pieces; but nonetheless they belong together on account of their contrast of feeling. Such a Mephisto can only spring from such a poodle!"[5] (The pieces were not published together until 1982.)

The reference is to Mephistopheles first entering Faust's life as a poodle—it is in such a disguise he breaches Faust's defenses (see p. 59). Mephisto's fatal presence is the back story to "Procession by Night"—he is not mentioned but he is entwined within Faust's psyche. In his letter Liszt is being ironic and characteristically self-denigrating. A few years later, in yet another plea for the two episodes not to be separated, he says he is even prepared for the "risk of boring the public for a few minutes with the 'Procession by Night.'"[6] Liszt's reference to the "contrast" set up by the two pieces, played together, is central to his concept, though the word hardly does justice to the seriousness of his intent.

It is major oversight in piano performance that the two pieces are so rarely performed as a unit—the justly celebrated First Mephisto Waltz ("first" on account of three more Mephisto Waltzes Liszt wrote in the last years of his life) gains immeasurably from the conjunction, however much it can stand as a masterpiece in its own right. Alone, the Mephisto Waltz is a piece of hair-raising musical entertainment. The *Two Episodes* together present a tragedy, a distillation of the Faust story that in a fine live performance can have the intensity of live theater. I have witnessed the *Two Episodes* played by the Swedish pianist Martin Sturfält that had the audience deeply shaken, transfixed in a manner far more intense than is ever the case after a performance of the First Mephisto by itself. Liszt's awareness of the "contrast in feeling" between the two pieces is an understatement concealing his acute awareness of what he had achieved in the *Two Episodes*, his psychological penetration of the myth, his understanding of its archetypal core. Sturfält's performance was a masterful example of the pianist as actor.

It is possible that Liszt took up Lenau not only on account of Faust but also because of the identification he felt with the poet's Hungarian origins. Lenau's life tragically disintegrated through mental illness. Elizabeth Butler wrote, "When the light of his beauty-loving mind began to flicker and then went out, poetry itself seemed temporarily extinguished for those who mourned his loss."[7]

LENAU'S EPISODES

Lenau cast his *Faust—Ein gedicht* ("Faust—A Poem") in twenty-four unconnected scenes. The first of Liszt's episodes is scene 11, "Der nächtliche Zug"

(Procession by Night), in which Faust watches a religious procession passing by and recognizes his terrifying loneliness, his inability ever again to connect with the "bright children's voices" of earthly happiness. It begins with a juxtaposition of heavy clouds looming over the forest—as if "listening and waiting"—with a "sweet springtime breeze" that accompanies all the living sounds of nature. No translation can do justice to the rhythm and rhyming of Lenau's poetry or the onomatopoeia of the German language. A brief example from the opening will give an idea of it:

> *Am Himmel schwere, dunkle Wolken hangen*
> *Und harrend schon zum Walde niederlauschen.*
> *Tiefnacht; doch weht ein süsses Frühlingshangen*
> *Im Wald, ein warmes, seelenvolles Rauschen.*
> *Die blüthentruknen Lüfte schwinden, schwellen,*
> *Und hörbar rieseln alle Lebensquellen.*
> *O Nachtigall, du theure, rufr, singe!*
> *Dein Wonnelied ein jedes Blatt durchdringe!*

> Heavy, dark clouds are hanging in the sky
> Waiting and listening to the deep night of the forest.
> A spring breeze hangs in the sweet air
> And in the the forest a warm, soulful rustling.
> The blooming air both fades and swells,
> And all the trickling sources of life are here.
> O you dear nightingale, call out, sing!
> Your song of joy penetrates every leaf![8]

But Faust cannot connect with the living world around him. The heavy clouds symbolize the darkness of his soul. His dislocation is made all the more disturbing by the way in which Lenau describes the natural beauty around him—the nightingale's song (to appear again in Liszt's second episode), the blossom-filled air, the glimmer of fireflies, the wind in the branches. Faust allows his horse to stroll along the edge of the wood, but he is frightened to go deeper into the trees. There are echoes of Dante's dark wood at the beginning of the "Inferno," with the difference that this is entirely Faust's hell, of his own making—a world of beauty is within reach but unavailable. It also has a human face: Faust witnesses a torch-lit procession of nuns in white habits, virgins "carrying wreaths of flowers in tender hands," and monks gently singing as if their solemn music "wanted to atone for all earthly suffering." The procession passes and Faust is left staring into the darkness. "He grips his faithful horse, and presses his face deep into its mane, weeping hot tears as he has never shed so bitterly before."

Figure A.1.   Cover of the first edition of the Mephisto Waltz, 1862.
(Public Domain).

Liszt's second episode, the Mephisto Waltz, takes Lenau's scene 6 as its text—"Der Tanz" (The Dance). The stage directions tell us we are in a village inn, and that there is a wedding party in progress with music and dance. Once again an English translation gets nowhere near the excitement of Lenau's verse, which in the cantering rhythms of the German, and the constant spring of the rhymes, mesmerizes the listeners in the same way as the seductive arts of Mephisto. A poor translation can leave us wondering what all the fuss is about—it seems we are in the presence of no more than a tawdry tale of seduction expressed in flat prose that repeatedly sinks into bathos. In the Henle translation, Faust says, on entering the inn,

> I know not what is happening to me,
> How all my senses are excited.
> My blood has never burnt so hot,
> I feel most peculiar.[9]

Whereas the German dramatizes his excitement and agitation:

> *Ich wieß nicht wie mir geschieht,*
> *Wie mich's an allen Sinnen zieht.*
> *So kochte niemals noch mein Blut,*
> *Mir ist ganz wunderlich zu Muth.*

Faust espies a village girl, and as in Goethe's Gretchen story he asks Mephisto to procure her for him, which Mephisto does with much scoffing at Faust's timidity. Mephistopheles snatches up a violin and whips the company up into a frenzy of dancing. Music itself becomes the embodiment of the demonic and it is not only the dancers who are possessed but the physical world too: the "trembling walls" of the tavern lament they cannot join the dancing. Faust leads his girl out into the forest in a whirl of passion, and they become "engulfed by a roaring ocean of pleasure." Out in the open the nightingale's song evokes dreams of love.

The best performances of the Mephisto Waltz capture this demonic element—and the sweetness of desire. In conjunction with "The Procession by Night" we have a keen sense that the pleasures instilled and controlled by Mephistopheles have terrifying consequences—the final page, which appears to bear no relation to the last lines of Lenau's dance scene, can be read as Faust's final demise—he is taken by the devil. (In Lenau, in contrast to Goethe, Faust is not redeemed: the last scene is titled "Faust's Death.") A great performance of the Mephisto Waltz can evoke the "roaring ocean" not as one of pleasure but of terror.

As a virtuoso display, the Mephisto Waltz is magnificent; its themes have an immediate identity and impact.[10] But following "Procession by Night," a

different, more serious, dynamic is set up, in keeping with Liszt's life-long
concern with literary meaning. The two episodes are part of a complete picture, the deep agony of the first episode impinges unforgettably on the bac-
chanalian character of the second. The entertaining Mephisto Waltz becomes
a devastating comment on the nature of temptation, sexual allure, and the
powers of musical virtuosity. If music can be erotic, the theme of seduction
in the Mephisto Waltz is the exemplar (figure A.2). Indeed it is possible that
Liszt's concern for his two episodes to be published together was a sign of
his unease with his achievement in capturing the power of Mephisto in the
waltz—he felt perhaps that he had given Mephisto too much power, that
indeed the devil had the best tunes.

Figure A.2. Mephisto Waltz, mm. 341–380.
First Edition, J. Schuberth & Co., n.d. (1862).

In a report on a Liszt recital in Paris in 1844, Heinrich Heine pinpointed the extraordinary effects of Liszt on the concert platform:

> The electric effect of a demonic nature on a crowd that is all pressed together, the infectious power of ecstasy, and perhaps the magnetism of music itself, this spiritual illness of the age, which vibrates in almost all of us—I have never encountered these phenomena so distinctly and so frighteningly as in the concert by Liszt.[11]

In a letter from 1877 Liszt wrote of music as "at once the divine and satanic art that more than all the other arts leads us into temptation."[12] In *Two Episodes from Lenau's Faust*, he was enacting his own psychology. At some level he was dramatizing the conflicts within himself.

* * *

THE TWO SAINT FRANCIS LEGENDS

Liszt combined stories from two different saints, St. Francis of Assisi and St. Francis of Paola, in these great piano compositions from the 1860s. He originally intended them for piano and orchestra, but only the piano solo versions were published in his lifetime. He attached extensive texts to both pieces. *St. Francis of Assisi* tells of the saint preaching to "a well-nigh numberless multitude of birds." Liszt begins his preface:

> That which one might call the "spiritual motive" of the following composition is taken from one of the most touching episodes in the life of St. Francis of Assisi, recounted with inimitable and naïve grace in the Fioretti di San Francesco, a slender volume which has become one of the classics of the Italian language.[13]

The *Fioretti* [Little Flowers] *di San Francesco* was compiled in the fourteenth century, relating the many events associated with the saint's life. Liszt quotes the whole tale.

> Saint Francis took delight and pleasure with them, amazed at their large number, at their beauteous variety, at their attention and trustfulness: for which he devotedly praised the creator in them. . . . When he had ended his sermon . . . at once all the birds flew into the sky with wondrous songs.[14]

Saint Francis of Paolo recounts the story of the saint walking across the Straights of Messina (between Italy and Sicily). Liszt writes, "The sailers refused to emburden their boat with a person of such lowly aspect; he paid no attention and strode with firm step across the sea." He then quotes from an Italian account of the legend:

> Our saint spread his cloak upon the waves, blessed them in the name of God, lifted part of the cloak to form a low sail suspended from his walking stick as a mast, stepped with his companions onto the miraculous launch, and sailed away to the amazement of the people.[15]

There is an aspect of Liszt that fits with "the inimitable and naive grace" that he found in the *Fioretti di San Francesco*. The strange charm and beauty of the *Two Legends* comes from the unerring simplicity of his response to the two stories that is the absolute opposite of his Faustian side—which is not to say that there is anything simple in the music itself. The opening pages of *Saint Francis of Assisi* tell us at once that this is a musical rendition of twittering, chattering birds, yet the complexity and originality of the imagination that created these sounds are by any standards extraordinary.

Liszt's pupil August Stradal, who was close to him at the end of his life, describes him in a manner that captures for us many of the characteristics of the Lisztian enigma:

> His religious outlook is all encompassing, embracing many philosophical systems, but having nothing in common with a man like Bruckner, who clings to the religion of his forebears. But Liszt, too, is a strict believer, and the epiphany of our Saviour is his guiding star as, trusting in God like St. Francis of Paolo, he battles against life's tempests. Nor does he fear death, or complain about spiteful attacks or the non appreciation of his works. Yet it would be an error to believe that Liszt might abandon his free-thinking ways because of clerical influence, for to him everything in art is progress: he knows of no "being" only "becoming"; his motto is "ever onwards towards the light of truth." Liberal and conservative feelings combine within him to produce the noble, kind, and high-minded man that he is.[16]

* * *

Thomas Wyatts's translation of Petrarch's sonnet "Pace non trovo":

> I find no peace and all my war is done.
> I fear and hope, I burn and freeze like ice.
> I fly above the wind yet can I not arise.
> And naught I have and all the world I seize on.
> That looseth nor locketh, holdeth me in prison

And holdeth me not, yet can I scape no wise;
Nor letteth me live nor die at my device
And yet of death it giveth me occasion.
Without eyen I see and without tongue I plain.
I desire to perish and yet I ask health.
I love another and thus I hate myself.
I feed me in sorrow and laugh in all my pain.
Likewise displeaseth me both death and life,
And my delight is causer of this strife.[17]

* * *

A NOTE ON "MAZEPPA"—AND AN AFTERTHOUGHT

We saw in the introduction how proud Liszt was of his friendship with Victor Hugo, a major and charismatic figure of French Romanticism, and how he spent time with him in the early 1830s. I quoted Elenor Perényi's assertion that "[i]f Byron and Victor Hugo had never lived, there would have been no Liszt."[18]

Hugo's poem "Mazeppa" was published in his collection *Les orientales* of 1829. Liszt was as fascinated by the Mazeppa story as were many of his contemporaries; he would have known it not only from Hugo but from Byron's *Mazeppa* of 1818, Hugo's model. Liszt was planning a Mazeppa étude as early as 1832[19]—which became part of the twenty-four *Grandes Études* of 1838 (and the *Etudes d'exécution transcendantes* of 1851, as well as the Symphonic Poem of the same year).

At the beginning of this book, I observed that Liszt's literary references are always clearly displayed at the front of his compositions. This is not the case with "Mazeppa," where Liszt quotes (misquotes) the final line of Victor Hugo's poem under the concluding bar: *Il tombe enfin—et se relève roi—* "Finally he falls, and rises a king."[20]

My final thought is not about the nature of Hugo's poem, or what it meant to Liszt, but rather the curious fact of Liszt placing the quotation at the end of his piece, and not at the beginning. It would not call for any comment except for the fact that this was Debussy's practice in his piano Preludes—words on a page (in parenthesis) placed at the end of each piece. Liszt's tiny quotation from Hugo is either a straw in the wind, or of no significance at all—perhaps he is simply drawing attention to what happens at the end of the poem, and so to what he wants to happen at the end of his étude, the rising of a king. But insignificant or not, his quotation does lead back to questions of musical meaning and to the purpose of literary references; and it enables a conversation about music. I am reminded of a comment by Vladimir Jankélévitch in his book *Music and the Ineffable,* in which he muses on the nature of program music in relation to Debussy's titles (at the end) and Liszt's quotations (at the front). The comment is Jankélévitch at his most rhapsodic, and it repays several readings:

> Liszt . . . though he announces all big "programs" in advance, gets to the centre, the soul and the heart, by some means other than his poet's poems: by means of an unimaginable, divine, troubling something, nowhere present in Goethe's Faust, or Petrarch's sonnets, or Victor Hugo's Mazeppa, but that . . . will have explained the deepest essence of the literary text.[21]

"By some means other than his poet's poems"—it occurs to me that this is what I have been trying to say all along.

Notes

EPIGRAPH

1. Vladimir Jankélévitch, *Music and the Ineffable*, trans. Carolyn Abbate (Princeton: Princeton University Press, 2003), 11.
2. Franz Liszt, *An Artist's Journey*, *Lettres d'un bachelier ès musique, 1835–1841*, translated and annotated by Charles Suttoni (Cambridge: University of Cambridge Press, 1989), 201–2. Liszt ends this thought with a phrase characteristic of the Romantic milieu in which he moved at this period: "[E]verything that stirs in the inaccessible depths of imperishable desires and feelings for the infinite." For Liszt and Romanticism see chapter 6 below.
3. Felix Mendelssohn, Letter to Marc André Souchay, October 15, 1842, in *Music and Aesthetics in the Eighteenth and Early-Nineteenth Centuries* (Cambridge: Cambridge University Press, 1988), 311.

INTRODUCTION: MAKING A SOUND

1. Eleanor Perényi, *Liszt, The Artist as Romantic Hero* (Boston: Little, Brown and Company, 1974), 50.
2. Perényi married into the Hungarian nobility. Her biography of Liszt is now much out of date, but her account of his character and the nature of his literary milieu are presented with immense liveliness and insight. Her book was treated with disdain when it first came out in 1974, it seems largely due to misogyny and for the fact that Perényi was known for a book on gardening.
3. Letter to Pierre Wolff, May 1832, in *Franz Liszt, Selected Letters*, trans. and ed. Adrian Williams (Oxford: Clarendon Press, 1998), 7–8. The poem is "A mes Amis"— To My Friends—by Victor Hugo, from *Les Feuilles d'automne* (Autumn Leaves), which had been published the previous year. One of the friends addressed is the writer and critic Sainte-Beuve, who became a friend of Liszt's, and the other the painter Louis Boulanger, whom Liszt would also have met at Hugo's home.
4. Letter to Marie d'Agoult, June 10, 1841, in *Franz Liszt, Selected Letters*, trans. and ed. Adrian Williams (Oxford: Clarendon Press, 1998), 160.

5. Ludwig Rellstab, in Allan Keiler, "Ludwig Rellstab's Biographical Sketch of Liszt" in *Franz Liszt and His World*, ed. Christopher H. Gibbs and Dana Gooley (Princeton: Princeton University Press, 2006), 352.

6. In Adrian Williams, *Portrait of Liszt by Himself and His Contemporaries* (Oxford: Clarendon Press, 1990), 48–49.

7. Susan Youens, "Heine, Liszt, and the Song of the Future," in *Franz Liszt and His World*, ed. Christopher H. Gibbs and Dana Gooley (Princeton: Princeton University Press, 2006), 41.

8. Lawrence Kramer, *Interpreting Music* (Berkeley: University of California Press, 2011), 3.

9. Peter Brook, *The Empty Space* (London: Penguin, 1972), 43, emphasis added.

10. Franz Liszt, *An Artist's Journey, Lettres d'un bachelier ès musique, 1835–1841*, translated and annotated by Charles Suttoni (Cambridge: University of Cambridge Press, 1989), 18–19.

11. Adrian Williams, *Portrait of Liszt by Himself and His Contemporaries* (Oxford: Clarendon Press, 1990), 39–98; Clara Schumann, in Alan Walker, *Franz Liszt: The Weimar Years 1848–1861* (London: Faber, 1989), 138.

12. Jens Zimmermann, *Hermeneutics: A Very Short Introduction* (Oxford: Oxford University Press, 2015), 65. For more on hermeneutics see "Hermeneutics" in Lawrence Kramer, *Interpreting Music* (Berkeley: University of California Press, 2011), 1–19.

CHAPTER 1: LIFE, LITERATURE, AND MUSIC

1. *Correspondence of Wagner and Liszt*, ed. Francis Hueffer (Cambridge: Cambridge University Press, 2009), Volume 1, 221.

2. Alan Walker, *Reflections on Liszt* (Ithaca: Cornell University Press, 2005), 239.

3. In Eleanor Perényi, *Liszt, The Artist as Romantic Hero* (Boston: Little, Brown and Company), 41.

4. Franz Liszt, *An Artist's Journey, Lettres d'un bachelier ès musique, 1835–1841*, translated and annotated by Charles Suttoni (Cambridge: University of Cambridge Press, 1989), 18–19.

5. Lawrence Kramer, *Interpreting Music* (Berkeley: University of California Press, 2011), 1.

6. Jens Zimmermann, *Hermeneutics: A Very Short Introduction* (Oxford: Oxford University Press, 2015), 65.

7. Ferrucio Busoni, *The Essence of Music and Other Papers*, trans. Rosamond Ley (London: Rockliff, 1957), 139.

8. I discuss these two pieces in "Impressions: Ravel and Liszt," in Paul Roberts, *Reflections: The Piano Music of Maurice Ravel* (Lanham: Amadeus Press, 2012), 21–35.

9. Vladimir Jankélévitch, *Music and the Ineffable*, trans. Carolyn Abbate (Princeton: Princeton University Press, 2003), 29.

10. Lawrence Kramer, *Interpreting Music* (Berkeley: University of California Press, 2011), 251.

11. *The White Crow*, written by David Hare, directed by Ralph Fiennes, premiered in Colorado and London in 2018. Nureyev was played by Oleg Ivenko; his teacher, Alexander Pushkin, was played by Ralph Fiennes.

12. Hare, *The White Crow*, 18.

13. Alfred Brendel, *Music Sounded Out* (London: Robson Books, 1990), 157.

14. For the whole episode recounting Donizetti's *Lucrezia Borgia*, see Franz Liszt, *An Artist's Journey, Lettres d'un bachelier ès musique, 1835–1841*, translated and annotated by Charles Suttoni (Cambridge: University of Cambridge Press, 1989), 221.

15. David Trippett, "An Uncrossable Rubicon: Liszt's Sardanapalo Revisited," *Journal of the Royal Musical Association* 143, no. 2 (2018): 143.

16. Liszt's preface can be found in Franz Liszt, *An Artist's Journey, Lettres d'un bachelier ès musique, 1835–1841*, translated and annotated by Charles Suttoni (Cambridge: University of Cambridge Press, 1989), 201–02.

CHAPTER 2: THE PIANIST AS ACTOR

1. Friedrich Nietzsche, *The Case Of Wagner, Nietzsche Contra Wagner, Selected Aphorisms*, trans. Anthony M. Ludovici (Edinburgh: T. N. Foulis, 1911), 33.

2. This can be found in no. 33 of the "Epigrams and Arrows" in Nietzsche's late book *Twilight of the Idols*.

3. Nietzsche, *The Birth of Tragedy*, trans. Shaun Whiteside, ed. Michael Tanner (London: Penguin, 1993). The original title was *The Birth of Tragedy Out of the Spirit of Music*.

4. Letter to Friedrich Nietzsche, February 29, 1872, in *Franz Liszt, Selected Letters*, trans. and ed. Adrian Williams (Oxford: Clarendon Press, 1998), 742.

5. Friedrich Nietzsche, in *Franz Liszt, Selected Letters*, trans. and ed. Adrian Williams (Oxford: Clarendon Press, 1998), 741.

6. Friedrich Nietzsche, *The Case Of Wagner, Nietzsche Contra Wagner, Selected Aphorisms*, trans. Anthony M. Ludovici (Edinburgh: T. N. Foulis, 1911), 33 and 19.

7. Dana Gooley, *The Virtuoso Liszt* (Cambridge: Cambridge University, 2004), 209. Alessandro Volta invented the first battery in 1800. Liszt mentions him in an article from Italy for the *Gazette musicale* in 1838, airing his knowledge of history, literature, and science. Volta was born and died near Lake Como: "Carried away by the enjoyment of the present, one loves to tell oneself that this is where the two Plinys may have written their finest pages . . . that, farther on beneath those trees, is where Volta's ashes rest." Franz Liszt, *An Artist's Journey, Lettres d'un bachelier ès musique, 1835–1841*, translated and annotated by Charles Suttoni (Cambridge: University of Cambridge Press, 1989), 70.

8. Friedrich Wieck, in Dana Gooley, *The Virtuoso Liszt* (Cambridge: Cambridge University, 2004), 108.

9. Pablo Picasso "Statement to Marius de Zayas," in "Picasso Speaks," *The Arts*, New York, May 1923, 315–26.

10. Heine, fascinated and appalled in equal measure by the Liszt phenomenon, coined the term Lisztomania to describe the effect Liszt had on his audiences. See

"Heinrich Heine on Liszt," selected and edited by Rainer Kleinertz, translated by Susan Gillespie, in *Franz Liszt and His World*, ed. Christopher H. Gibbs and Dana Gooley (Princeton: Princeton University Press, 2006), 458.

11. Quoted in Dana Gooley, *The Virtuoso Liszt* (Cambridge: Cambridge University, 2004), 28.

12. Marie d'Agoult, quoted in Adrian Williams, *Portrait of Liszt* (Oxford: Clarendon Press, 1990), 73.

13. Leon Botstein, "A Mirror to the Nineteenth Century: Reflections on Franz Liszt," in *Franz Liszt and His World*, ed. Christopher H. Gibbs and Dana Gooley (Princeton: Princeton University Press, 2006), 528.

14. Quoted in Dana Gooley, *The Virtuoso Liszt* (Cambridge: Cambridge University, 2004), 47–48.

15. In a report on the Paris music season for 1844 Heine wrote, "He is here, the modern-day Homer. . . . He is here, the Attila, the scourge of God and all Erard pianos, which already trembled at the mere news of his coming, and which now, under his hand, twitch, bleed and whimper." See "Heinrich Heine on Liszt," selected and edited by Rainer Kleinertz, translated by Susan Gillespie, in *Franz Liszt and His World*, ed. Christopher H. Gibbs and Dana Gooley (Princeton: Princeton University Press, 2006), 458.

16. Robert Schumann, in *Robert Schumann on Music and Musicians*, ed. Konrad Wolff, trans. Paul Rosenfield (Berkeley: University of California Press, 1983), 156.

17. Peter Hall, *Shakespeare's Advice to the Players* (London: Oberon, 2003), 13.

18. Friedrich Nietzsche, *The Case Of Wagner, Nietzsche Contra Wagner, Selected Aphorisms*, trans. Anthony M. Ludovici (Edinburgh: T. N. Foulis, 1911), 24.

CHAPTER 3: THE MUSIC OF DESIRE—PETRARCH SONNETS

1. William Shakespeare, *Twelfth Night*, act 1, scene 1, 1–7

2. See Adrian Williams, *Portrait of Liszt By Himself and His Contemporaries* (Oxford: Clarendon Press, 1990), 91. Williams writes, "Different versions of this utterance haunt the literature."

3. Jennifer Rushworth, *Petrarch and the Literary Culture of Nineteenth-Century France* (Woodbridge: Boydell & Brewer, 2017), 1. Rushworth writes, "Temporally his life spanned the end of the Middle Ages and the start of the Renaissance, and he has accordingly been hailed both as 'the last troubadour' and 'the first modern man.'"

4. Jennifer Rushworth, *Petrarch and the Literary Culture of Nineteenth-Century France* (Woodbridge: Boydell & Brewer, 2017), 7.

5. Jennifer Rushworth, *Petrarch and the Literary Culture of Nineteenth-Century France* (Woodbridge: Boydell & Brewer, 2017), 18–19.

6. Sacheverell Sitwell, *Liszt* (Boston: Houghton Mifflin, 1934), 70.

7. Mark Musa, *Petrarch, Selections from the Canzoniere and Other Works* (Oxford: Oxford University Press, 1985), xiv.

8. I have been unable to discover the origin of these words. The sentence appears to be a subtitle for the *Canzoniere* as a whole, possibly from some edition of the po-

ems that Liszt had consulted. In the Henle edition of *Années de pèlerinage—Italie* the words are reprinted underneath the main heading *Tre Sonetti di Petrarca.*

9. Now gathered under one heading as *An Artist's Journey, Lettres d'un bachelier ès musique, 1835–1841*, translated and annotated by Charles Suttoni (Cambridge: University of Cambridge Press, 1989).

10. Heinrich Heine, *Gazette musicale*, February 4, 1838, 41–44, in Franz Liszt, *An Artist's Journey, Lettres d'un bachelier ès musique, 1835–1841*, translated and annotated by Charles Suttoni (Cambridge: University of Cambridge Press, 1989), 221. Heine continues: "Loving to stick his nose into all the pots in which God is cooking up the future of mankind, it is easy to understand why Liszt is not the placid pianist to entertain peaceable citizens and sensible cotton bonnets."

11. Franz Liszt, *An Artist's Journey, Lettres d'un bachelier ès musique, 1835–1841*, translated and annotated by Charles Suttoni (Cambridge: University of Cambridge Press, 1989), 91.

12. Franz Liszt, *An Artist's Journey, Lettres d'un bachelier ès musique, 1835–1841*, translated and annotated by Charles Suttoni (Cambridge: University of Cambridge Press, 1989), 28.

13. Alan Walker, *Franz Liszt, The Virtuoso Years* (Ithaca: Cornell University Press, 1987), 269.

14. *Petrarch: Selections from the Canzoniere and Other Works*, translated with an introduction and notes by Mark Musa (Oxford: Oxford University Press, 1985), 50.

15. Dante Alighieri, *The Divine Comedy*, trans. Allen Mandelbaum (New York: Everyman's Library, Alfred A. Knopf, 1995), 60.

16. Rena Mueller, "The Lieder of Liszt," in *The Cambridge Companion to the Lied* (Cambridge: Cambridge University Press, 2004), 170–71. See also Rena Mueller, "From the Biographer's Workshop: Lina Ramann's Questionaires to Liszt," in *Franz Liszt and His World*, ed. Christopher H. Gibbs and Dana Gooley (Princeton: Princeton University Press, 2006), 380, n. 5. In this long note Mueller spells out the circumstances of Liszt's discovery of Hugo's poem, to which his attention had been drawn by Marie d'Agoult.

17. Giuseppe Mazzotta, "The 'Canzoniere' and the Language of the Self," in *Studies in Philology* (Chapel Hill: University of North Carolina Press, 1978), 292–93. Mazotta writes of Petrarch's "ironic awareness that there is not a proper name for desire. We must not, however, minimize the fact that desire for Petrarch has a name, bears indeed the proper name of Laura." See also Unna Falkeid, "Petrarch's Laura and the Critics," in *Essays in Honor of Giuseppe Mazzotta*, Modern Language Notes (Baltimore: The Johns Hopkins University Press, 2012), S69.

18. Letter to Marie d'Agoult, October 8, 1846, in *Franz Liszt, Selected Letters*, trans. and ed. Adrian Williams (Oxford: Clarendon Press, 1998), 238.

19. Rena Mueller, "The Lieder of Liszt" in *The Cambridge Companion to the Lied* (Cambridge: Cambridge University Press, 2004), 171.

20. "The Death of Daniel Liszt," in Alan Walker, *Liszt: The Weimar Years, 1848–1861* (London: Faber 1989), 474–79; "The Death of Blandine, 1862," in Alan Walker, *Franz Liszt: The Final Years, 1861–1886* (London: Faber, 1997), 47–53.

21. Robert M. Durling, *Petrarch's Lyric Poems* (Cambridge: Harvard University Press), 27. Durling is actually referring to poem 23, not a sonnet but a *canzone* and the longest poem of the *Canzoniere*. But his words can also apply to the whole collection.

22. *Petrarch: Selections from the Canzoniere and Other Works*, translated with an introduction and notes by Mark Musa (Oxford: Oxford University Press, 1985), 35.

23. Charles Rosen, *Music and Sentiment* (New Haven: Yale University Press, 2010), 5–6.

24. Claude Debussy, letter to Paul Dukas, February 11, 1901, in *Debussy Letters*, selected and edited by Francois Lesure and Roger Nichols, trans. Roger Nichols (London: Faber, 1987), 118.

25. Wallace Stevens, *The Necessary Angel* (New York: Random House, 1951), 126.

26. T. S. Eliot, *Selected Essays 1917–1932* (New York: Harcourt Brace, 1932), 238.

CHAPTER 4: THE QUESTION OF GOETHE'S *FAUST*— SONATA IN B MINOR

1. Johann Wolfgang von Goethe, *Faust Part 1*, translated with an introduction and notes by David Luke (Oxford: Oxford University Press, 1987), l. 1754–5.

2. F. J. Lamport, *German Classical Drama: Theatre, Humanity and Nation 1750–1870* (Cambridge: Cambridge University Press, 1990), 132.

3. See the Barenreiter edition of the Sonata in B minor, ed. Michael Kube, vii.

4. August Stradal in Adrian Williams, *Portrait of Liszt by Himself and His Contemporaries* (Oxford: Clarendon Press, 1990), 650.

5. Samuel Taylor Coleridge, letter to Byron, Easter week, 1815, in *Collected Letters of Coleridge Letters*, ed. Earl Leslie Griggs, 6 vols. (Oxford: Clarendon Press, 1956–1971), Vol. III, 528.

6. Osman Durrani, *Faust* (Robertsbridge: Helm Information Ltd., 2004), 8.

7. Osman Durrani, *Faust* (Robertsbridge: Helm Information Ltd., 2004), 166.

8. Osman Durrani, *Faust* (Robertsbridge: Helm Information Ltd., 2004), 543.

9. Among many, see especially the Russian film director Alexander Sukurov's *Faust* from 2011; and, at the end of the twentieth century, see the translation by Robert David MacDonald for staged versions by Glasgow Citizens'Theatre and London's Lyric Hammersmith. See note 18 below.

10. Elizabeth M. Butler, *The Fortunes of Faust* (Stroud: Sutton, 1998), 157.

11. *Faust Part 1*, scene 5, l.1112–17.

12. Jacques Barzun, *Berlioz and the Romantic Century*, Volume 1 (Boston: Little, Brown, 1950), 87.

13. Johann Wolfgang von Goethe, *Faust Part 1*, translated with an introduction and notes by David Luke (Oxford: Oxford University Press, 1987), xxvii.

14. Nicholas Boyle, *Goethe: The Poet and the Age—Volume II, Revolution and Renunciation, 1790–1803* (Oxford: Clarendon Press, 2000), 509.

15. Elizabeth M. Butler, *The Fortunes of Faust* (Stroud: Sutton, 1998), 137.

16. David Luke has: "Oh why was I born, at such a cost!" *Faust Part 1*, l.4596.

17. *Faust Part 1*, scene 26, p. 141.

18. The term was coined by Oswald Spengler in his seminal work *The Decline of the West, 1918–22.*

19. Orson Welles played the leading role in Marlowe's *Dr. Faustus* in New York in 1937, at the age of twenty-one. Thereafter his career had a Faustian trajectory, an identification with Faustian man. His most famous film, *Citizen Kane,* loosely based on the life of newspaper proprietor Randolph Hearst, dramatizes a version of the Faust story.

20. *Faust I,* scene 6, l.1237.

21. *Faust Part 1,* scene 16, l.3188–94.

22. "The truly Goethean, the truly human divine Moment would be a paradoxical synthesis of contemplation and action, a union of complete satisfaction with continued longing, and intersection of the timeless with time." David Luke, *Faust Part 1,* translated with an introduction and notes by David Luke (Oxford: Oxford University Press, 1987), xxxviii.

23. *The Memoirs of Hector Berlioz,* trans. and ed. David Cairns (London: Victor Gollancz, 1969), 139. In a letter to his father, December 6, 1830, the day after the premier, Berlioz wrote, "Liszt, the well-known pianist, literally dragged me off to have dinner at his house and overwhelmed me with the vigour of his enthusiasm." In his *Memoirs,* Berlioz wrote how Nerval's *Faust* translation "made a strange and deep impression on me. The marvellous book fascinated me from the first. I could not put it down. I read it incessantly, at meals, at the theatre, in the street." *Memoirs,* 125.

24. *Faust 1,* scene 2, l.146–49.

25. Liszt wrote in an open letter to George Sand, "I would sooner have been anything in the world than a musician in the service of the Great Lords, patronised and paid by them on a par with a juggler or the performing dog Munito." Franz Liszt, *An Artist's Journey, Lettres d'un bachelier ès musique, 1835–1841,* translated and annotated by Charles Suttoni (Cambridge: University of Cambridge Press, 1989), 16.

26. *Faust 1,* scene 5, l.1072–83.

27. Franz Liszt, "Berlioz and His 'Harold' Symphony," in Oliver Strunk, *Source Readings in Music History* (London: Faber, 1982), 107–33. Music and poetry, Liszt wrote, "feel themselves mutually attracted and striving for inner union." Strunk's introduction perpetrates misunderstandings about Liszt's authorship of his writings, errors that have long since been corrected. See especially "The Scribe of Weimar" in Alan Walker, *Liszt: The Weimar Years, 1848–1861* (London: Faber 1989), 368–96; "Liszt the Writer," in Alan Walker, *Reflections on* Liszt (Ithaca: Cornell University Press, 2005), 217–38; "Liszt as Author," in Franz Liszt, *An Artist's Journey, Lettres d'un bachelier ès musique, 1835–1841,* translated and annotated by Charles Suttoni (Cambridge: University of Cambridge Press, 1989), 238–45; "Liszt on the Artist in Society," introduced and translated by Ralph P. Locke, in *Franz Liszt and His World,* ed. Christopher H. Gibbs and Dana Gooley (Princeton: Princeton University Press, 2006), 291–302.

28. Franz Liszt, "Berlioz and His 'Harold' Symphony," in Oliver Strunk, Source Readings in Music History (London: Faber, 1982), 123. For Liszt the art of piano playing was also a form of thought. Virtuosity, he wrote, "brings ideas to realization. . . . To call [composition] 'a product of thought' and [performance] a 'product of mechanical dexterity' is totally absurd." See David Larkin, "Dancing to the Devil's Tune," *19th-Century Music* 38, no. 3 (Spring 2015): 216.

29. Joseph Horowitz, *Conversations with Arrau* (London: Collins, 1982), 137.

30. Alan Walker, *Liszt: The Weimar Years, 1848–1861* (London: Faber 1989), 327.

31. See the letter to Louis Köhle, May 1854, quoted in the Barenreiter edition of the Sonata in B minor, ed. Michael Kube, p. vi.

32. Ernst Burger, *Franz Liszt: A Chronicle of His Life in Pictures and Documents*, trans. Stewart Spencer, foreword Alfred Brendel (Princeton: Princeton University Press, 1989), 196.

33. August Göllerich, *The Piano Master Classes of Franz Liszt 1884–1886*, ed. Wilhelm Jerger, trans. Richard Louis Zimdars (Bloomington: Indian University Press, 1996), 33.

34. August Göllerich, *The Piano Master Classes of Franz Liszt 1884–1886*, ed. Wilhelm Jerger, trans. Richard Louis Zimdars (Bloomington: Indian University Press, 1996).

35. Letter to Carolyne von Sayn-Wittgenstein, December 27, 1871, in Ernst Burger, *Franz Liszt: A Chronicle of His Life in Pictures and Documents*, trans. Stewart Spencer, foreword Alfred Brendel (Princeton: Princeton University Press, 1989), 286.

36. Alan Walker, *Liszt: The Weimar Years, 1848–1861* (London: Faber 1989), 393–94.

CHAPTER 5: MUSIC AS METAPHOR—SONATA IN B MINOR

1. Alfred Cortot, *Liszt Sonata in B minor* (Paris: Salabert, 1949).

2. Alfred Cortot, *Liszt Sonata in B minor* (Paris: Salabert, 1949).

3. Alfred Brendel, *Music Sounded Out* (London: Robson Books, 1990), 175.

4. Alfred Brendel, *Naivety and Irony: Goethe's Musical Needs*, English Goethe Society Wilkinson-Willoughby Lecture, January 21, 2021.

5. Kenneth Hamilton, *Liszt Sonata in B minor* (Cambridge: Cambridge University Press, 1996), 46.

6. Kenneth Hamilton, *Liszt Sonata in B minor* (Cambridge: Cambridge University Press, 1996), 54.

7. Kenneth Hamilton, *Liszt Sonata in B minor* (Cambridge: Cambridge University Press, 1996), 38, 34, 45.

8. Carl Lachmund, *Living with Liszt, from the Diary of an American Pupil of Liszt, 1882–1884*, edited, annotated and introduced by Alan Walker (Stuyvesant: Pendragon Press, 1995), 14.

9. Alan Walker, *Liszt: The Weimar Years, 1848–1861* (London: Faber 1989), 247.

10. Kenneth Hamilton, *Liszt Sonata in B minor* (Cambridge: Cambridge University Press, 1996), 48.

11. Lina Ramann "Lina Ramann: Liszt Pädagogium," trans. Viktor Schoner, *Journal of the American Liszt Society* 49 (Spring 2001), 39.

12. Adrian Williams, *Portrait of Liszt by Himself and His Contemporaries* (Oxford: Clarendon Press, 1990), 251–52. Liszt had in fact composed a transcription, listed as S739 in Searle's catalogue, "probably lost." See also Tibor Szász (with Gerard Carter and Martin Adler), "Towards a New Edition of Liszt's B minor," *Journal of the American Liszt Society* 68 (2017): 78, n. 15.

13. See Tibor Szász (with Gerard Carter and Martin Adler), "Towards a New Edition of Liszt's Sonata in B minor," *Journal of the American Liszt Society* 68 (2017).

14. Tibor Szász (with Gerard Carter and Martin Adler), "Towards a New Edition of Liszt's Sonata in B minor," *Journal of the American Liszt Society* 68 (2017): 13.

15. Kenneth Hamilton, *Liszt Sonata in B minor* (Cambridge: Cambridge University Press, 1996), 51.

16. Kenneth Hamilton, *Liszt Sonata in B minor* (Cambridge: Cambridge University Press, 1996), 36.

17. Alfred Cortot, *Liszt Sonata in B minor* (Paris: Salabert, 1949).

18. Klaus König, oboist, in the film *Traces to Nowhere: The Conductor Carlos Kleiber*, Euro Arts, https://www.youtube.com/watch?v=Ta8Tqjn7Suo&list=RDTa8Tqjn7Suo&start_radio=1&t=28.

19. Edwin Fischer, in Eva and Paul Badura-Skoda, *Interpreting Mozart on the Keyboard* (London: Barrie and Rockliff, 1962), 5.

20. See especially the work of pediatrician and psychoanalyst Donald Winnicot, especially his celebrated book *Playing and Reality*, completed just before he died in 1971. "Where the will to meaning does the work of the imagination," writes the psychotherapist Adam Phillips, "something essential is lost." Adam Phillips, *In Writing* (London: Penguin, 2019), 230. Phillips is citing the work of Donald Winnicott, especially his celebrated *Playing and Reality* (London: Tavistock, 1971).

21. Alfred Brendel, *Music Sounded Out* (London: Robson Books, 1990), 174.

22. J. M. Coetzee, "What Is a Classic," in *Stranger Shores: Literary Essay 1986–1999* (London: Penguin, 2001), 9. See also chapter 4, note 27, above.

23. Joseph Horowitz, *Conversations with Arrau* (London: Collins, 1982), 137; Alfred Brendel, *Music Sounded Out* (London: Robson Books, 1990), 175.

24. Stéphane Mallarmé, *Oeuvres complètes* (Paris: Pléiade, 1965), 869. *Nommer un objet, c'est supprimer les trois quarts de la jouissance du poème . . . le suggérer, voilà le rêve.*

25. Alfred Brendel, *Alfred Brendel On Music: His Collected Essays* (London: JR Books, 2007), 125–26.

26. *Faust 1*, scene 6, l.1349–51.

27. Alfred Brendel, *Music Sounded Out* (Londong: Robson Books, 1990), 177.

28. Lewis Lockward, *Beethoven: The Music and the Life* (New York: Norton, 2003), 115. Beethoven's famous words come from a letter to his old friend Dr. Franz Wegeler, November 16, 1801, recounting the continuing disintegration of his hearing. Lockward calls the remark "a sentence for the ages . . . the artist in him will win out."

29. Oswald Spengler, in Osman Duranni, *Faust* (Robertsbridge: Helm Information Ltd., 2004), 166.

30. One might change the metaphor here: my own private indulgence is a vision of the birth of Venus, in Botticelli's painting, stepping from her seashell.

31. Charles Rosen, *The Romantic Generation* (London: HarperCollins, 1996), 491.

32. Charles Rosen, *The Romantic Generation* (London: HarperCollins, 1996).

33. Kenneth Hamilton, *Liszt Sonata in B minor* (Cambridge: Cambridge University Press, 1996), 56.

34. Adrian Williams, *Portrait of Liszt by Himself and His Contemporaries* (Oxford: Clarendon Press, 1990), 308.

35. George Henry Lewes, *The Life of Goethe*, in Osman Durrani, *Faust* (Robertsbridge: Helm Information Ltd., 2004), 192.

CHAPTER 6: THE ROMANTIC IMAGE—"VALLÉE D'OBERMANN"

1. Gautier, *Histoire de Romantisme*, in Eleanor Perényi, *Liszt, The Artist as Romantic Hero* (Boston: Little, Brown and Company), 1974, 28.

2. Etienne de Sénancour, *Obermann, avec une Préface de Sainte-Beuve* (Paris: Ledoux, 1833), volume 2, 99.

3. Isaiah Berlin, *The Roots of Romanticism* (Princeton: Princeton University Press, 2001), 1–2.

4. Kazuo Ishiguro, *Never Let Me Go* (London: Faber, 2005), 173. The emphasis is Ishiguro's.

5. *Robert Schumann on Music and Musicians*, ed. Konrad Wolff, trans. Paul Rosenfield (Berkeley: University of California Press, 1983), 147.

6. *Letters of Dupuis and Cotonet* by Alfred de Musset, in *Romanticism and Realism* by Charles Rosen and Henri Zerner (London: Faber 1984), 19–20.

7. Isaiah Berlin, *The Roots of Romanticism* (Princeton: Princeton University Press, 2001), 105.

8. "The First Biography: Joseph d'Ortigue on Franz Liszt," introduced and edited by Benjamin Walton, translated by Vincent Giroud, in *Franz Liszt and His World*, ed. Christopher H. Gibbs and Dana Gooley (Princeton: Princeton University Press, 2006), 324.

9. "Le poème étrange et douloureux." George Sand, "Obermann," in *Revue des Deux Mondes,* Deuxième série, Vol. 2, No. 6 (June 15, 1833), 680. Sand's essay became the preface to the third edition of *Obermann*, published in 1840.

10. Letters to Marie d'Agoult, 1833, in *Franz Liszt, Selected Letters*, trans. and ed. Adrian Williams (Oxford: Clarendon Press, 1998), 10–20.

11. Letter to Marie d'Agoult, 1833, in *Franz Liszt, Selected Letters*, trans. and ed. Adrian Williams (Oxford: Clarendon Press, 1998), 14.

12. Etienne de Sénancour, *Obermann, avec une Préface de Sainte-Beuve* (Paris: Ledoux, 1833), volume 2, 5.

13. "On verra dans ces lettres l'expression d'un homme qui sent, et non d'un homme qui travaille." Etienne de Sénancour, *Obermann, avec une Préface de Sainte-Beuve*, volume 1 (Paris: Ledoux, 1833), 3.

14. "Une individualité nette, une image dont les traits bien arretés n'ont de modèle, et de copie nulle part." George Sand, "Obermann," in *Revue des Deux Mondes,* Deuxième série, Vol. 2, No. 6 (June 15, 1833), 681.

15. George Sand, "Obermann" in *Revue des Deux Mondes*, Deuxième série, Vol. 2, No. 6 (15 Juin 1833), 682–83. Sand draws attention, in italics, to the climax of the quotation: "[J']ai dévoré dix années de ma vie" (I devoured, this night, ten years of my life).

16. Letter to Marie d'Agoult, July 4, 1834, in *Franz Liszt, Selected Letters*, trans. and ed. Adrian Williams (Oxford: Clarendon Press, 1998), 30–31.

17. "Tout ce qui me passe par la tête, tout ce qui je dirais en jasant . . . tout ce que je pense, tout ce que je sens." *Obermann*, volume 1, letter 37, 244.

18. *Obermann*, volume 1, letter 5, 67.

19. Jessica Peabody Fotheringham, *Obermann, Selections from Letters to a Friend by Etienne Pivert de Sénancour* (Cambridge: Riverside Press, 1901), xiv.

20. Sainte-Beuve had a deep knowledge of the English Romantic poets, and especially Wordsworth; his own novel *Volupté* shows the influence of both Wordsworth and *Obermann*. See chapter 7, "The Aura of Byron," for the influence of Wordsworth on Byron. No doubt it was through Marie d'Agoult's friendship with Sainte-Beuve that she introduced Wordsworth into the extensive reading she and Liszt undertook together. Winklhofer lists, among others, Dante, Sénancour, Sand, Goethe, Byron, Hugo, and Wordsworth. See Sharon Winklhofer, "Liszt, Marie d'Agoult, and the 'Dante' Sonata," *19th-Century Music* 1, no. 1 (1977): 23.

21. George Sand, "Obermann," in *Revue des Deux Mondes,* Deuxième série, Vol. 2, No. 6 (June 15, 1833), 681.

22. *Obermann,* volume 1, note A, 407.

23. Sainte-Beuve in Etienne de Sénancour, *Obermann, avec une Préface de Sainte-Beuve* (Paris: Ledoux, 1833), volume 1, v.

24. *Obermann,* volume 2, letter 63, 98.

25. Alan Walker, *Franz Liszt, The Virtuoso Years* (Ithaca: Cornell University Press, 1987), 269.

26. "Ce sentiment exquis de la poèsie." George Sand, "Obermann" in *Revue des Deux Mondes*, Deuxième série, Vol. 2, No. 6 (15 Juin 1833), 683.

27. *Obermann,* volume 1, letter 4, 46–49.

28. Isaiah Berlin, *The Roots of Romanticism* (Princeton: Princeton University Press, 2001), 105.

29. *Obermann,* volume 1, letter 4, 51–52.

CHAPTER 7: THE AURA OF BYRON—
ANNÉES DE PÈLERINAGE—SUISSE

1. The context of this remark is a letter to Marie d'Agoult on January 24, 1842, in which Liszt extols Lord Byron, for whom he still feels "the same liking, the same passion. . . . Hugo called Virgil the moon of Homer; when I flatter myself, I tell myself that I shall perhaps one day be B's." *Franz Liszt, Selected Letters*, trans. and ed. Adrian Williams (Oxford: Clarendon Press, 1998), 178.

2. Kenneth Hamilton wonders if the scene might be a reference to the famous occasion, recorded by Berlioz, when Liszt played Beethoven's "Moonlight" Sonata by candlelight. Kenneth Hamilton, *After the Golden Age: Romantic Pianism and Modern Performance* (Oxford: Oxford University Press, 2008), 83–85.

3. Christopher H. Gibbs, "'Just Two Words. Enormous Success': Liszt's 1838 Vienna Concerts," in *Franz Liszt and His World*, ed. Christopher H. Gibbs and Dana Gooley (Princeton: Princeton University Press, 2006), 184 and 198.

4. The is an important statement, albeit only in the words of Marie d'Agoult (from her *Mémoires*): *Ma mission à moi sera d'avoir le premier mis avec quelque éclat la poésie dans la musique de piano,* quoted in English in Franz Liszt, *An Artist's Journey, Lettres*

d'un bachelier ès musique, 1835–1841, translated and annotated by Charles Suttoni (Cambridge: University of Cambridge Press, 1989), 183. There is no reason to suppose it is not an accurate recollection of what Liszt would have said. By "*avec quelque éclat*," it appears he wants to distinguish himself from the kind of intimate "poetry" that his contemporaries (notably Heine) found in Chopin. Liszt's "poetry" would be altogether more dramatic, redolent of Hugo and Byron. Chopin, for Heine, was "able to reveal the poetry that lives in his soul." See Suttoni, Liszt, *An Artist's Journey*, 224.

5. Stendhal, in Jonathan Keates, *Stendhal* (London: Sinclair-Stevenson, 1994), 186.

6. In Adrian Williams, *Portrait of Liszt By Himself and His Contemporaries* (Oxford: Clarendon Press, 1990), 58.

7. Ludwig Rellstab, in Allan Keiler, *Ludwig Rellstab's Biographical Sketch of Liszt;* in *Franz Liszt and His World*, ed. Christopher H. Gibbs and Dana Gooley (Princeton: Princeton University Press, 2006), 352.

8. Ludwig Rellstab, in Adrian Williams, *Portrait of Liszt by Himself and His Contemporaries* (Oxford: Clarendon Press, 1990), 177.

9. Letter to Marie d'Agoult, September 16, 1840, in Adrian Williams, *Portrait of Liszt by Himself and His Contemporaries* (Oxford: Clarendon Press, 1990), 143.

10. Letter to Marie d'Agoult, September 16, 1840, in Adrian Williams, *Portrait of Liszt by Himself and His Contemporaries* (Oxford: Clarendon Press, 1990), 143.

11. David Trippett, "An Uncrossable Rubicon: Liszt's *Sardanapalo* Revisited," *Journal of the Royal Musical Association* 143, no. 2 (2018): 361–432.

12. Gillen D'Arcy Wood, *Romanticism and Music Culture in Britain, 1770–1840—Virtue and Virtuosity* (Cambridge: Cambridge University Press, 2010), 207.

13. For a detailed account of the different publications, titles, and disputed dates see György Kroó, "Années de Pèlerinage, Première Année: Versions and Variants. A Challenge to the Thematic Catalogue," *Studia Musicologica Academiae Scientiarum Hungaricae* 34, no. 3/4 (1992): 405–26. Kroó makes it clear that the plan for three books of *Années de pèlerinage* was already in embryo in 1840.

14. Ludwig Rellstab, in Allan Keiler, *Ludwig Rellstab's Biographical Sketch of Liszt;* in *Franz Liszt and His World*, ed. Christopher H. Gibbs and Dana Gooley (Princeton: Princeton University Press, 2006), 349.

15. Terence Cave, *Mignon's Afterlives: Crossing Cultures from Goethe to the Twenty-First Century* (Oxford: Oxford University Press, 2011). One of Liszt's early songs was a setting of the celebrated "Do you know the land where the lemon trees grow"—"Kennst du das Land, wo die Zitronen blühn?"—one of Mignon's songs from *Wilhelm Meisters Lehrjahre*.

16. *La Belgique musicale*, March 9, 1843; Franz Liszt, *An Artist's Journey, Lettres d'un bachelier ès musique, 1835–1841*, translated and annotated by Charles Suttoni (Cambridge: University of Cambridge Press, 1989), xii, n.4.

17. Franz Liszt, *An Artist's Journey, Lettres d'un bachelier ès musique, 1835–1841*, translated and annotated by Charles Suttoni (Cambridge: University of Cambridge Press, 1989), 85.

18. Ernst Burger, *Franz Liszt: A Chronicle of His Life in Pictures and Documents*, trans. Stewart Spencer, foreword Alfred Brendel (Princeton: Princeton University Press, 1989), 147.

19. Franz Liszt, *An Artist's Journey, Lettres d'un bachelier ès musique, 1835–1841*, translated and annotated by Charles Suttoni (Cambridge: University of Cambridge Press, 1989), 201.

20. George Sand in Brigitte Diaz, "Poetics of the Letter in the *Letters of a Traveler*," *Research & Works* 70 (2007): 41–54.

21. The sentence has echoes of the style of Goethe's first novel *The Sufferings of Young Werther*, widely read by Liszt's generation, and Werther's proud attempts to write "periodic sentences." See Johann Wolfgang von Goethe, *The Sufferings of Young Werther*, translated and edited by Stanley Corngold (New York: Norton 2013), 47, n. 1.

22. See chapter 4, note 26.

23. Byron, *Le Corsair*, verse 11, l. 77–82.

24. *Ce soit peut-être le plus magnifique élan de son génie.* George Sand, "Essai sur le Drame Fantasque: Goethe, Byron, Mickiewicz," in *Souvenirs et Impressions Littéraires* (Paris: Hetzel et Lacroix, 1862), 4.

25. Franz Liszt, letter to Therese von Helldorff, September 22, 1869, in Alan Walker, ed., *Liszt: The Man and His Music* (London: Barrie & Jenkins, 1970), 304.

26. Richard Cardwell, *The Reception of Byron in Europe* (London: Thoemmes Continuum, 2004), 2.

27. Dana Gooley, "Warhorses: Liszt, Weber's *Konzertstücke*, and the Cult of Napoleon," in *The Virtuoso Liszt* (Cambridge: Cambridge University, 2004).

28. *Correspondance de Liszt et de Marie d'Agoult*, ed. Daniel Ollivier (Paris, 1933–35), vol. I, 447. Quoted in Dana Gooley, *The Virtuoso Liszt* (Cambridge: Cambridge University, 2004), 88.

29. Walter Scott in *The Poetical Works of Lord Byron*, vol. 3 (Cambridge: The Riverside Press, 1879), 145. Scott's long account of *The Corsair* is quoted as a footnote in this complete edition of Byron's works. At the head of canto 1, Byron quotes as an epigraph, in Italian, lines from Dante's "Inferno": "There is no greater sorrow / than thinking back upon a happy time / in misery."

30. Lord Macaulay in a review for the *Edinburgh Review* of the 1842 edition of Byron's works. See Richard Cardwell, *The Reception of Byron in Europe* (London: Thoemmes Continuum, 2004), 2.

31. Gillen D'Arcy Wood, *Romanticism and Music Culture in Britain, 1770–1840—Virtue and Virtuosity* (Cambridge: Cambridge University Press, 2010), 192. I am indebted to D'Arcy Wood's essay in this volume, "The Byron of the piano." He suggests that Liszt was "perhaps the closest reader of *Childe Harold* in the nineteenth century."

32. Liszt's compositions for voice and piano, among his greatest works, show an acute understanding of the sound and psychology of language. See Susan Youens, "Heine, Liszt, and the Song of the Future," in *Franz Liszt and His World*, ed. Christopher H. Gibbs and Dana Gooley (Princeton: Princeton University Press, 2006).

33. Frederick W. Shilstone, "Byron's 'Mental Theatre' and the German Classical Precedent," *Comparative Drama* 10, no. 3 (Fall 1976): 189.

34. *Lord Byron: The Major Works*, edited with an introduction and notes by Jerome J. McGann (Oxford: Oxford University Press, 2000), xxi.

35. Richard Holmes, *Shelley: The Pursuit* (London: HarperCollins, 1994), 337. It is a shame Liszt did not grapple with Shelley. Holmes calls the latter "a Dante among

English poets, an image of Faustian daring." See especially chapter 13, "The Byron Summer: Switzerland 1816," pp. 319–46.

36. Byron, *Childe Harold's Pilgrimage*, canto 3, verse 102.

37. Byron, *Childe Harold's Pilgrimage*, canto 3, verse 72.

38. Byron, *Childe Harold's Pilgrimage*, canto 3, verse 71.

39. For Byron, Wordsworth was a challenge in terms of poetic genius, an anxiety that needed to be dismissed. Byron was able to embrace Rousseau because he represented the humanist values of the Enlightenment. Wordsworth's liberal politics had by this time soured into conservatism.

40. Franz Liszt, *An Artist's Journey, Lettres d'un bachelier ès musique, 1835–1841*, translated and annotated by Charles Suttoni (Cambridge: University of Cambridge Press, 1989), 201.

41. Byron, *Childe Harold's Pilgrimage*, canto 3, verse 72.

42. Johann Wolfgang von Goethe, quoted in Rupert Christiansen, *Romantic Affinities* (London: Bodley Head), 214–15.

43. "A Mirror to the Nineteenth Century: Reflections on Franz Liszt" by Leon Botstein, in *Franz Liszt and His World*, ed. Christopher H. Gibbs and Dana Gooley (Princeton: Princeton University Press, 2006), 525.

44. Johann Wolfgang von Goethe, quoted in Rupert Christiansen, *Romantic Affinities* (London: Bodley Head), 217–18.

45. Goethe, quoted in Rupert Christiansen, *Romantic Affinities* (London: Bodley Head), 218.

CHAPTER 8: MENTAL THEATER—*ANNÉES DE PÈLERINAGE—SUISSE*

1. Byron, *Childe Harold's Pilgrimage*, canto 3, verse 72.

2. "One for all, or all for one we gage," is a line from Shakespeare's narrative poem *The Rape of Lucrece*; it can be discounted as a source for it has a quite different meaning in the context of the poem, concerned at this point with the single-minded pursuit of desire which will let nothing stand in its way.

3. "On Goethe's Tragedy, Egmont" (Über Egmont, Trauerspiel von Goethe) by Friedrich Schiller, 1788. Schiller's adaptation of Egmont is usually taken as the start of what came to be known at Weimar Classicism, the movement away from *sturm und drang*.

4. Franz Liszt, letter to Princess Belgiojoso, June 4, 1839, in *Selected Letters*, trans. and ed. Adrian Williams (Oxford: Clarendon Press, 1998), 106–7.

5. Byron, *Childe Harold's Pilgrimage*, canto 3, verse 85.

6. Marie d'Agoult, quoted in Adrian Williams, *Portrait of Liszt by Himself and His Contemporaries* (Oxford: Clarendon Press, 1990), 68.

7. Alfred Brendel, *Music Sounded Out* (London: Robson Books, 1990), 168.

8. Marie d'Agoult, quoted in Adrian Williams, *Portrait of Liszt By Himself and His Contemporaries* (Oxford: Clarendon Press, 1990), 68.

9. Friedrich Schiller, *Der Flüchtling*. My translation comes from Alfred Brendel, *Music Sounded Out* (London: Robson Books, 1990), 169. For a German and Eng-

lish text of the complete poem see Oxford Lieder: https://www.oxfordlieder.co.uk /song/2947.

10. Byron, *Childe Harold's Pilgrimage*, canto 3, verse 96.

11. Byron, *Childe Harold's Pilgrimage*, canto 3, verse 94.

12. Lord Byron: *The Major Works* (Oxford: Oxford University Press, 2000), edited with and Introduction and Notes by Jerome J. McGann, 143.

13. Byron, *Childe Harold's Pilgrimage*, canto 3, verse 93.

14. Byron, *Childe Harold's Pilgrimage*, canto 3, verse 97.

15. Byron, *Childe Harold's Pilgrimage*, canto 3, verse 98.

16. *Obermann*, volume 1, 258–66 "Troisième fragment."

17. *Obermann*, volume 1, 263.

18. Lord Byron: *The Major Works* (Oxford: Oxford University Press, 2000), edited with and Introduction and Notes by Jerome J. McGann, 143.

19. Byron, *Childe Harold's Pilgrimage*, canto 3, stanza 72.

20. Byron, *Childe Harold's Pilgrimage*, canto 3, stanza 102.

CHAPTER 9: MUSIC AND POETRY—THE DANTE SONATA

1. T. S . Eliot, "What Dante Means to Me," in *To Criticize the Critic* (London: Faber, 1965), 134.

2. August Stradal in Adrian Williams, *Portrait of Liszt By Himself and His Contemporaries* (Oxford: Clarendon Press, 1990), 650.

3. Thomas Love Peacock, *Headlong Hall & Nightmare Abbey* (Wordsworth Classics, Ware: 1995), 107.

4. For "the Dante cult" in France at this period see Sharon Winklhofer, "Liszt, Marie d'Agoult, and the 'Dante' Sonata," *19th-Century Music* 1, no. 1 (1977): 21. Winklhofer points out that Liszt's and d'Agoult's initial enthusiasm for Dante was on account of the poet's early collection of poems *La Vita Nuova* recounting his love for Beatrice.

5. T. S. Eliot, "What Dante Means to Me," in *To Criticize the Critic* (London: Faber, 1965), 134.

6. Lord Byron, journal entry for January 31, 1821, in *Life Letters and Journals of Lord Byron, with Notices of his Life*, by Thomas Moore (London: John Murray, 1838), 485. The rediscovery of Dante is well under way in Byron's journals. The context of this reference reads, "Why they talk Dante—write Dante—and think and dream Dante at this moment (1821) to an excess which would be ridiculous, but that he deserves it. . . . There is gentleness in Dante beyond all gentleness, when he is tender. It is true, that treating of the Christian Hades, or Hell, there is not much scope or site for gentleness—but who *but* Dante could have introduced any 'gentleness' at all in *Hell?*"

7. David Trippett, "Après une Lecture de Liszt: Virtuosity and *Werktreue* in the 'Dante' Sonata," *19th-Century Music* 32, no. 1 (2008): pp. 52–93.

8. Anna Harrell Celenza, "Liszt, Italy and the Republic of the Imagination," in *Franz Liszt and His World*, ed. Christopher H. Gibbs and Dana Gooley (Princeton: Princeton University Press, 2006), 28–29.

9. David Trippett, "Après une Lecture de Liszt: Virtuosity and *Werktreue* in the 'Dante' Sonata," *19th-Century Music* 32, no. 1 (2008): 54. Trippett points out how the Dante Sonata was "a piece born expressly from acts of performance." He argues that it "interweaves hours and hours of improvisation with a gradual process of revision on a more abstracted, conceptual level."

10. Franz Liszt, in *An Artist's Journey, Lettres d'un bachelier ès musique, 1835–1841*, translated and annotated by Charles Suttoni (Cambridge: University of Cambridge Press, 1989), 186.

11. T. S. Eliot, "Dante," in *T. S. Eliot, Selected Essays 1917–1932* (New York: Harcourt Brace, 1932), 204.

12. Alfred Brendel, "Liszt Misunderstood" in *Musical Thoughts & Afterthoughts* (London: Robson Books, 1976), 79–80.

13. Alan Walker, *Franz Liszt, The Virtuoso Years* (Ithaca: Cornell University Press, 1987), 277.

14. Dante Alighieri, *The Divine Comedy*, trans. Allen Mandelbaum (New York: Everyman's Library, Alfred A. Knopf, 1995), "Paradiso," 1.70–71.

15. "Inferno," 2.55.

16. "Purgatorio," 1.13–14.

17. "Paradiso," 27.88–96.

18. "Introduction to *Paradiso*" by Rachel Jacoff, in *The Cambridge Guide to Dante*, ed. Rachel Jacoff (Cambridge: Cambridge University Press, 2007), 118.

19. Richard Wagner, letter to Franz Liszt in *Correspondence of Wagner and Liszt*, ed. Francis Hueffer (Cambridge: Cambridge University Press, 2009), Volume 2, 92–93.

20. Franz Liszt, in *An Artist's Journey, Lettres d'un bachelier ès musique, 1835–1841*, translated and annotated by Charles Suttoni (Cambridge: University of Cambridge Press, 1989), 18–19.

21. Dante Alighieri, *The Divine Comedy*, trans. Allen Mandelbaum (New York: Everyman's Library, Alfred A. Knopf, 1995), "Inferno," 1, 1–3.

22. Dante Alighieri, *The Divine Comedy*, trans. Allen Mandelbaum (New York: Everyman's Library, Alfred A. Knopf, 1995), "Inferno," 3, 1–9.

23. For courtly love, see Sharon Winklhofer, "Liszt, Marie d'Agoult, and the 'Dante' Sonata," *19th-Century Music* 1, no. 1 (1977): 22. Winklhofer points out that "[a]n important aspect of the Romantic conception of love was its stress on love as a transcendent state of existence." See also Dante Alighieri, *The Divine Comedy*, trans. Allen Mandelbaum (New York: Everyman's Library, Alfred A. Knopf, 1995), 556–58.

24. Dante Alighieri, *The Divine Comedy*, trans. Allen Mandelbaum (New York: Everyman's Library, Alfred A. Knopf, 1995), "Inferno," 5, 121–23. See also chapter 7, note 27.

25. *Dante: The Divine Comedy*, trans. Clive James (London: Picador, 2013), canto 5, l. 149–62.

26. Madame Germaine de Staël, *Corinne—ou Italie*. See Sharon Winklhofer, "Liszt, Marie d'Agoult, and the 'Dante' Sonata." *19th-Century Music* 1, no. 1 1977, 21.

27. *Dante: The Divine Comedy*, trans. Clive James (London: Picador, 2013), xiii.

28. Charles Rosen, *Music and Sentiment* (New Haven: Yale University Press, 2010), 5–6.

APPENDIX: LAMARTINE; TWO EPISODES FROM LENAU'S *FAUST*;
THE TWO ST. FRANCIS LEGENDS; THOMAS WYATT'S TRANSLATION
OF PETRARCH'S SONNET "PACE NON TROVO"; A NOTE ON
"MAZEPPA" AND AN AFTERTHOUGHT

1. Richard Cardwell, *The Reception of Byron in Europe* (London: Thoemmes Continuum, 2004), 24.

2. Heinrich Heine, *Gazette* musicale, 4 February 1838, 41–44, in Franz Liszt, *An Artist's Journey, Lettres d'un bachelier ès musique, 1835–1841*, translated and annotated by Charles Suttoni (Cambridge: University of Cambridge Press, 1989), 221. See chapter 4, note 9.

3. Elizabeth M. Butler, *The Fortunes of Faust* (Stroud: Sutton, 1998), 284–24.

4. "5 seconds with the manuscript will assure you that Liszt's input is mighty and considerable," says Leslie Howard in his YouTube video presentation on *Two Episodes from Lenau's Faust*. See also Franz Liszt, *The Procession by Night; Mephisto Waltz No.1*, ed. Leslie Howard (London: Peters, 2007); and *Mephisto-Waltzer*, ed. Veronika Giglberger and Norbert Gertsch (Munich: G. Henle Verlag).

5. Franz Liszt, "Letter to Franz Brendel," August 29, 1862, in La Mara, *Franz Liszts Briefe*, vol. 2 (Leipzig, 1893). Quoted in *Mephisto-Waltzer*, ed. Veronika Giglberger and Norbert Gertsch (Munich: G. Henle Verlag, 2008), vii.

6. Franz Liszt, letter to Max Edmannsdörfer, in La Mara, September 16, 1873, in *Mephisto-Waltzer*, ed. Veronika Giglberger and Norbert Gertsch (Munich: G. Henle Verlag, 2008), vii.

7. Elizabeth M. Butler, *The Fortunes of Faust* (Stroud: Sutton, 1998), 284.

8. Nikolaus Lenau, *Faust: Ein Gedicht*, scene 11, translation by the author. See also, Franz Liszt, "The Procession of the Night; Mephisto Waltz, No. 1," ed. Leslie Howard (London: Peters, 2007).

9. Nikolaus Lenau, *Faust: Ein Gedicht*, Scene 6, trans. Timothy Motz in *Mephisto-Waltzer* ed. Veronika Giglberger and Norbert Gertsch (Munich: G. Henle Verlag), xiii.

10. For the various programmatic interpretations of the Mephisto Waltz, see David Larkin's detailed essay "Dancing to the Devil's Tune," *19th-Century Music* 38, no. 3 (Spring 2015): 193–218.

11. Cited in "Heinrich Heine on Liszt," ed. Rainer Kleinert, trans. Susan Gillespie, in *Franz Liszt and His World*, ed. Christopher H. Gibbs and Dan Gooley (Princeton: Princeton University Press, 2006), 460. See also Clara Schumann, p. 5 above.

12. Franz Liszt, letter to Carolyne von Sayn-Wittgenstein, 1877, in David Larkin, "Dancing to the Devil's Tune," *19th-Century Music* 38, no. 3 (Spring 2015): 214. Larkin shows in this essay that even after giving up his recital career Liszt remained wedded to his own need for "demonic" virtuosity. I am indebted to David Larkin for galvanizing my thoughts on this superb music.

13. Franz Liszt, Zwei Legenden, preface by Maria Eckhardt (Munich: G. Henle Verlag 2004), 34–35.

14. Franz Liszt, Zwei Legenden, preface by Maria Eckhardt (Munich: G. Henle Verlag 2004), 34–35.

15. Liszt, *Zwei Legenden*, 35.

16. Ernst Burger, *Franz Liszt: A Chronicle of His Life in Pictures and Documents*, trans. Stewart Spencer, foreword Alfred Brendel (Princeton: Princeton University Press, 1989), 292.

17. *Sir Thomas Wyatt—The Complete Poems*, ed. R. A. Rebholz (London: Penguin, 1978), 80.

18. Eleanor Perényi, Liszt, *The Artist as Romantic Hero* (Boston: Little, Brown and Company), 50.

19. Albert Brussee, "Franz Liszt's Mazeppa Sketch in His Sketchbook N6," *Studia Musicologica* 55, no. 1/2 (2014): 27–42.

20. Hugo's lines are as follows: En fin le terme arrive . . . il court, il vol, il tombe / Et se relève, roi. (Finally the time comes . . . he runs, he flies, he falls / And rises a king.)

21. Vladimir Jankélévitch, *Music and the Ineffable*, trans. Carolyn Abbate (Princeton: Princeton University Press, 2003), 59.

Select Bibliography

Alighieri, Dante. *The Divine Comedy.* Trans. Allen Mandelbaum, with an introduction by Eugenio Montale and notes by Peter Armour. New York: Everyman's Library, Alfred A. Knopf, 1995.

Arnold, Ben. *The Liszt Companion.* London: Greenwood Press, 2002.

Berlin, Isaiah. *The Roots of Romanticism.* Princeton: Princeton University Press, 2001.

Berlioz, Hector. *The Memoirs of Hector Berlioz.* Trans. and ed. David Cairns. London: Victor Gollancz, 1969.

Botstein, Leon. "A Mirror to the Nineteenth Century: Reflections on Franz Liszt." In *Franz Liszt and His World.* Ed. Christopher H. Gibbs and Dana Gooley. Princeton: Princeton University Press, 2006.

Boyle, Nicholas. *Goethe: The Poet and the Age—Volume II, Revolution and Renunciation, 1790–1803.* Oxford: Clarendon Press, 2000.

Brendel, Alfred. *Musical Thoughts & Afterthoughts.* London: Robson Books, 1976.

———. *Music Sounded Out.* London: Robson Books, 1990.

———. *Alfred Brendel on Music: His Collected Essays.* London: JR Books, 2007.

Brook, Peter. *The Empty Space.* London: Penguin, 1972.

Brookner, Anita. *Romanticism and Its Discontents.* London: Viking Penguin, 2000.

Brussee, Albert. "Franz Liszt's Mazeppa Sketch in His Sketchbook N6." *Studia Musicologica* 55, no. 1/2 (2014): 27–42.

Burger, Ernst. *Franz Liszt: A Chronicle of His Life in Pictures and Documents.* Trans. Stewart Spencer, foreword by Alfred Brendel. Princeton: Princeton University Press, 1989.

Busoni, Ferrucio. *The Essence of Music and Other Papers.* Trans. Rosamond Ley. London: Rockliff, 1957.

Butler, Elizabeth M. *The Fortunes of Faust.* Stroud: Sutton, 1998.

Byron, Lord George Gordon. *Life Letters and Journals of Lord Byron, with Notices of His Life.* Ed. Thomas Moore. London: John Murray, 1838.

———. *The Poetical Works of Lord Byron.* Cambridge: The Riverside Press, 1879.

———. *Lord Byron: The Major Works.* Edited with an introduction and notes by Jerome J. McGann. Oxford: Oxford University Press, 2000.

Cardwell, Richard. *The Reception of Byron in Europe.* London: Thoemmes Continuum, 2004.

Cave, Terence. *Mignon's Afterlives: Crossing Cultures from Goethe to the Twenty-First Century*. Oxford: Oxford University Press, 2011.

Christiansen, Rupert. *Romantic Affinities*. London: Bodley Head, 1988.

Cortot, Alfred. *Liszt Sonata in B minor*. Paris: Salabert, 1949.

Dalmonte, Rossana. "Rethinking the Influence of Italian Poetry and Music on Liszt: The Petrarca Sonnet 'Benedetto Sia 'l Giorno.'" *Studia Musicologica* 54, no. 2 (2013): 177–97. http://www.jstor.org/stable/43289715.

D'Arcy Wood, Gillen. *Romanticism and Music Culture in Britain, 1770–1840—Virtue and Virtuosity*. Cambridge: Cambridge University Press, 2010.

Diaz, Brigitte. "Poetics of the Letter in the Letters of a Traveler." *Research & Works*, 70 (2007), 41–54.

Durling, Robert M. *Petrarch's Lyric Poems: The* Rime sparse *and Other Lyrics*. Trans. and ed. Robert M. Durling. Cambridge: Harvard University Press, 1976.

Durrani, Osman. *Faust*. Robertsbridge: Helm Information Ltd., 2004.

Eliot, T. S. *Selected Essays 1917–1932*. New York: Harcourt Brace, 1932.

———. *To Criticize the Critic*. London: Faber, 1965.

Gibbs, Christopher H. "'Just Two Words. Enormous Success': Liszt's 1838 Vienna Concerts." In *Franz Liszt and His World*. Ed. Christopher H. Gibbs and Dana Gooley. Princeton: Princeton University Press, 2006.

Goethe, Johann Wolfgang von. *The Sufferings of Young Werther*. Trans. and ed. by Stanley Corngold. New York: Norton, 2013.

Göllerich, August. *The Piano Master Classes of Franz Liszt 1884–1886*. Ed. Wilhelm Jerger, trans. Richard Louis Zimdars. Bloomington: Indian University Press, 1996.

Gooley, Dana. *The Virtuoso Liszt*. Cambridge: Cambridge University, 2004.

Hamilton, Kenneth. *Liszt Sonata in B minor*. Cambridge: Cambridge University Press, 1996.

———. *After the Golden Age: Romantic Pianism and Modern Performance*. Oxford: Oxford University Press, 2008.

Horowitz, Joseph. *Conversations with Arrau*. London: Collins, 1982.

Jacoff, Rachel. "Introduction to *Paradiso*." In *The Cambridge Guide to Dante*. Ed. Rachel Jacoff. Cambridge: Cambridge University Press, 2007.

Jankélévitch, Vladimir. *Music and the Ineffable*. Trans. Carolyn Abbate. Princeton: Princeton University Press, 2003.

Jensen, Eric Frederick. "Liszt, Nerval, and 'Faust.'" *19th-Century Music* 6, no. 2 (1982): 151–58. https://doi.org/10.2307/746273.

Keiler, Allan. "Ludwig Rellstab's Biographical Sketch of Liszt." In *Franz Liszt and His World*. Ed. Christopher H. Gibbs and Dana Gooley. Princeton: Princeton University Press, 2006.

Kleinertz, Rainer. "Heinrich Heine on Liszt." Selected and edited by Rainer Kleinertz, translated by Susan Gillespie. In *Franz Liszt and His World*. Ed. Christopher H. Gibbs and Dana Gooley. Princeton: Princeton University Press, 2006.

Kramer, Lawrence. "Dangerous Liaisons: The Literary Text in Musical Criticism." *19th-Century Music* 13, no. 2 (1989): 159–67. https://doi.org/10.2307/746653.

———. *Interpreting Music*. Berkeley: University of California Press, 2011.

Kroó, György. "Années de Pèlerinage, Première Année: Versions and Variants. A Challenge to the Thematic Catalogue." *Studia Musicologica Academiae Scientiarum Hungaricae* 34, no. 3/4 (1992): 405–26. https://doi.org/10.2307/902291.

Lachmund, Carl. *Living with Liszt, from the Diary of an American Pupil of Liszt, 1882–1884.* Edited, annotated, and introduced by Alan Walker. Stuyvesant: Pendragon Press, 1995.

Lamport, F. J. *German Classical Drama: Theatre, Humanity and Nation 1750–1870.* Cambridge: Cambridge University Press, 1990.

Larkin, David. "Dancing to the Devil's Tune." *19th-Century Music* 38, no. 3 (Spring 2015): 193–218.

Liszt, Franz. *An Artist's Journey, Lettres d'un bachelier ès musique, 1835–1841.* Translated and annotated by Charles Suttoni. Cambridge: University of Cambridge Press, 1989.

———. *Selected Letters.* Trans. and ed. Adrian Williams. Oxford: Clarendon Press, 1998.

Le Hurray, Peter, and James Day. *Music and Aesthetics in the Eighteenth and Early-Nineteenth Centuries.* Cambridge: Cambridge University Press, 1988.

———, and Richard Wagner. *Correspondence of Wagner and Liszt.* Ed. Francis Hueffer. Cambridge: Cambridge University Press, 2009.

Lockward, Lewis. *Beethoven: The Music and the Life.* New York: Norton, 2003.

Luke, David. *Faust Part 1*, by Johann Wolfgang von Goethe. Translated with an introduction and notes by David Luke. Oxford: Oxford University Press, 1987.

Mazzotta, Giuseppe. "The 'Canzoniere' and the Language of the Self." *Studies in Philology* 75, no. 3 (1978): 271–96. http://www.jstor.org/stable/4173972.

Mueller, Rena. "The Lieder of Liszt." In *The Cambridge Companion to the Lied.* Cambridge: Cambridge University Press, 2004.

———. "From the Biographer's Workshop: Lina Ramann's Questionaires to Liszt." In *Franz Liszt and His World.* Ed. Christopher H. Gibbs and Dana Gooley. Princeton: Princeton University Press, 2006.

Musa, Mark. *Petrarch, Selections from the Canzoniere and Other Works.* Trans. Mark Musa. Oxford: Oxford University Press, 1985.

Nietzsche, Friedrich. *The Case of Wagner, Nietzsche Contra Wagner, Selected Aphorisms.* Trans. Anthony M. Ludovici. Edinburgh: T. N. Foulis, 1911.

———. *The Birth of Tragedy.* Trans. Shaun Whiteside, ed. Michael Tanner. London: Penguin, 1993.

d'Ortigue, Joseph. "The First Biography: On Franz Liszt." Trans. Vincent Giroud, introduced and edited by Benjamin Walton. In *Franz Liszt and His World.* Ed. Christopher H. Gibbs and Dana Gooley. Princeton: Princeton University Press, 2006.

Perényi, Eleanor. *Liszt, The Artist as Romantic Hero.* Boston: Little, Brown and Company, 1974.

Roberts, Paul. *Reflections: The Piano Music of Maurice Ravel.* Lanham: Amadeus Press, 2012.

Rosen, Charles. *The Romantic Generation.* London: HarperCollins, 1996.

———. *Music and Sentiment.* New Haven: Yale University Press, 2010.

Rosen, Charles, and Henri Zerner. *Romanticism and Realism.* London: Faber 1984.

Rushworth, Jennifer. *Petrarch and the Literary Culture of Nineteenth-Century France.* Woodbridge: Boydell & Brewer, 2017.

Sand, George. *Obermann.* Revue des Deux Mondes, Deuxième série, Vol. 2, No. 6 (June 15, 1833): 677–90.

———. *Souvenirs et Impressions Littéraires.* Paris: Hetzel et Lacroix, 1862.

Searle, Humphrey. *The Music of Liszt.* New York: Dover, 1966.

Sénancour, Etienne de. *Obermann, avec une Préface de Sainte-Beuve.* Paris: Ledoux, 1833.

———. *Obermann, Selections from Letters to a Friend.* Trans. Jessica Peabody Fotheringham. Cambridge: Riverside Press, 1901.

Shilstone, Frederick W. "Byron's 'Mental Theatre' and the German Classical Precedent." *Comparative Drama* 10, no. 3 (1976): 187–99. http://www.jstor.org/stable/41152687.

Sitwell, Sacheverell. *Liszt.* Boston: Houghton Mifflin, 1934.

Stevens, Wallace. *The Necessary Angel: Essays on Reality and the Imagination.* New York: Random House, 1951.

Szász, Tibor, with Gerard Carter and Martin Adler. "Towards a New Edition of Liszt's Sonata in B minor." *Journal of the American Liszt Society* 68 (2017).

Tanner, Mark. "The Power of Performance as an Alternative Analytical Discourse: The Liszt Sonata in B Minor." *19th-Century Music* 24, no. 2 (2000): 173–92. https://doi.org/10.2307/746841.

Trippett, David. "An Uncrossable Rubicon: Liszt's Sardanapalo Revisited." *Journal of the Royal Musical Association* 143, no. 2 (2018): 361–432. https://search.ebscohost.com/login.aspx?direct=true&db=rft&AN=A1950001&site=eds-live.

Walker, Alan. *Franz Liszt, The Virtuoso Years.* Ithaca: Cornell University Press, 1987.

———. *Franz Liszt: The Weimar Years 1848–1861.* London: Faber, 1989.

———. *Franz Liszt: The Final Years, 1861–1886.* London: Faber, 1997.

———. *Reflections on Liszt.* Ithaca: Cornell University Press, 2005.

Williams, Adrian. *Portrait of Liszt by Himself and His Contemporaries.* Oxford: Clarendon Press, 1990.

Winklhofer, Sharon. "Liszt, Marie d'Agoult, and the 'Dante' Sonata." *19th-Century Music* 1, no. 1 (1977): 15–32.

Winnicott, D. W. *Playing and Reality.* London: Tavistock, 1971.

Youens, Susan. "Heine, Liszt, and the Song of the Future." In *Franz Liszt and His World.* Ed. Christopher H. Gibbs and Dana Gooley. Princeton: Princeton University Press, 2006.

Zimmermann, Jens. *Hermeneutics: A Very Short Introduction.* Oxford: Oxford University Press, 2015.

Index

Page references for figures are italicized

d'Agoult, Marie, 2, 27, 40, 95, *96*, 102, 129–30, 131, 161n16, 166n16, 167n4, 170n6; Liszt's correspondence with, 3, 33–35, 83–84, 98, 104, 108–109, 167n1; on Liszt, 5, 21–22, 97, 119–21
Alighieri, Dante. *See* Dante
Arrau, Claudio, 61–62, 69, 71–73

Bach, J. S., 3, 36, 70
Beethoven, Ludwig van, 10, 45, 54, 58, 77, 91, 95–96, *96*, 117, 125, 134, 139, 146, 165n28; *Corialan* Overture, 66–67, 73, 102; piano works, 3, 5, 15, 21, 63, 167n2
Bellini, Vincenzo, 118, 121
Berlin, Isaiah, 79–83, 89, 136
Berlioz, Hector, 4, 5, 45, 54, 61, 67, 80, 82, 112, 134; and *Faust*, 56, 57–58, 62, 163n23
Bonaparte, Napoleon, 103–104, 117, 131
Botstein, Leon, 22, 112–13
Brendel, Alfred, 17, 121, 124; and the Romantic fragment, 135–36; and the *Sonata in B Minor*, 65–66, 69, 70–73, 77
Brook, Peter, 4, 6
Brontë, Charlotte, 103
Brontë, Emily, 103
Busoni, Ferrucio, 12

Byron, Lord, 3, 50, 54, 77, 82–83, 95, *96*, 100–103, 145, 167n1, 170n39; and the Byronic hero, 2, 30, 87, 88, 96, 97, 103–106, 107, 113, 117, 126; *Childe Harold's Pilgrimage*, 77, 89, 96–99, 106–121, 124–130; *The Corsair*, 103, 106, 168n29; and Dante, 131, 133, 137, 168n29, 170n6; *Don Juan*, 107; *The Giaour*, 136; *Manfred*, 97, 103, 106, 107; and nature, 107, 108–112, 115, 120, 124, 129; *Sardanapalus*, 62, 98, 113

Cardwell, Richard, 104
Chateaubriand, François-René de, 82–84
Chopin, Frédéric, 41, 77, 83, 167n4
Coetzee, J.M., 70
Coleridge, Samuel Taylor, 50, 54, 131
Collin, Heinrich Joseph von, 67
Cornelius, Peter von, *55*
Cortot, Alfred, 49, 65, 69

dance, 16, 42, 120–21, 151
Danhauser, Josef, 95–96, *96*, 98
Dante, 27, 92, 97, 112, 171n6; *Divine Comedy*, 6, 28, 32, 34, 50, 131–144, 149; *La Vita Nuova*, 171n4. *See also* Romanticism, and Dante
Dante Sonata. *See* Liszt, Franz, Solo piano works

About the Author

British pianist **Paul Roberts** has written seminal books on impressionist piano music—*Images: The Piano Music of Claude Debussy* and *Reflections: The Piano Music of Maurice Ravel*, both for Amadeus Press—and has recorded the music of Debussy, Ravel, and Liszt. Before embarking on his concert career, he took a degree in English literature at the University of York. He has long had a fascination for the correspondences between music, poetry, and painting, which are a feature of his acclaimed lecture recitals throughout America and Europe. In the United States he has given lectures and master classes at Juilliard and Peabody; at the International Keyboard Festival in New York, San Francisco Conservatory, University of Washington, and Portland Piano International; and in Europe at the Theo and Petra Lieven Foundation in Vienna, and Piano Visions in Stockholm. He is director of the International Piano Summer School in southwest France, Music at Chateau d'Aix, a fellow of the Guildhall School of Music and Drama in London, and an associate of the Royal Academy of Music.

CPSIA information can be obtained
at www.ICGtesting.com
Printed in the USA
BVHW090251220322
632037BV00001B/2